Athenian Identity
and Civic Ideology

Athenian Identity
and Civic Ideology

EDITED BY

Alan L. Boegehold

AND

Adele C. Scafuro

The Johns Hopkins University Press

BALTIMORE AND LONDON

The Johns Hopkins University Press
2715 North Charles Street
Baltimore, Maryland 21218-4139
The Johns Hopkins Press Ltd., London

Library of Congress Cataloging-in-Publication Data

Athenian identity and civic ideology / edited by Alan L.
Boegehold and Adele C. Scafuro.
p.   cm.
Includes bibliographical references.
ISBN 0-8018-4578-5
1. Citizenship—Greece—Athens. I. Boegehold, Alan L.
(Alan Lindley) II. Scafuro, Adele C.
JC75.C5A85   1993
323.6'0938'5—dc20   92-46746

A catalog record for this book is
available from the British Library.

Contents

Acknowledgments

The editors of this volume wish to extend thanks to those who made possible the conference at which most of these essays were first presented: the Brown University Faculty Lectures and Charles P. Sisson Memorial Lectureship Funds, the Department of Classics, the Program of Ancient Studies, and the Rhode Island Committee for the Humanities.

Introduction: Bifurcations
and Intersections

🮑🮑🮑🮑🮑🮑🮑🮑🮑🮑🮑🮑🮑🮑

ADELE C. SCAFURO

Most of the essays presented here were first delivered as talks at a conference, organized by the editors of this volume, at Brown University in April 1990; a few were solicited from commentators at that event. In organizing the conference, our goal was to bring together scholars who had addressed questions about the nature and meaning of Athenian citizenship and civic ideology in the course of their research. It was an appropriate time to assemble such a group because of the approach of the 2,500th birthday of the Athenian administrative reforms that made possible the first democracy. It was also an opportune time because scholars of diverse interests had been exploring new perspectives in the study of citizenship with the result that we were now beginning to have both a broader and more detailed picture. In particular, the fields of archeology, anthropology, women's studies, semiotics, and the history of religion had all made valuable contributions to a topic that is frequently viewed as the privileged property of political and constitutional historians. We began planning the conference before the momentous events in Eastern Europe and the former Soviet Union had taken an observable shape in late 1989. Those events—the toppling of totalitarian regimes and the establishment of new democracies—have brought a vivid meaningfulness to the issues treated by the authors in this volume. In particular, as large polities dissolve into smaller ones, we cannot fail to see the uneasy relationship between political and cultural identity, and we cannot help but ask: What is it that shapes the identity of individuals into citizens of a particular state? And what happens to individuals who resist that definition of communality?

Television cameras and newspapers have sensationally pictorialized the process of emerging statehood and the creation of new democratic identities and ideologies in Eastern Europe; modern historians of ancient Athens have less colorful and less ample documentation. Of central importance to the study of ancient citizenship since its discovery a century ago is the Aristotelian *Constitution of Athenians* (*Athenaion Politeia,* abbreviated *AP* throughout this volume). The first two-thirds of the treatise is an account of changes in Athenian government from the time of kings to the end of the fifth century; the last third (roughly) is a description of institutions and their functions in the author's own day (c. 333–325 B.C.). The corpus of fifth- and fourth-century Attic orators provides a detailed if tendentious picture of the functioning of the Assembly (*ekklesia*) and courts (*dikasteria*), both significant locales of active participation in civic life. Historians, poets, and philosophers have left in their work a rich but not unproblematic quarry for historians of citizenship and civic ideology. Epigraphic texts and other physical remains, such as buildings, memorials for the dead, and painted scenes on vases, add significant details.[1]

These various sources are helpful in ways that depend on the sorts of question asked about citizenship and the definition given by scholars to citizenship in the first place. Sealey has provided an apt summation of the traditional questions posed by scholars: "In the study of citizenship two questions can be asked. One is the question of 'extent': it asks, who had citizenship? It includes questions about the bearing of marriage on the status of children in Athens, about the relationship of *politeia* to *anchisteia,* about admission to the phratry and to the deme, and about enfranchisement of aliens. Many studies have been devoted to this group of questions. The other question is that of 'content': what rights, privileges, capacities and material advantages constituted citizenship?"[2] Sealey's description of the bifurcated nature of citizenship studies accurately reflects earlier scholarship. One point, perhaps, needs clarification: some of the older works on citizenship, such as those of Busolt and Swoboda, Kahrstedt, and Paoli, did consider both sets of questions, even if they considered them under different headings.[3] A similar bifurcation of treatment is evident in many current studies of citizenship; the new perspectives taken in these studies to some degree depend upon which set of questions historians have chosen to pursue.

Earlier scholarship on citizenship is frequently perceived as "constitutionalist" (with various connotations), that is, as focusing on the legal criteria of status and on the citizen's involvement with formal institutions of government. Several factors contribute to that perception. First, as Sealey's description indicates, a strong tradition of juridical studies of citizenship and civic institutions does exist; its methodological perspective is positivistic, and its style can be compendious.[4] Second, the discovery of *AP* only a century ago summoned scholars to focus critical attention on the sources of that work and the Atthidographers in general as the foundation for Athenian constitutional history.[5] Third, diachronic histories of Greece often have not provided full (insofar as the range of sources in a given period might allow) synchronic discussions of citizenship that go beyond summary treatment within the parameters established by legal historians.[6] In particular, until recently there has been a noticeable neglect of discussions about the definition and conditions for citizenship (or lack thereof) before Perikles' citizenship law of 451/0.[7]

The perception of these earlier works as constitutionalist does not quite do justice to their breadth of inquiry and analysis. Not always by virtue of an explicit intention on the part of earlier historians, but rather because of the character of the particular animal so positivistically examined, studies of Athenian citizenship have always had to incorporate social phenomena when posing Sealey's first question, that of "extent."[8] One would be hard put, for example, to omit discussion of the role of phratries in civic life; and once the phratry enters discussion, one has entered the realm, willy-nilly, of social and family relations. Some historians, such as Busolt and Swoboda and Kahrstedt, have written important chapters on the role of the family and other social institutions in their studies of citizenship. The realm of the second set of questions, however, might seem less promising if one is looking for more than a juridical assessment. Yet Kahrstedt devoted a long section of his work to an analysis of protections and rights of citizens which was far more than a mere catalogue; having sifted masterfully through the laws of Athens, he pointed to *patterns* of protection, for example, in the realm of private ownership, which seemed to signal the special concerns of Athenian citizens.[9] Here is a nucleus of civic ideology.

Nevertheless, the description of a study as "constitutionalist" or as "focused on institutions" nowadays commonly insinuates narrowness. In several of the essays collected here, for example, the constitutionalist perspective comes under fire: Manville selects this perspective ("that Athenian citizenship was a legal status, defined by a fixed set of juridical criteria") and the related institutional one ("that the manifestation of Athenian citizenship is primarily to be understood through institutional contexts") as two propositions belonging to an older paradigm of citizenship that is no longer tenable; Connor attacks the notion that "citizenship is best approached through law"; Patterson's essay is a full-scale demonstration of the failure of constitutionalists to account for the position of Athenian women in the public life of the polis. In earlier work, Ober has criticized the view "that we can best understand the Athenian democracy as a 'constitution' and that we can best understand this constitution, and the principles on which it was based, by analyzing the relations between formal institutions of government," and he continues with a warning that "students of Athenian history must come to grips with the constraints that these 'constitutionalist' assumptions place upon the analysis of political life."[10] When Ober examines the subject of Athenian citizenship in his essay in this volume, the subject leads him immediately to an investigation of civic ideology; one starting point for him is that "the political identity of the citizen was articulated in a civic ideology that was defined by a public discourse that was hegemonic and the source of political power for the ordinary citizen."

What accounts for the perception of earlier scholarship as being *narrowly* constitutionalist and inadequate? Clearly it is not simply due to the factors cited earlier: while it is true that *Quellenkritik* of *AP* has absorbed a great deal of scholarly attention and that older diachronic histories have not been expansive on the topic of citizenship, earlier historians have not utterly confined their studies to strictly political institutions and juridical criteria. Rather, many of the questions that are now being asked about citizenship are different from those asked sixty years ago. Interestingly, the questions derive from the same bifurcated set of interests. The explicit integration of the topic of "civic ideology" into the study of citizenship is firmly rooted in the study of the *content* of citizenship (i.e., its "rights, privileges, capacities and material advantages").[11] The study of citizenship has accordingly become more intimately connected with the study of the development of democratic ideals and of democratic sociology.[12] No longer is it sufficient, for example, to catalogue the protections and rights offered to citizens; those protections and rights must be analyzed in an explicitly articulated ideological framework and new sets of questions posed: What social, moral, and political values do they presuppose?[13] What social inequalities do they compensate or exacerbate?[14] What is the relationship of the political sphere to the social, or the public to the private—and how are these spheres defined?[15]

The last question has become increasingly important in studies of citizenship that start from the question of extent. At the heart of the matter is the meaning of the word *citizen*. When they speak of the classical age, constitutionalists frequently advert to Aristotle's definition, in *Politics* 3, that a citizen is one who shares in the offices of juror (*dikastes*) and assemblyman (*ekklesiastes*).[16] Some might add or subjoin to that definition certain obligations that citizenship so defined carried with it.[17] Others, however, might insist on broader membership and an even wider sphere of activity when they consider Aristotle's reference to Perikles' citizenship law of 451/o B.C.: "Whoever was not born of two *astoi* would

4

have no share of the *polis*" (*AP* 26.4).[18] Patterson, for example, argues that "the relevant Athenian notion is . . . that of 'sharing in' (*metechein*) the city or being a member of the Athenian family."[19] Patterson's formulation calls attention to the lack of precise and strict "political" terminology in the very law that states the requirement for citizenship: two *astoi* (not "two *politai*" or "a *polites* and a *politis*" or "a *polites* and an *aste*") produce those who share in the polis. Patterson's attention to the terminology of citizenship in the fifth and fourth centuries leads her to conclude that "while *Athenaios* (and especially *hoi Athenaioi*) and *polites* had a primarily male, political reference, *Attikos/e* and *astos/e* applied to those, male or female, with an inherited, communal and familial connection with the Athenian *polis*. Membership in the classical Athenian *polis* can be understood as a double-stranded bond, one strand built of traditional family relationships, the other of those new individual and egalitarian political relationships emphasized by Aristotle."[20] Our English word *citizenship*, then, does not do justice to the duality that Patterson has identified in the Athenian notion of citizenship. A comparison of Patterson's metaphor of the "double-stranded bond" with Sealey's formulation of two traditionally separate sets of questions suggests a major difference of perspective. The separation of family and politics, private and public, has become more problematic; it is not clear, from Patterson's perspective, that the questions of extent and content can continue to be regarded as entirely discrete.[21]

Two long-term and related factors have contributed to the broadening of citizenship studies and the articulation of its new questions. First, a shift in modern views of political systems has created a different nexus of interests, away "from institutions to extra-institutional forces such as political groups, public opinion and social structure."[22] Second, developments in anthropology and sociology over the last century have begun to have an effect on ancient historians, particularly in the fields of political history and law.[23] An organic component of both factors and a characteristic that distinguishes many current studies of citizenship is a readiness to perceive as problematic the categories (e.g., public and private, political and social, citizen and noncitizen) according to which the phenomena of ancient societies have been studied in the past.[24] The present recognition of the complex interaction of phenomena in turn corresponds with a far more self-conscious reflection on the boundaries separating modern disciplines and on the assumptions underlying them.[25] What is at stake in recent studies that have been influenced by these factors is not only the meaning of citizenship but also a view of the society inhabited by the citizen.

Historians in the last two decades who have tried to demarcate and define the political in society have come up with varying answers. In his essay "Cities of Reason," first published in 1987, Oswyn Murray took up a related and traditional question: "How rational was the Greek *polis?*"[26] Murray observed that answers to the question always seemed to fall within either (1) a Weberian tradition, which focused on the political self-consciousness of the Greeks and the separation of the principles of state organization and of political discourse from general traditional skills of community life; or (2) a Durkheimian tradition that claimed there was no absolute dividing line between public and private spheres of activity and that "the political institutions of the ancient city are to be understood in terms of the totality of forms of social interaction."[27] Murray explained this phenomenon by maintaining that the question of how rational the polis was actually involved two different (but not unconnected) questions: (1) how far the Greeks had achieved a separation of politics from other spheres, and (2) how coherent and systematic Greek thought was about political life. Depending upon which question was asked, the answer would correspond with the Weberian ("politically separatist") or Durkheimian ("holistic") tradition. Murray eschewed an approach that would apply a Durkheimian analysis to archaic society and a Weberian analysis to classical Athens. At the end of his essay, he instead embraced the holistic approach with a slight modification: the collective consciousness of the Greeks—and *not* socially refracted religion—was the central organizing principle of the polis. Viewed thus,

> we can see how it is that the *polis* dominates religion and the family and gentile structures, rituals of death, military organisation and rites of commensality; we can understand how it is that the political life of the city develops as a set of ritual practices concerned with decision-making, why tradition counts and yet is manipulated as a rational tradition. Such a viewpoint explains why there are no significant aspects of Greek culture which appear independent of its political structures, in contrast to other societies, which may be organised around different centres, such as religion or warfare, or which may have a more complex polyvalent structure.[28]

How one defines and hierarchizes the interrelationships of activities in the polis, then, will necessarily affect the portrait one paints of citizenship and civic ideology. An outstanding virtue of Murray's essay is his strenuous insistence on the validity of the questions posed by both traditions.

For the politically separatist tradition—nurtured within the bifurcation of constitutionalist historiography—is by no means an artifact of the past. Its current adherents have even been an immediate catalyst for the reception of the different perspectives and methods of other disciplines.

The strength of the politically separatist tradition lies in what might be called its faculty for the quantitative measurement of polis institutionalization in the developed Athenian democracy. Mogens H. Hansen has documented this measure more thoroughly than any earlier historian and has taken an eloquent part in contemporary debate over the significance of this phenomenon.[29] Hansen takes the most extreme separatist position: for him, the polis is coextensive with its *politai;* it is "a state, not a fusion of state and society."[30] The most concrete testimony for the absence of fusion is the evidence for clearly defined areas of Athenian life from which the operation of polis institutions was disallowed.[31] In an essay written to defend the importance of institutions for studies of democracy, Hansen ends with a glance at the broad picture of Athenian society and divides it up accordingly: "In the Greek *polis* political life was separated from social life by being the prerogative of the *politai*. In the social sphere citizens mingled with metics and often even with slaves; and some social activities were open to women as well as to men. . . . But to attend an *ekklesia* or to be a juror was a mark of honour that distinguished even a poor citizen from a rich metic. The isolationism of the citizens in the political sphere was bound up with the institutions from which women, foreigners and slaves were banned, and the isolationism underlines the importance of the political institutions."[32]

The two views of the relationship between the political and social spheres that have been adumbrated here represent the most extreme ones. Along the spectrum ranging from "total fusion" (Murray) to the "utter separation" (Hansen) of the political and the social, there are intermediary positions. Some historians have taken what might be called, for lack of any conventional term, a position of sociopolitical fluidity and linkage. While seeing significant links between the political and private spheres as holists do, these historians do not insist that the two spheres be entirely fused together in Athenian life; and while seeing gaps between the two spheres and recognizing the uniqueness of Athenian institutions as political separatists do, they do not draw a heavy black line between the political activity of a citizen and his private life. Instead, they recognize the fluidity of private and political activity in different aspects of Athenian life (e.g., law, economics, religion, art); the same phenomena will appear to be private in one context and political in another.[33] Intersections of the two, such as Patterson's identification of the double-stranded bond in Perikles' citizenship law, are of particular interest for suggesting the breadth of Athenian notions of membership in the polis and the ideology of sharing in it.

Examining links between private and public spheres in the areas of law, economics, religion, and art has proved useful for many scholars; it has produced, for example, interesting discussions of laws that have been traditionally viewed as infringements upon private freedoms, and it has considerably broadened a traditional and more restricted view of the "political."[34] In the area of law, for example, the following two claims have been made by scholars: (1) wherever legislation has the effect of regulating social conduct in a way that supports the constitutional make-up of the polis, that linkage is sociopolitical; (2) social institutions that support the *politeia* are sociopolitical. The most important law that fulfills the first criterion has already been mentioned—Perikles' law on citizenship. Laws about inheritance likewise fulfill it; such laws support the privileged position of the *polites,* reject the *nothos,* and sanction the marriage of *astos* with *aste.* The social institution of citizen marriage is sociopolitical at its core because it is at least the standard venue for the production of *politai.*[35] Another link between citizenship and what might be called, in Patterson's terminology, the public ideology of the *oikos* is evident in the *graphe moikheias* (public action for seduction and adultery): a polites who has successfully prosecuted his wife's paramour and who then does not divorce her is subject to *atimia* (disfranchisement).[36]

It is difficult to think of any of these laws as not being intimately linked with the polis and its politeia; difficult, likewise, to think of them as unimportant.[37] Considered collectively, such examples are useful in formulating a much larger view of civic ideology, a view that allows for greater interplay of the social and political, of private and public, of family and state. Other laws could likewise be brought into the picture— laws that do not so directly impinge upon the constitutional make-up of the polis, but that nevertheless, through the intersection of public and private, suggest the values of the polis and its citizens. Here we would want to include, for example, the law that forbade *epheboi* (young men who served two years of military service) from suing or being sued in court "so that they might not request leave—except in cases of disputes over inheritance and *epikleroi,* or if a priesthood hereditary in their families, became theirs" (*AP* 42.5).

While the specific links between society (or the *oikos*) and the polis suggested here are not exhaustive, they are sufficient to show that the law is a good testing rod by which to measure them. While political and social phenomena may not be completely fused in Athens, the extent of the linkages is significant enough not only to warrant investigation but also to incorporate the pathways of interrelationship into the definition of the polites as a polites.

It should be readily apparent how heuristically useful and polemically powerful these different views are for historians of citizenship and civic ideology. The essays in this volume have not been tailored to endorse one view or another. Indeed, we did not set any particular agenda—neither for the papers that were presented at the conference in 1990 nor for the additional essays that were solicited for this volume—other than that they treat issues of Athenian citizenship. Nevertheless, the range of topics attests the broad vision of the concepts of citizenship and civic ideology in a society in which the boundary between public and private is not always easily discernible. The first two essays (Manville's "Toward a New Paradigm of Athenian Citizenship" and Connor's "The Problem of Athenian Civic Identity") are critiques of the study of citizenship and expand in different directions some of the issues that have been raised here. In "Aspects of Early Athenian Citizenship," Frost examines pre-Cleisthenic notions of citizenship. In "Perikles' Citizenship Law of 451/0 B.C.," Boegehold considers social and economic motivations for the passage of that important law. The next three essays treat different aspects of civic ideology. Morris ("Everyman's Grave") and Ober ("Civic Ideology and Counterhegemonic Discourse") consider evidence for changes in that ideology in the fifth and fourth centuries—Morris by examining its visual aspect in funeral monuments, Ober by offering an interpretation of Thucydides' history as a discourse that actively resists hegemonic public discourse. On the other hand, Wallace ("Private Lives and Private Enemies") examines what might be perceived as contradictions within civic ideology, namely, alleged infringements of intellectual freedom.

With the last three essays in this volume, we turn our attention to the fourth and (possibly) early third centuries. Scafuro ("Witnessing and False Witnessing") examines the process of citizen identification in Athenian society. She links deficiencies in the bureaucratic system (i.e., that there was no central archive for birth or marriage records) with the importance attached to the appearance of witnesses at communal events and concludes that "witnessed participation in communal events as a function of being born Athenian was perceived by Athenians as tantamount to 'being Athenian.'" Patterson ("The Case against Neaira and the Public Ideology of the Athenian Family") examines the position held by women in the maintenance of civic ideology. Konstan ("Premarital Sex, Illegitimacy, and Male Anxiety in Menander and Athens") considers the relationship between sexual attitudes and civic status. The three essays have an extraordinary similarity of focus: the centrality of the oikos and its important relationship to the polis. That similarity may at first seem surprising because of the chronological spread of the material used by these authors. The orations that form much of the subject matter of Scafuro's and Patterson's essays predate what scholars call New Comedy. We do not know when Menander wrote *Epitrepontes* (the subject of Konstan's essay); while scholars usually assign the play to a late position in Menander's corpus on the grounds of its ethical refinement and mature stagecraft, those are not vital historical reasons.[38] Menander's writing career appears to have begun in the late 320s and presumably ended with his death around 290.[39] It was a period of great political change in Athens.[40] Even so, the social structures and cultural notions that are evident in fourth-century oratory have left their mark on New Comedy.[41]

Most of the essays in this volume were completed in 1991. With few exceptions, publications appearing after the early months of that year could not be taken into consideration. A note on the rationale of spelling is in order. We have, for the most part, used transliterated Greek spellings for proper names of historical individuals, fictive characters, and places (with exceptions for the most commonly used names; e.g., Athens, Corinth). We have retained conventional Latinate spellings for well-known authors and the titles of their works (with conventional inconsistencies, such as the use of English titles for some Aristophanic comedies). The more obscure authors who appear in this volume are for the most part historians and philosophers whose works are fragmentary; the titles of their works, when known, do not often have a standard Latin translation, and so we have retained Greek spellings for both author and work. We have transliterated χ as *kh* rather than *c*, except in cases where the spelling of a lesser known author has become conventional (e.g., Philochoros). We have transliterated υ as *u*, except in proper names, where we have used *y*. Adjectives based on proper or ethnic names have been anglicized (e.g., Periclean and Plataean), on the grounds that these are not Greek words. While at times the use of both Greek and Latinate spellings will undoubtedly have an odd look, it struck us as odder to Latinize all Greek names or to anglicize all place-names, including quite unfamiliar ones; hence we made our decision. Attika remains conventionally hybrid.

Notes

1. An excellent brief summary of literary and epigraphical evidence appears in Hansen 1991, 4–26. On the limitations of epigraphical evidence, see Connor 1974, 33.

2. Sealey 1983, 97.

3. On the other hand, Müller 1899 and Ledl 1907 and 1908 focus on "extent."

4. E.g., Schömann 1838 and Müller 1899 (both writing before the discovery of *AP*); Ledl 1907 and 1908; Busolt and Swoboda 1920–26; Paoli 1930, 197–339; Kahrstedt 1934.

5. Wilamowitz 1893; de Sanctis 1912; Jacoby 1949; Hignett 1952; Day and Chambers 1962. Lengthy *Quellenkritiken* of *AP* occasionally appear in dia-

chronic histories, e.g., Beloch 1926, 318–33; Busolt 1895, 32–54. For a survey of earlier scholarly views on the sources of *AP,* see Rhodes 1981, 1–58.

6. See, e.g., *CAH* V, 1927; Bengtson 1965.

7. Work that has focused (in part or entirely) on the early period: Meier 1980 and 1984; Patterson 1981; Sealey 1983; Manville 1990; and see Frost's essay in this volume.

8. Broad generalizations about the character of earlier scholarship must be fearlessly superficial and are prone to misrepresentation. The constitutional historians mentioned in n. 4 above, for example, (from whom we might, in this context, exclude Schömann), while often focused on juridical criteria, did not overlook the citizen's relationship to social organization. See further, n. 25 below. The sociological dimension of citizenship, moreover, often appears in Paoli's essays that are not specifically designated studies of citizenship (see, e.g., Paoli 1976c [= 1950]). Among early studies of institutions that contributed to the sociological or social historical dimension of citizenship: Haussoullier 1884; Glotz 1904; Sundwall 1906. Haussoullier's study, for example, focused on the activities of demesmen within deme and polis. One would be ill-advised to label such a work as the "history of an institution"—if one meant by such a designation a static and limited account of one institution's tasks and functions without regard to that institution's relationship to the community in general. The vigor of Haussoullier's account is best attested to by the absence of successors for a century until the appearance of Robin Osborne's *Demos: The Discovery of Classical Attika* (1985) and David Whitehead's magisterial *The Demes of Attica* (1986). Both works, though differing in conception and thesis, nevertheless once again reveal the potential breadth of institutional history, seeing the political dimension of demesmen as intricately connected with land tenure, religion, and family.

9. Kahrstedt 1934, 132–91.

10. Ober 1989b, 324.

11. On the problems of defining "ideology," see the succinct discussion by Strauss 1990, 101–3, citing relevant bibliography; also Ober's essay in this volume and 1989a, 38–40, where he quotes the following useful definition of "political ideology" from Washburn 1982, 261: "Individuals' relatively stable, more or less integrated set of beliefs, values, feelings, and attitudes about the nature of human beings and society and their associated orientations toward the existing distribution of social rewards, and the uses of power and authority to create, maintain, or change them."

12. E.g., Hansen 1991, 73–85, centers his discussion of democratic political ideology on liberty and equality, which involves an analysis of protections provided to citizens (due process, freedom from torture, protection of home, property, and speech). Cf. Ober 1989a, 296–99 for an astute analysis of the antithetical nature of individual freedom (esp. of speech) and political consensus, both of which he sees as components of democratic ideology; these ideas form an important foundation for his essay in this volume. The concluding section of Morris' essay here offers a different view of "egalitarian ideology" in the fifth century.

13. E.g., Raaflaub 1985, 289–93, 331–32 and 1983 sees individual political rights and freedoms as "parts of a system which can represent and guarantee freedom only as a whole" (1983, 521). He also thinks that "democratic freedom was not only political freedom but also the supreme realization of the personal freedom of the free man" (522). These observations lead him to conclude: "Democracy was the only constitution that took seriously the only qualities the poor and low-born citizen possessed, namely his citizenship and his personal freedom. Athenian 'liberties,' therefore, as far as they were perceived at all, strongly emphasized social aspects: they were as much social liberties as they were political liberties" (522 with n. 25).

14. Delineating the tension between political equality and social inequality is an important component of the analyses of Raaflaub 1983 and 1985; Meier 1988, 67–89; Ober 1989a. In his essay in this volume, Morris offers a sociological analysis of the "polis iconography" of death memorials and argues that the elite has appropriated what had previously been "polis-only symbols."

15. E.g., Osborne 1985, 6–10. Where to draw the boundary between public and private spheres of activity has become extremely important for those treating the problem of what has traditionally been viewed as the law's infringements upon the private domain. See Cohen 1991 and Wallace's essay in this volume.

16. Aristotle Politics 3.1275a 20–32. Cf. Hansen 1991, 97 with n. 119, referring to the passage in the Politics: "The principal privilege of an Athenian citizen was his political rights; in fact, they were more than just a 'privilege': they constituted the essence of citizenship. In contrast to metics and slaves, every adult male Athenian citizen had the right to attend the Assembly, and every Athenian citizen over thirty the further right to be a magistrate (arche) or a legislator (nomothetes) or a juror (dikastes)." Cf. Kahrstedt 1934, 129.

17. E.g., Kahrstedt 1934, 130–32; Sinclair 1988, 49–76 points out that the terms "obligations" and "responsibilities" should "not be interpreted too narrowly"; a "whole complex of personal, religious and social reasons" (53) is involved. Hansen 1991, 99–101 makes the interesting observation that "neither military service nor liability to taxation was a duty exclusive to citizens, for metics also had to do military service and pay the property tax." He then points out that "the only duties devolving exclusively on citizens were in the sphere of marriage, certain kinds of personal conduct and family life" and indicates specifically what these duties were. In the realm of family life, he points out that it was an offense for a citizen to squander his ancestral wealth and to neglect the duties owed his parents. He concludes: "Here the Athenian state was, indeed, legislating about private conduct, but these were all matters which, though private, directly affected the maintenance and quality of the citizen body." Hansen's observations are a very precise pinpointing of an important intersection of private and political life.

18. [Aristotle] AP 26.4: καὶ τρίτωι μετὰ τοῦτον ἐπὶ Ἀντιδότου διὰ τὸ πλῆθος τῶν πολιτῶν Περικλέους εἰπόντος ἔγνωσαν μὴ μετέχειν τῆς πόλεως ὃς ἂν μὴ ἐξ ἀμφοῖν ἀστοῖν ἦι γεγονώς.

19. Patterson 1987, 49. Manville 1990, 7 (and cf. 13–14) also calls attention to the generality of the Aristotelian statement "sharing in the *polis*," but without drawing the same set of implications as Patterson.

20. Patterson 1987, 50 (see also Patterson 1981, 161–76). Patterson's observation has a firm root in constitutionalist historiography; consider Busolt and Swoboda 1920–26, 954: "Das erste soziale Element der athenischen Bürgerschaft war nach gemeingriechischem Gewohnheits- und Gesetzesrecht die auf der rechten Ehe mit einer förmlich 'in die Hand gegebenen' Ehefrau beruhende Familien- und Hausgenossenschaft (1:239)"; and Kahrstedt 1934, 269: "Der stark zurückgedrängten Stellung der Familie im öffentlichen Recht entspricht es, dass die Frau unmittelbar mit staatlichen Organen in Berührung kommt und dass der Staat allenthalben von ihr Notiz nimmt. Wie o. S. 61ff. gesehen, ist seit dem Bürgergesetz des 5. Jhdts. bei der Bestimmung des politischen Standes des Sohnes die Mutter ebenso wichtig wie der Vater." Where Patterson opens up a new perspective is in her questioning of the oikos sphere as an essentially private one; hence the radicalness of her phrase, used in the title of her essay in this volume.

21. In recent literature on democracy, there is a tendency to minimalize treatment of the family and of the extent of citizenship and to focus attention on political institutions and ideology. See, e.g., Bleicken 1986; Sinclair 1988; Hansen 1991. Sealey 1987 is somewhat exceptional in this regard, with a chapter (pp. 5–31) devoted to these issues. On the other hand, the past two decades have seen a profusion (in comparison with the past) of books on women. The traditional bifurcation of studies still reigns.

22. See Hansen 1989a (the quote appears on p. 107); Ober 1989a and 1989b.

23. Humphreys 1985; Todd and Millett 1990, 14–18, with notes citing relevant bibliography.

24. Schmitt-Pantel 1990, for example, has designated certain activities such as the *symposion* and religious celebrations as "collective activities" that belong to the "common domain" (*koinon*) of polis society. While in archaic societies such activities are part of the concept of citizenship, in fifth-century Athens, they lie "neither in the political sphere (political life is only one of the elements of the common domain), nor in the private domain (*idion*)." For Schmitt-Pantel, "these collective activities are part of the *koina* which define a city without constituting its political requirements" (208) Whether we agree with Schmitt-Pantel's final assessment, her work demonstrates how important and reflective the question of boundaries has become. Indeed, the observations of the fluidity of the collective, the private, and the political lead the author to call for historians to see "the points of contact between areas normally regarded as different, such as the history of institutions, political history, social history, and the history of customs and behaviour" (211). On the significance of the public/private boundary in other recent discussions: Humphreys 1978, 193–202; 1983c and d; Foley 1981; Saxonhouse 1983 and 1992, 9–15; Musti 1985; Hansen 1989b, 1990, 231–33, and 1991, 79–81; Strauss 1990; Cohen

1991, 70–97. Moore 1984, 81–167 is amateurish and somewhat ignorant on points of fourth-century history, but collects many useful passages from the orators.

25. Humphreys 1985, 241–42 calls attention to the history of the formation of different disciplines; after pointing out that a number of important nineteenth-century scholars (such as Bachofen, Maine, Fustel de Coulanges, Morgan, McLennan) worked "in the borderland between history and law," she writes: "The idea that differences between societies and changes in social structure could be studied under the rubric of 'constitutional law' had, of course, a long history before Savigny began to write. . . . The nineteenth century had widened this perspective to include kinship and family, economic institutions and, as Maine said, the 'whole view of life' of past societies. Though we look back now to the second half of the nineteenth century as the period when some of the basic principles round which modern academic disciplines organise their identities were formulated, we must remember that it was an age of holistic purviews rather than hard boundaries. Philosophy, psychology, economics, law, history and sociology were closely interconnected. The passage from unselfconscious assumptions about the nature of man and society to formal theory was taking place in parallel along different axes of thought; changes in contemporary society, the educational system and the organisation of the professions provided a common background and plenty of opportunities for the exchange of ideas." It is more than mildly amusing that Foucault, subverter of academic taxonomies, took as his starting point in *The Order of Things* a passage from Borges, purporting to be a classification of animals from "a certain Chinese encyclopaedia."

26. The essay was later published in a volume edited by Murray and Price (1990). The later publication does not contain the appendix with Hansen's useful comments, some of which (see esp. "g" and "h") attempt to refute Murray's most persuasive arguments in behalf of the holistic approach. References to the essay in nn. 27 and 28 are to the later publication.

27. Murray 1990, 5–6. Fustel de Coulanges is sometimes mentioned as the head of this tradition (e.g., Hansen 1991, 61); for his influence on Durkheim and other sociologists and social anthropologists, see Humphreys 1983b, 140, and, more extensively, Lukes 1977, 58–63.

28. Murray 1990, 19.

29. A long list of Hansen's works are conveniently found in the bibliography of Hansen 1991.

30. Hansen 1989b, 17–21 (reiterated in 1991, 61–62); the quote is from p. 21. In this short treatise, Hansen addresses the issue of "separation" and asks: "Did the Athenians distinguish a public sphere from a private sphere, in which the democratic *polis* did not interfere, but allowed the citizens to live as they pleased?" (17). With some qualifications that are discounted, Hansen answers that indeed they did. The conclusion is derived from an explicit equation of the public sphere with the political sphere that is limited to *politai* acting in a narrowly defined "political" way. Hansen's view of the "political" tends toward the literal: social institutions are only political if they are run by the state. The

religious sphere is somewhat problematic; while admitting that "most of the cult festivals were organized by the *polis*' magistrates and connected with the *polis*," Hansen adds, by way of countering that admission, "but foreigners and slaves were mostly allowed to participate, and it is important to remember that the priests (*hiereis*) were not state officials (*archai*)" (21). The polis' interest in regulating religious belief is perhaps most notable through the availability of the *graphe asebeias;* see Cohen 1991, 203–17, and Wallace's essay in this volume.

31. Hansen 1989b, 12 lists regulations that "protected a citizen's person, his property and his home against violations inflicted by the *polis* and its officials." Cf. Cohen 1991, 218–40.

32. Hansen 1989a, 113. Meier 1990, 140–54 similarly presents a separatist view. In the context of his concepts of "political identity" and "civic presence," he writes: "A precondition for politics of this kind was that everything outside the political sphere be exempt from political control. The economy and society, educational conditions and religion, were quite simply given; they could not be subject to decision making and so provide a focus for the formation of factions. And they remained for the most part unchanged. It followed that all generally relevant change, that is, change that was of importance to everybody, was political" (152). And later, on the same page of meditation, he adds: "Because they [the citizens of Athens] politicized themselves, there could be no politicizing of their nonpolitical interests. Besides the *polis* virtually nothing existed except the house." Similarly, Meier 1988, 80–82.

33. David Cohen's illuminating discussion of the private and public dichotomy in his study *Law, Sexuality, and Society* might serve as the basis for some of these observations. He has pointed out that "Athenian sources express a gender-oriented distinction between public and private both in terms of persons, places, and, more abstractly, spheres of life." As for individuals, they distinguish between "private citizens" and "political leaders." As for spatial dimensions, they distinguish between "public space," where men gathered (e.g., the *ekklesia, boule, agora*) and "private space," which is largely viewed as "female." As for "spheres of life," "public" and "private" are not binary opposites (so that everything outside the house is viewed as "public"), but rather are "relational concepts standing in a 'complementary opposition' to one another." While the private sphere of life begins with the oikos, it can be represented as extending far beyond it. Likewise, the public sphere of life can extend beyond a narrow limitation to political leadership to include "the obligations of the citizen to the city" (77)—obligations that in one context might be portrayed as "public" and in another "private." A sociopolitical analysis such as Cohen's does not look for any absolute line that will distinguish the public and private in every aspect of society, but recognizes its fluidity.

34. For legal infringements and private freedoms, see Cohen 1991; for intersections of the political and private spheres with a considerable broadening of view of the former, see Humphreys 1983c and d (with important regard for variations in different periods); Goldhill 1986, 57–78; Strauss 1990.

35. Humphreys (who is interested in gaps as well as links between the two

spheres) 1983c, 4–5 likewise notes these laws (among others) as impinging upon the oikos. I am more concerned here with laws relating to the oikos that specifically support the constitution.

36. Cohen 1991, 122–25 has suggested that there may have been no public action for *moikheia;* he maintains that the *graphe moikheias* cited by [Aristotle] *AP* 59.3 in a partial list of *graphai* is the only classical source for the *graphe.* Rather than interpreting that graphe as a reference to an indictment that is not attested elsewhere, Cohen prefers to interpret it as an abbreviated reference to the graphe against the unlawful detention of an individual as a *moikhos* ([Dem.] 59 *Neaera* 66). Cohen is right in pointing out that there is no classical reference to a graphe moikheias to which a *definition* of the indictment is attached, and his argument is a salutary reminder of the often tenuous basis of our evidence for ancient Greek laws. But his argument is vitiated by his equation of the graphe moikheias of *AP* 59.3 with the law paraphrased in [Dem.] 59 *Neaera* 66. Anyone's careful reading of the latter law will show that the former citation cannot be a shorthand reference to it. Acceptance of the existence of the graphe moikheias does not, however, destroy Cohen's general argument about the law's treatment of sexual transgressions in Athens, that it only stepped in when "public order" was transgressed. "Public order" is transgressed by the (potential and deceptive) admission of nothoi into the citizenship body and among the legitimate heirs of the oikos. On the significance of nothoi in related contexts, see Konstan's essay in this volume.

37. Judgments about the relative importance of types of activity within the polis often appear in the historiography of citizenship. See, e.g., Meier 1990, 152, quoted in n. 32 above, and also Hansen 1989a, 113, quoted in the text above.

38. On the lack of data for dating this play, see Arnott 1979, 383–84.

39. For an excellent and succinct discussion of the dates of Menander's life and works, see Arnott 1979, xiii–xix.

40. On political change in Athens during this period, see Ferguson 1911 and Habicht 1979. On the functioning of law courts during this period, see Boegehold 1994, chap. 4.

41. This thesis plays an important role in many of Paoli's essays; see, e.g., Paoli 1976b and c; also Scafuro (n.d.).

Works Cited

Arnott, W. G. 1979. *Menander.* Vol. I. Cambridge, Mass.: Harvard University Press.

Beloch, Karl Julius. 1926. *Griechische Geschichte*² 1.2. Berlin and Leipzig: Walter de Gruyter.

Bengtson, Hermann. 1965. *Griechische Geschichte von den Anfängen bis in die römische Kaiserzeit*³. Munich: C. H. Beck'sche Verlagsbuchhandlung.

Bleicken, Jochen. 1986. *Die athenische Demokratie.* Paderborn: Ferdinand Schöningh Verlag.

Boegehold, Alan L. 1994. *Lawcourts at Athens: Sites, Buildings, Equipment, Procedure, and Testimonia.* Agora 28. Princeton. Forthcoming.

Busolt, Georg. 1895. *Griechische Geschichte bis zur Schlacht bei Chaeroneia.* 2². Gotha: Perthes.

Busolt, Georg, and Heinrich Swoboda. 1920–26. *Griechische Staatskunde.* 2 vols. Munich: C. H. Beck'sche Verlagsbuchhandlung.

Cohen, David. 1991. *Law, Sexuality, and Society: The Enforcement of Morals in Classical Athens.* Cambridge: Cambridge University Press.

Connor, W. Robert. 1974. "The Athenian Council: Method and Focus in Some Recent Scholarship." *CJ* 70:32–41.

Day, James, and Mortimer Chambers. 1962. *Aristotle's History of Athenian Democracy.* Vol. 73. University of California Publications in History. Berkeley: University of California Press.

de Sanctis, G. 1912. *Atthis: Storia della reppubblica Ateniese dalla origini alla eta di Pericle².* Turin: Bocca.

Ferguson, William S. 1911. *Hellenistic Athens.* London: MacMillan.

Foley, Helene P. 1981. "The Conception of Women in Athenian Drama." In *Reflections on Women in Antiquity,* edited by Helene P. Foley, 127–68. New York: Gordon and Breach Science Publications.

Foucault, Michel. 1970. *The Order of Things.* Translated by Alan Sheridan. London: Tavistock; New York: Pantheon. Originally published in 1966 as *Les mots et les choses.* Paris: Gallimard.

Glotz, Gustave. 1904. *La Solidarité de la Famille dans le Droit Criminel en Grèce.* Paris: Albert Fontemoing.

Goldhill, Simon. 1986. *Reading Greek Tragedy.* Cambridge: Cambridge University Press.

Habicht, Christian. 1979. *Untersuchungen zur politischen Geschichte Athens im 3. Jahrhundert v. Chr.* Munich: C. H. Beck'sche Verlagsbuchhandlung.

Hansen, Mogens H. 1987. *The Athenian Assembly in the Age of Demosthenes.* Oxford: Basil Blackwell.

———. 1989a. "On the Importance of Institutions in an Analysis of Athenian Democracy." *ClMed* 40:107–13.

———. 1989b. *Was Athens a Democracy? Popular Rule, Liberty and Equality in Ancient and Modern Political Thought.* Historisk-Filosofiske Meddelelser 59. Copenhagen: Royal Danish Academy of Sciences and Letters.

———. 1990. "The Political Powers of the People's Court in Fourth-Century Athens." In Murray and Price 1990:215–43.

———. 1991. *The Athenian Democracy in the Age of Demosthenes: Structures, Principles, and Ideology.* Oxford: Basil Blackwell.

Haussoullier, Bernard. 1884. *La Vie Municipale en Attique: Essai sur l'organisation des dèmes au quatrième siècle.* Paris.

Hignett, Charles. 1952. *A History of the Athenian Constitution to the End of the Fifth Century.* Oxford: Clarendon Press.

Humphreys, Sally C. 1978. *Anthropology and the Greeks.* London: Routledge and Kegan Paul.

17

————. 1983a. *The Family, Women, and Death: Comparative Studies.* London: Routledge and Kegan Paul.

————. 1983b. "Fustel de Coulanges, The Ancient City. Part II." In Humphreys 1983a:136–44.

————. 1983c. "*Oikos* and *Polis.*" In Humphreys 1983a:1–21.

————. 1983d. "Public and Private Interests in Classical Athens." In Humphreys 1983a:22–32.

————. 1985. "Law as Discourse." *History and Anthropology* 1:241–64.

Jacoby, Felix. 1949. *Atthis: The Local Chronicles of Ancient Athens.* Oxford: Clarendon Press.

Kahrstedt, Ulrich. 1934. *Staatsgebiet und Staatsangehörige in Athen. Studien zum öffentlichen Recht Athens.* Stuttgart-Berlin: Verlag W. Kohlhammer.

Ledl, Artur. 1907. "Das attische Bürgerrecht und die Frau I." *WS* 29:173–227.

————. 1908. "Das attische Bürgerrecht und die Frau II." *WS* 30:1–46.

————. 1908. "Das attische Bürgerrecht und die Frau III." *WS* 30:173–230.

Lukes, Steven. 1977. *Emile Durkheim: His Life and Work.* Middlesex, Eng.: Harmondsworth; New York: Penguin Books.

Manville, Philip Brook. 1990. *The Origins of Citizenship in Ancient Athens.* Princeton: Princeton University Press.

Meier, Christian. 1984. *Introduction à l'anthropologie politique de l'antiquité classique.* Paris: Presses Universitaires de France.

————. 1988. "Bürger-Identität und Demokratie." In *Kannten die Griechen die Demokratie?* 47–95. Berlin: Verlag Klaus Wagenbach.

————. 1990. *The Greek Discovery of Politics.* Translated by David McLintock. Cambridge, Mass.: Harvard University Press. First published in 1980 as *Die Entstehung des Politischen bei den Griechen.* Frankfurt am Main: Suhrkamp Verlag.

Moore, Barrington. 1984. *Privacy: Studies in Social and Cultural History.* Armonk, N.Y.: M. E. Sharpe.

Müller, O. 1899. "Untersuchungen zur Geschichte des attischen Bürger- und Eherechts." *Jahrbücher für classische Philologie* Suppl. 25:661–866.

Murray, Oswyn. 1990. "Cities of Reason." In Murray and Price 1990:1–25. First published in 1987, in *Archives Européennes de Sociologie—European Journal of Sociology* 28:325–46 (including comments by Mogens H. Hansen, pp. 341–45).

Murray, Oswyn, and Simon Price, eds. 1990. *The Greek City from Homer to Alexander.* Oxford: Clarendon Press.

Musti, D. 1985. "Pubblico e privato nella democrazia periclea." *Quaderni Urbinati,* n.s., 20:7–15.

Ober, Josiah. 1989a. *Mass and Elite in Democratic Athens: Rhetoric, Ideology, and the Power of the People.* Princeton: Princeton University Press.

————. 1989b. Review of Hansen (1987). "The Nature of Athenian Democracy." *CP* 84:322–34.

Osborne, Robin. 1985. *Demos: The Discovery of Classical Attika.* Cambridge: Cambridge University Press.

Paoli, Ugo Enrico. 1930. "Lo stato di cittadinànza in atene." In *Studi di diritto attico*, 197–339. Florence: R. Bemporad and Son.

————. 1976a. *Altri studi di diritto greco e romano*. With an introduction by Arnaldo Biscardi. Milan: Istituto Editoriale Cisalpino—La Goliardica.

————. 1976b. "Comici latini e diritto attico." In Paoli 1976a:31–78. First published in 1962 in *Quaderni di Studi Senesi* 8:iv–82.

————. 1976c. "Il reato di adulterio (*moikheia*) in diritto attico." In Paoli 1976a:251-308. First published in 1950, *SDHI* 16:123 ff.

Patterson, Cynthia. 1981. *Pericles' Citizenship Law of 451–0 B.C.* New York: Arno Press. Reprint. Salem, N.H.: Ayer, 1987.

————. 1987. "*Hai Attikai:* The Other Athenians." *Helios* 13:49–67.

————. 1990. "Those Athenian Bastards." *CA* 9:40–73.

Raaflaub, Kurt. 1983. "Democracy, Oligarchy, and the Concept of 'Free Citizen' in Late Fifth-Century Athens." *Political Theory* 11:517–44.

————. 1985. *Die Entdeckung der Freiheit*. Vestigia. Vol. 37. Munich: C. H. Beck'sche Verlagsbuchhandlung.

Rhodes, Peter J. 1981. *A Commentary on the Aristotelian* Athenaion Politeia. Oxford: Clarendon Press.

Saxonhouse, Arlene W. 1983. "Classical Greek Conceptions of Public and Private." In *Public and Private in Social Life*, edited by S. I. Bean and G. F. Gauss, 363–84. London: Croom Helm; New York: St. Martin's Press.

————. 1992. *Fear of Diversity: The Birth of Political Science in Ancient Greek Thought*. Chicago: University of Chicago Press.

Scafuro, Adele C. n.d. *The Forensic Stage: Settling Disputes in Graeco-Roman New Comedy*. Cambridge: Cambridge University Press. Forthcoming.

Schmitt-Pantel, Pauline. 1990. "Collective Activities and the Political in the Greek City." In Murray and Price 1990:199–214.

Schömann, G. F. 1838. *A Dissertation on the Assemblies of the Athenians*. Translation of *De Comitiis Atheniensium*, 1819. Cambridge: W. P. Grant.

Sealey, Raphael. 1983. "How Citizenship and the City Began in Athens." *AJAH* 8:97–129.

————. 1987. *The Athenian Republic*. University Park: Pennsylvania State Press.

Sinclair, R. K. 1988. *Democracy and Participation in Athens*. Cambridge: Cambridge University Press.

Strauss, Barry S. 1990. "*Oikos/Polis:* Towards a Theory of Athenian Paternal Ideology 450–399 B.C." In *Aspects of Athenian Democracy. Classica et Mediaevalia. Dissertationes* 11, 101–27. Copenhagen: Museum Tusculanum Press.

Sundwall, Johannes. 1906. *Epigraphische Beiträge zur sozial-politischen Geschichte Athens im Zeitalter des Demosthenes. Klio* Beiheft 4.

Todd, Stephen, and Paul Millett. 1990. "Law, Society and Athens." In *Nomos: Essays in Athenian Law, Politics and Society*, edited by Paul Cartledge, Paul Millett, and Stephen Todd, 1–18. Cambridge: Cambridge University Press.

Washburn, Philo C. 1982. *Political Sociology: Approaches, Concepts, Hypotheses.* Englewood Cliffs, N.J.: Prentice-Hall.
Whitehead, David. 1986. *The Demes of Attica 508/7–ca. 250 B.C.* Princeton: Princeton University Press.
Wilamowitz-Moellendorff, Ulrich von. 1893. *Aristoteles und Athen.* Berlin: Weidmann.

Toward a New Paradigm
of Athenian Citizenship

PHILIP BROOK MANVILLE

This essay describes an approach and a set of conceptualizing assumptions for understanding ancient Athenian citizenship. It attempts to identify a new paradigm, representing an emerging set of ideas about this topic, and describes a decided shift from an older paradigm. Readers of my recent *Origins of Athenian Citizenship* will recognize much of what follows, but it is not my aim here to restate and defend the book's several propositions, nor merely to rename them as "a new paradigm."[1] Instead, I would like to sketch out an evolving conceptual framework, indeed represented in my book, but also perceptible to varying degrees throughout the work of many other scholars (and typically those "on whose shoulders I have gratefully stood"). Understanding both the old and new paradigms can be a mirror for all of us that we may better understand Athenian citizenship per se, and further, the boundaries of our historical thinking, past, present, and future.

The first task is to be clear about the terminology and meaning of "paradigms" and the like. A good starting point, and the inspiration for much of my own thinking, is the recent work of Josiah Ober.[2] In various publications, Ober has argued that historians inevitably use—consciously or unconsciously—models to explain the past. As Ober suggests, in the same way that a map models a geographical region, so does any historical narrative or analysis impose some model (or models) upon past events and phenomena. Every model necessarily carries with it what Ober calls an ideology: "assumptions about human nature and behavior, opinions on morality and ethics, general political principles, and attitudes towards social relations."[3] By means of models, historians endeavor to explain various aspects of past societies and relate them to current phenomena.

The heuristic usefulness of the models chosen will determine the degree to which any piece of historical work will be seen as relevant and meaningful today.

As Ober further holds, historical analysis and narrative usually imply not one but several explanatory models, which, when integrated, can be described as a paradigm. Borrowing from Thomas Kuhn's analysis of scientific knowledge, Ober proposes that the history of historical knowledge in any one field is a progression of paradigms: practitioners adhere to the current dominant paradigm until a new one emerges and the old is discarded.[4] For scientists, the evolution of the new paradigm is a response to mounting new data that does not fit the old. The danger for ancient historians, as Ober argues, is that our discipline does not include a large enough flow of new data to force with any frequency the development of new paradigms, and therefore the clearing and pruning of the old. For ancient history, staleness is an occupational hazard, and we would do well to reflect periodically upon the freshness and relevance of those paradigms that are by tradition held dear.

What, then, is the prevailing paradigm of Athenian citizenship? Scholarly thought about the topic is in transition. Although the new paradigm seems to be gaining adherents, the influence of what I am calling the old paradigm remains strong. Charting the shift is made all the more difficult because the transition I am postulating is not black and white: most of the work in this area falls somewhere along a spectrum between end points represented by the two paradigms. Furthermore, the field under consideration needs to be defined rather broadly because almost any research on Athenian government or society embodies, at least implicitly, a set of assumptions about citizenship: what it was, what it meant to Athenians, and "how it worked."

It is not my purpose here to segment and quantify all categories of historians' mind-sets on this topic, or to navigate through all the gradations of various assumption sets. At the risk of simplifying generalization, I nonetheless propose that we can identify a loosely coordinated set of models and ideologies in much of the older scholarship; and, similarly, that over the last decade or so those models and ideologies have begun to give way to another set that are quite different. To highlight the change, I will first sketch and comment upon the older paradigm. The following are some of the main tenets of this habit of thought:

1. *Athenian citizenship was a legal status, defined by a fixed set of juridical criteria.* Clearly, certain characteristics and activities separated Athenians from non-Athenians in the classical age. But how sharply, and when were the lines drawn? And when we talk of precise legal distinctions are we fairly coloring the nature of "law" itself in the Attic commu-

nity? Generations of scholars have thought so, and with these assumptions have labored against such "problems" as the hierarchy of legal privilege between *gene* and phratries, whether bastards (i.e., those born out of wedlock to two Athenian parents) were Athenian citizens, and whether all Athenian citizens after the reforms of Kleisthenes (508/7) "were required" or "not required" to belong to phratries as well as demes.[5] As is increasingly understood, however, the historical task in each of these (and other comparable) cases may not be to refine relentlessly and more subtly the limited evidence to find "the answer," but rather to ask whether inquiry based upon hard-edged constructs, concise distinctions, and legal requirements indeed represents the appropriate set of questions.[6]

2. *Athenian citizenship was an individual identity representing privileges and protection in opposition to an impersonal entity, the "state."* In its most extreme form, this model can be seen in the work of those Marxist commentators who portray the Athenian "state" as an agent of control, dominated by a ruling elite who wield power over the means of production.[7] The same idea in more moderate form underlies the "traditional liberal" view of democracy protecting the individual from the encroachment of the state.[8] In the majority of contemporary treatments some of this mentality almost always creeps in, even if the historian may concede that the polis and the citizens were one and the same and that the polis was not a "state" in the modern sense of the word, but rather a unique kind of sociopolitical organization.[9] Despite such assurances from commentators, falling into the trap of the language, as well as the thinking, of politics in the modern state is common; the framework assumed is one of an adversarial relationship between individuals and authority, with an essentially negative portrayal of an omnipotent and impersonal bureaucracy. Thus, in otherwise sensible treatments, one reads such comments as "the public laws of Solon led . . . to greater control of the polis over the lives of its inhabitants," hears of "personal liberty" as a principle established by "the Athenian political experience," or finds citizenship linked to discussions of "public authority in the state."[10]

3. *The manifestation of Athenian citizenship is primarily to be understood through institutional contexts.* This assumption, well challenged by Ober, pervades the scholarship that approaches Athenian history from the standpoint of its "constitution" and "government bodies."[11] Inevitably, it stresses the political over the social or, in the extreme, excludes the latter altogether in representing the polis. The perspective defines the citizenry primarily in terms of its access and privileges in governing entities (*ekklesia, boule,* archonship, etc.) and the role of such entities in determining political sovereignty. Overall, the approach reflects the

"active" side of the model of citizenship and is complemented by the view that *politeia* in its passive aspect was a purely legal status. The challenge of the historian here is not to deny the importance of law and institutions in the structuring of society, but rather to ask whether such things should be seen as the sole or even critical determinants of the phenomenon of citizenship.

4. *Although many Athenian citizens concerned themselves with moral issues, citizenship in general was a value-free concept.* This assumption is a strong corollary of the view that citizenship was primarily a legal construction, which in turn stems from our modern assumptions—alien to most of Greek culture—that law and morality are strictly distinct spheres. In this spirit, many standard handbooks on Greek institutions and law treat citizenship in a moral vacuum.[12] Similarly, when scholars describe the "rights" and "responsibilities" of citizenship, their discussion is often couched in terms of statutory obligations rather than moral action grounded in social norms. Thus, Athenians "had to serve in the army" or "were expected to attend the democratic assembly," rather than "did so to improve themselves and the polis that they comprised."[13] Once again, this mentality can be traced to an essentially negative view of the "state." An analogous perspective can be found in one scholarly initiative that tried to strip the concept of justice—clearly central to the concept of the polis—of all moral connotations.[14] By that view, citizen participation in the courts was only an objectively legal exercise.

For the sake of a label, we might describe the paradigm characterized by these kinds of assumptions as the "modern and inorganic." At the theoretical extreme, it frames Athenian citizenship in terms that are rational, value-free, and relatively static. This paradigm understands events in a world supposed to be orderly and formally hierarchical, in which the private sphere is sharply and meaningfully distinguished from the public, and in which that public sphere is largely known through the struggle for institutional power, with legal milestones standing as the mark of success for those striving for sovereignty. Politics and law stand in contrast to society and are similarly divorced from morality.

Over the last several years, in contrast, the new paradigm that has begun to emerge is one that we might now call the "premodern and organic." This paradigm is a habit of thought that sees Athenian citizenship spanning both *politics* (in the contemporary sense of the word) and society; it is grounded in a world in which the private sphere is often difficult to distinguish from, and frequently overlaps with, the public.[15] In the premodern and organic, there is no abstract "state"; citizenship and the polis are one and the same, growing out of a dynamic and constantly evolving association of families and kinship groups. Although the "true citizens" are the adult Athenian males, their political life is constantly shadowed by their networks of social relations. As the label I have given it suggests, the paradigm understands the Athenian polis with an ideology comparable to that represented by anthropological studies of preindustrial societies: a simpler world with minimal bureaucracy, defined by personal interactions, and a continuing interplay of people, ideas, and sociopolitical structures.[16]

The new paradigm is less rational, as well as looser for its greater tolerance of inconsistency and sometimes fuzzy boundaries. Its more tendentious proponents—and here I count myself—further assume that intangible values and moral principles offset the lack of sharp legal boundaries while also informing a collective spirit of the society.[17] Thus it portrays laws not as purely negative preventions but as guidelines with moral purpose that ultimately reflect and define shared values of the members of the political community. Citizenship by this view, synonymous with the life of the polis, was not value-free, but aimed at some common good. Similarly, political activity was not a simple struggle for power, but rather, at least as the democratic ideal evolved, was seen to benefit the individuals who engaged themselves and thus, at the same time, to benefit the overall association of citizens.

To provide some further texture to the difference between the paradigms as I have described them, let us look briefly at three traditional turning points in the history of Athenian citizenship: Solon's establishment of *tele* in 594/3, the Cleisthenic revolution of 508/7, and Perikles' citizenship law of 451/0. It will be instructive to look at representative approaches to each of these events which are indicative of the two paradigms.

According to Aristotle and other sources, in the year of his archonship, Solon divided the Athenian population into four economically based groupings, or tele.[18] Under the old paradigm, these tele represented a new distribution of political rights throughout society, awarding privilege on the basis of wealth rather than aristocratic birth. The tele, determined according to "measures dry or liquid," are portrayed as centrally measured categories that reallocated most of the power of government from aristocrats by birth to "new men" of wealth and, through the wider conferral of political prerogatives, began a constitutional movement toward (eventual) democracy.[19] By the new paradigm, however, the tele were sociopolitical segments of society that, taken as a whole, represented a new definition of the polis, and thus citizenship. The degree of public participation indeed varied according to wealth, but distinctions were imprecise and were even left to citizens themselves to determine (or defend) through public process. The case has been made, for example, that only the *pentakosiomedimnoi* were defined in terms of produce and that military classifications—perhaps the *hippeis* and *zeugitai*—were self-selected by individuals according to their patriotism.[20] If we accept this framework, duty rather than illegality became the key issue; those who aspired to offices beyond their means were prevented only by the civic challenge of their fellow citizens. Thus the approval or censure of the community, rather than some tax assessor's measurement, determined eligibility—and how indeed the community would govern itself.[21]

In 508/7, in the aftermath of the collapse of the Peisistratid tyranny and ensuing factional strife between aristocratic factions, Kleisthenes "took the people into partnership," *apodidous toi plethei ten politeian* (which I have translated as "by rendering to all Athenians what was their due: citizenship").[22] The reforms that emerged through the course of this revolution are seen by the old paradigm as either the fruits of a conniving leader intending to break the geographic, tribally based political power of his rivals, or, under the cry of *isonomia,* another decisive step toward the democratic government of the fifth century (or some similar combination of these two interpretations).[23] The new paradigm instead stresses socio-political evolution, as well as the organization of demes and new public bodies that better provided for the definition and participation of a community marked by demographic or spiritual change over the preceding generations.[24] The old paradigm looks at a leader and his motives in simply creating institutions; the new emphasizes the overall renewal of a society, with institutions reflecting the social and ideological transformation of the community. The new paradigm does not reject political change, but rather views it in the broader context of *politics* in the Greek sense of the word: the world of the polis. New people and new ideas had changed what the community was, so the community had to change the basis by which it organized itself.

Under the old paradigm, Perikles' law of 451/0 has similarly been told as a tale of narrow political manipulation or legal renegotiation.[25] That is, the law determining Athenian citizenship on the basis of birth from two Athenian parents is seen as a shift in the statutory requirement of citizenship from one set of criteria to another, motivated by a leader determined to thwart political opponents born of mixed marriages, or by the collective impulse of a high-riding *demos* jealous of sharing its impe-rial perks with current or future "half-breeds" (or again, some combina-tion of these or similar explanations). The new paradigm sees the law in a wider setting, with less of a cynical and modern-style set of motives at work. The personal aim of Perikles the politician is put aside as separate and less important than the consciousness and behavior of the general community that accepted him as their leader. The law itself becomes less significant than the thought processes of the citizens that would lead to its being either enforced or ignored—an interpretation we may call ideological.[26]

By this view, Aristotle's explanation of the measure, *dia to plethos ton politon* ("because of the mass of citizens," *AP* 26.4), is taken at face value and is read to represent several interconnected motives reflective of the subsurface attitudes and beliefs of polis ideology. The new paradigm thus stresses the complexity of group feelings and values—on the assumption that ideology emerging from people's everyday social, economic, and political experience superseded that derived from any ruling elite.[27] In the premodern and organic world of the polis, men would vote to restrict citizenship more tightly—not a shift from one set of legal criteria to another, but rather a movement toward a group-established definition of the polis that was more bounded and socially homogeneous than the previous form of the community.

It has been shown that the Attic population had been growing in the first half of the fifth century, and there is sufficient evidence for irregularity and lack of controls about non-Athenians becoming citizens to paint a scenario of perceived—irrespective of absolute numbers—encroachments by "outsiders."[28] What the new paradigm focuses on, however, is an apparent and gradual breakdown of group values. Thus the people's willingness to support the measure stemmed from anxiety not only about sharing perks but also about losing the small scale of the political association that allowed for meaningful and beneficial public activity by every citizen. Athenians were becoming too many in number, as Aristotle says. Therefore, the intangible as well as the tangible benefits of polis life were at risk when the community grew too big. Here, we see that in the premodern and the organic, law is interpreted in terms of ideology; in the modern and the inorganic, it is vice versa.

The skeptic will say that this "new paradigm" represents no more than the swing of the pendulum from legal and political history through the extremes of anthropologically guided social history and back to a midpoint that happily combines the two; it is more "heuristically useful" only because it better fits the available evidence.[29] Others will say that there is no new paradigm, but really only a rediscovery, now with more professional trappings, of broader-based ideas about the polis from an earlier age of historical inquiry.[30] I will not deny that each of these points of view has its merit. But whatever label we choose to use—if not a "new paradigm," perhaps "social history revisionism" or "back-to-basics generalism"—a shift of thinking in the current generation of scholarship seems very clear. And the reason is that the new (or renewed) paradigm may have greater resonance than the old for the lives of thoughtful students of citizenship today. Some speculation about why that might be so is appropriate.

We live in a world with an expanding enthusiasm for the concept of democracy, surrounded as we are by the collapse of totalitarian regimes and many new countries' search for a viable form of government. It is also a world in which more mature democracies, such as we have in the United States, are being questioned for their accountability and effectiveness. In such a world, it is hard to think about the Athenian polis without thinking about one's own citizenship, as well as the nature and meaning of membership in a democratic political entity. The new paradigm, with its focus on social and ideological issues in addition to legal prerogatives, may represent an ideal more keenly in tune with the interests of today's historically minded observers.

As the labels I have chosen suggest, the modern and the inorganic hark back to a way of thinking that is rationally contemporary, cynical, and scientific. In this paradigm's political dimensions, one sees the shadow of the modern nation-state, with its well-organized legal systems, harsh frontiers, and impersonal relationship with citizens. Although one can hardly say that the nation-state as an institutional entity is disappearing, it is clearly under pressure as the world economy globalizes and as national boundaries are challenged by the accelerating movements of both people and information.[31] At the same time, the public press and commentary are rife with reports and perceptions of citizens' political alienation, as well as a sense that the huge and legally complex bureaucracies of modern republics are less and less responsive to the needs of individuals. Not surprisingly, in the United States at least, voter participation in elections has steadily declined over the last three decades.[32]

As one news commentator said, the United States "is increasingly disaffected. There's a sense that the government is not addressing the real problems of people: how they live, how they get to work, how they pay their bills. There's no sense of cohesion, no national purpose, no sense of here are the three problems we're going to solve in the next ten years. Increasingly the spotlight is shifting more towards state and local governments."[33] Another commentator spoke of civic alienation in terms of an overall decline of "socially cooperative behavior," arguing for a link between such social phenomena as rising crime, the disintegration of the nuclear family, and increasing separation of individuals from the communities in which they were raised.[34]

Under such conditions, it may be only natural that those who look to the past for inspiration and understanding will increasingly shy away from the models of modernity and open their eyes to the evidence of a political world that was smaller, less narrowly legalistic, and more reflective of human endeavor in its search for purpose and values. Thus, the new paradigm, which I have also called the premodern for its inspiration from anthropological studies of simpler cultures, may really represent something postmodern: indicative of today's sensibility that rejects the large, bureaucratic, and mechanical in favor of the more human, spirited, and personal. Only history will tell how and if such a vision will be realized anew in our futures.

Notes

This essay develops remarks I made at a conference at Brown University. I thank fellow conference participants for helping to stimulate my thinking on this topic, as well as Johns Hopkins University Press' anonymous reader and Professors Josiah Ober and Adele C. Scafuro for helpful suggestions made on earlier drafts. In my essay, all three figure dates are B.C.

1. Manville 1990.
2. E.g., Ober 1989a, xiii–xiv, 38–40; 1989b; 1989c.
3. Ober 1989b, 134.
4. Ober 1989b, 136; cf. Kuhn 1970.
5. For some typical examples (citing other scholarship on such controversies), see Andrewes 1961; Rhodes 1981, 496–97; Whitehead 1986, 97–98 n. 55.
6. See Manville 1990, 24–27; cf. Humphreys 1983a; 1985; Osborne 1985a; Connor's essay in this volume.
7. See, e.g., Runciman 1982; for discussion and critique of the Marxist case, see Starr 1986, 42 ff.
8. For a recent defense of this view, citing previous scholarship, see Hansen 1989.
9. Manville 1990, 35–54, citing earlier scholarship. (On rereading my own book, I see I have not completely escaped the same mind-set that I am here criticizing!) On the contrast between the polis and modern states, see esp. Holmes 1979; Maio 1983; Meier 1984; Osborne 1985a, 8–10; Ostwald 1986, xix ff.; Ober 1989a, 7–10; Euben 1989.
10. Gagarin 1986, 140; Roebuck 1966, 269; Stroud 1990.
11. Ober 1989c, 332 ff.
12. Some typical examples are Hignett 1952, 117–22; MacDowell 1978, 67–73; Rhodes 1981, 331–32, 496–500. A moral dimension of citizenship is often ignored in many other treatments bearing on the topic, e.g., Davies 1977–78; Snodgrass 1980, 91–94.
13. For the nuances of "obligation" appropriate to Athenian political society, see Sinclair 1988, 49–53.
14. Gagarin 1973; 1974. In fairness, Gagarin's main arguments focus on the preclassical polis. He also seems to moderate his position in 1986, 47, 99–101; and 1987.

15. For treatments along this line of thought (suggesting, to varying degrees, some overlap between public and private): Humphreys 1983a; 1983d; 1983e; Rahe 1984; Goldhill 1986, 69–74; Garner 1987, 12 ff.; Herman 1987, 1–9, 116 ff.; Sinclair 1988, 50 ff.; Foxhall 1989; Ober 1989a; Scafuro's essay in this volume. For an extreme opposite view, Hansen 1989.

16. Cf. the remarks of Connor 1986; also his essay in this volume. There are many scholars who might identify some or all of this perspective in their work, but a few of the more vocal adherents include those cited in n. 15 above, as well as Roussel 1976; Finley 1981; Snodgrass 1986; Osborne 1985a, 6 ff.; Morris 1987, 1–8; Ober 1989a, 3–15. For an interesting attempt to synthesize opposing paradigms of the polis analogous to those I am describing for citizenship (more or less, though framed in terms of the traditions of Weber and Durkheim), see Murray 1990.

17. See, e.g., Rahe 1984; Starr 1986, 35; Hansen 1987, 9; Sinclair 1988, 49 ff.; Goldhill 1986, 57 ff.; Garner 1987, 11 ff.; Ober 1989a.

18. AP 7.3–4. For other sources and discussion, see Manville 1990, 144 ff.

19. See, e.g., Hignett 1952, 99–107; Forrest 1966, 161–74.

20. An unpublished article of G. E. M. de Ste. Croix quoted by Rhodes 1981, 143; cf. MacDowell 1978, 160; Connor 1987, 47–48.

21. Contrast this view, e.g., with that of Chrimes 1932; Thiel 1950.

22. Manville 1990, 185–88, and, more generally, 173 ff. for sources and scholarship on the Cleisthenic reforms.

23. E.g., Lewis 1963; Forrest 1966, 197–200.

24. For some examples: Whitehead 1986, 23 ff.; Morris 1987, 9, 209–10; Ober 1989a, 70 ff.; Manville 1990, 173 ff.; Meier 1980, 129–38.

25. For a summary of the most important traditional views, see Patterson 1981, 105 ff.; see also Rhodes 1981, 331–35; Walters 1983; Sinclair 1988, 24–27.

26. Ober 1989a, 23; cf. Finley 1973, 23.

27. Cf. Washburn 1982, 257. This perspective actually goes beyond the view I expressed in 1990, 217, but I believe it represents a valid complement to what I said there. For some other views in the same general spirit, see: Sealey 1983; Ober 1989a, 80–81, 260–66; Loraux 1986, 150 ff.

28. Patterson 1981, 96 ff. For other treatments of the vexed question of the size of the Athenian population, see references cited in Manville 1990, 19 n. 65. Cf. Boegehold's essay in this volume; Boegehold argues that "too many citizens" was a perception based on pressure on the land and the court system that adjudicated claims.

29. Cf. remarks of Connor 1986; Ober 1989a, 35–52; Manville 1990, 3–34. For some interesting and more general remarks about the evolution of interpretative frameworks in history, see Novick 1988.

30. Indeed, much of this "new paradigm" can be traced back to seminal earlier works, e.g., Jaeger 1946; Ehrenberg 1969.

31. Ohmae 1990.

32. Knack 1990.

33. David Gergen, speaking on the PBS "McNeil-Lehrer News Hour," 28 December 1990.
34. Knack 1990.

Works Cited

Andrewes, A. 1961. "Philochoros on Phratries." *JHS* 81:1–15.
Chrimes, Kathleen M. T. 1932. "On Solon's Property Classes." *CR* 46:2–4.
Connor, W. Robert. 1986. "The New Classical Humanities and the Old." *CJ* 81:337–47.
———. 1987. "Tribes, Festivals and Processions: Civic Ceremonial and Political Manipulation." *JHS* 107:47–48.
Davies, John K. 1977–78. "Athenian Citizenship: The Descent Group and the Alternatives." *CJ* 73:105–21.
Ehrenberg, Victor. 1969. *The Greek State*. 2d ed. London: Methuen.
Euben, Peter. 1989. *The Tragedy of Political Theory*. Princeton: Princeton University Press.
Finley, Moses I. 1973. *Democracy Ancient and Modern*. New Brunswick, N.J.: Rutgers University Press.
———. 1981. "The Freedom of the Citizen in the Greek World." In *Economy and Society in Ancient Greece*, edited by B. Shaw and R. Saller, 77–94. New York: Viking Press.
Forrest, W. George. 1966. *The Emergence of Greek Democracy*. New York: McGraw-Hill.
Foxhall, Lin. 1989. "Households, Gender and Property in Classical Athens." *CQ* 39:22–44.
Gagarin, Michael. 1973. "Dike in the *Works and Days*." *CP* 68:81–94.
———. 1974. "Dike in Archaic Greek Thought." *CP* 69:186–97.
———. 1986. *Early Greek Law*. Berkeley: University of California Press.
———. 1987. "Morality in Homer." *CP* 82:285–306.
Garner, Richard. 1987. *Law and Society in Classical Athens*. London: Croom Helm.
Goldhill, Simon. 1986. *Reading Greek Tragedy*. Cambridge: Cambridge University Press.
Hansen, Mogens H. 1987. *The Athenian Assembly in the Age of Demosthenes*. Oxford and New York: Basil Blackwell.
———. 1989b. *Was Athens a Democracy? Popular Rule, Liberty and Equality in Ancient and Modern Political Thought*. Historisk-Filosofiske Meddelelser 59. Copenhagen: Royal Danish Academy of Sciences and Letters.
Herman, Gabriel. 1987. *Ritualised Friendship and the Greek City*. Cambridge: Cambridge University Press.
Hignett, Charles. 1952. *A History of the Athenian Constitution to the End of the Fifth Century*. Oxford: Clarendon Press.
Holmes, Stephen T. 1979. "Aristippus in and out of Athens." *American Political Science Review* 73:113–28.

Humphreys, Sally C. 1983a. "The Evolution of Legal Process in Ancient Attica." In *Tria Corda: Scritti in onore di Arnaldo Momigliano*, edited by E.
Gabba, 229–56. Como: Edizioni New Press.

———. 1983b. *The Family, Women, and Death: Comparative Studies*. London: Routledge and Kegan Paul.

———. 1983c. "The Family in Classical Athens: The Search for a Perspective." In Humphreys 1983b: 55–78.

———. 1983d. "Oikos and Polis." In Humphreys 1983b: 1–21.

———. 1983e. "Public and Private Interests in Classical Athens." In Humphreys 1983b: 22–32.

———. 1985. "Law as Discourse." *History and Anthropology* 1:241–64.

Jaeger, Werner. 1946. *Paideia*. 2d ed. Oxford: Oxford University Press.

Knack, Steven. 1990. "Why We Don't Vote—Or Say 'Thank You.'" *Wall Street
Journal*, 31 December, 6.

Kuhn, Thomas. 1970. *The Structure of Scientific Revolutions*. 2d ed. Chicago:
University of Chicago Press.

Lewis, David M. 1963. "Cleisthenes and Attica." *Historia* 12:22–40.

Loraux, Nichole. 1986. *The Invention of Athens: The Funeral Oration in the
Classical City*. Cambridge, Mass.: Harvard University Press.

MacDowell, Douglas M. 1978. *The Law of Classical Athens*. Ithaca: Cornell
University Press.

Maio, Dennis P. 1983. "Politeia and Adjudication in Fourth-Century B.C.
Athens." *American Journal of Jurisprudence* 28:16–45.

Manville, Philip Brook. 1990. *The Origins of Citizenship in Ancient Athens*.
Princeton: Princeton University Press.

Meier, Christian. 1980. *Die Entstehung des Politischen bei den Griechen*.
Frankfurt am Main: Suhrkamp Verlag.

———. 1984. *Introduction à l'anthropologie politique de l'antiquité classique*. Paris: Presses Universitaires de France.

Morris, Ian. 1987. *Burial and Ancient Society*. Cambridge: Cambridge University Press.

Murray, Oswyn. 1990. "Cities of Reason." In *The Greek City From Homer to
Aristotle*, edited by O. Murray and S. Price, 1–25. Oxford: Clarendon Press.

Novick, Peter. 1988. *That Noble Dream: The Objectivity Question and the
American Historical Profession*. Cambridge: Cambridge University Press.

Ober, Josiah. 1989a. *Mass and Elite in Democratic Athens: Rhetoric, Ideology,
and the Power of the People*. Princeton: Princeton University Press.

———. 1989b. "Models and Paradigms in Ancient History." *Ancient History
Bulletin* 3.6:134–37.

———. 1989c. Review of Mogens H. Hansen (1987). "The Nature of Athenian Democracy." *CP* 84:322–34.

Ohmae, Kenichi. 1990. *Beyond National Borders*. New York: Dow Jones-
Irwin.

Osborne, Robin. 1985a. *Demos: The Discovery of Classical Attika*. Cambridge: Cambridge University Press.

———. 1985b. "Law in Action in Classical Athens." *JHS* 105:40–58.

Ostwald, Martin. 1986. *From Popular Sovereignty to the Rule of Law: Law, Society, and Politics in Fifth-Century Athens.* Berkeley: University of California Press.

Patterson, Cynthia. 1981. *Pericles' Citizenship Law of 451/0.* New York: Arno Press. Reprint, Salem, N.H.: Ayer, 1987.

Rahe, Paul. 1984. "The Primacy of Politics in Ancient Greece." *AHR* 89:265–93.

Rhodes, Peter J. 1981. *A Commentary on the Aristotelian Athenaion Politeia.* Oxford: Clarendon Press.

Roebuck, Carl. 1966. *The World of Ancient Times.* New York: Scribner.

Roussel, Denis. 1976. *Tribu et Cité.* Paris: Annales littéraires de l'Université de Besançon.

Runciman, W. G. 1982. "Origins of States: The Case of Archaic Greece." *CSSH* 24:351–77.

Sealey, Raphael. 1983. "How Citizenship and the City Began in Athens." *AJAH* 8:97–129.

Sinclair, R. K. 1988. *Democracy and Participation in Athens.* Cambridge: Cambridge University Press.

Snodgrass, Anthony M. 1980. *Archaic Greece: The Age of Experiment.* Berkeley: University of California Press.

————. 1986. "Interaction by Design: The Greek City-State." In *Peer Polity Interaction and Socio-Political Change,* edited by C. Renfrew and J. Cherry, 47–58. Cambridge: Cambridge University Press.

Starr, Chester. 1986. *Individual and Community: The Rise of the Polis 800–500 B.C.* New York: Oxford University Press.

Stroud, Ronald. 1990. "Citizenship in Early Athenian Lawgivers." Paper read at Brown University Conference on Constructions and Reconstructions of Civic Ideology in Ancient Athens. April 20.

Thiel, J. 1950. "Solon's Property Classes." *Mnemosyne* 4.3:1–11.

Walters, Kenneth R. 1983. "Pericles' Citizenship Law." *CA* 2:314–36.

Washburn, Philo C. 1982. *Political Sociology: Approaches, Concepts, Hypotheses.* Englewood Cliffs, N.J.: Prentice-Hall.

Whitehead, David. 1986. *The Demes of Attica, 508/7–ca. 250 B.C.* Princeton: Princeton University Press.

The Problem of Athenian
Civic Identity

回回回回回回回回回回回回回回回

W. R O B E R T C O N N O R

The study of Athenian civic identity has to date largely been based on the understanding of Athenian citizenship, and this in turn has to a large extent been based on three widely held views. First, the Athenians, by and large, were the descendants of the original inhabitants of the land. Grants of citizenship to individuals or groups with a special claim on the Athenians were rare. "Classical Athens defined the membership of its citizen body . . . rigorously in terms of descent," as John K. Davies remarked.[1] Although descent could be fictionalized, that was surely exceptional; most citizens were descendants of the original inhabitants of Attika. Our sources express this consensus through the myth of autochthony, which represents their understanding that, insofar as they could trace their family histories, they were all rooted in Attika.[2]

Second, the Athenians were both politically and culturally homogeneous. The ancient sources often present this through legends; for example, the story of the synoecism of Attika. The interpretation of this legend may be controversial in detail, but its broad significance is clear enough. The story that King Theseus synoecized separate townships in Attika into a single polis, whatever its origin, chronology, or other implications, affirms the cultural unity of the citizens of Attika. This is thought to be corroborated by shared dialect, festivals, pottery styles, and, in the classical period at least, burial patterns. Athenian civic identity, then, is in this view essentially nonproblematic.

Third, it is widely assumed that citizenship is best approached through law. It was a carefully guarded privilege, defined by decree and regulated by elaborate legal procedures. It is sometimes suggested that the success of Athenian democracy depended to a large extent on its

34

ability to draw a sharp line between citizens and all noncitizens.[3] Because citizenship was legally defined, those who wish to understand what citizenship meant in ancient Athens need only look at these legal criteria and procedures.

This essay challenges all three of these tenets. Far from being premises upon which we can base further analysis, they are all misapprehensions based on partial or inadequate readings of our sources. After examining each of them, this essay will suggest an alternative view of Athenian citizenship and an alternative approach to the difficult problem of Athenian civic identity.

I.

First, consider indigenous descent. That is precisely what the Athenian encomiasts, especially those in the epideictic tradition, encourage their audiences to believe existed. Perikles began with the ancestors: "They dwelt in the country without break in the succession from generation to generation and handed it down free to the present time by their valor" (Thucydides 2.36.1, trans. Crawley). Thucydides seems to confirm this at the beginning of the "Archaeology" when he asserts that whereas other parts of Greece were often invaded, "Attika, from the poverty of its soil enjoying from a very remote period freedom from faction, never changed its inhabitants" (1.2.5, trans. Crawley).

Thucydides goes on, however, in a way that shows that he meant that Attika was never *conquered,* not that its population consisted only of the descendants of the original inhabitants: "The most powerful victims of war or faction from the rest of Hellas took refuge with the Athenians as a safe retreat, and at an early period, becoming citizens, swelled the already large population of the city to such a height that Attika became too small to hold them and they had at last to send out colonies to Ionia" (1.2.6, trans. Crawley, modified). One might object, to be sure, that Thucydides meant that the Ionian colonizers were the descendants of precisely those immigrants who "took refuge with the Athenians," presumably the former inhabitants of Akhaia, often alleged to be the ancestors of the Ionians. Yet if this is what he meant, why does he say "from the rest of Hellas" and not "from one region of Hellas"? And why would he then remark that they "became citizens" (*politai gignomenoi*) and emphasize that the colonization took place only "at last" (*husteron*)? Surely it is more plausible that Thucydides meant that immigrants from many regions of Greece came to Attika, were assimilated, and that eventually the colonization of Ionia followed after the population reached new levels.

Perhaps Thucydides knew no more than the rest of us about the much fictionalized Ionian migration. But if we dismiss his comments, we must still confront the traditions that prominent Athenian families had originally immigrated to Attika,[4] and the assertions that those displaced from other cities had found refuge there.[5] Moreover, Attic oratory is sometimes convincing in its arguments that in the fourth century the children of slaves, foreigners, those with illegitimate unions, and so forth managed to pass as citizens.[6] We know that marriages with foreigners were not uncommon among members of the Athenian elite. As we move down the social scale, and to progressively earlier periods, our evidence becomes less precise, but it seems likely that infusions of non-Attic blood were not uncommon in both the Archaic and the classical period.

In many cases citizenship and even place of residence must have been unclear. For example, shepherds must often have moved across the boundary line between Attika and Boiotia, or between Attika and Megara, as they searched for good pasture, or moved from summer to winter meadows. Craftsmen are known to have traveled from city to city. "A large percentage of the artists of Peisistratid Athens . . . were not [Athenians]. Sculptors seem to have been especially mobile. . . . Potters and painters once established, were a more sedentary lot, yet signatures on Attic vases of the Peisistratid era tell much the same tale of immigration."[7] Solon is reported in Plutarch *Solon* 23–24 to have granted citizenship to exiles and permission to practice a trade to the heads of families relocating in Attika. In classical times we would expect such immigrants to be given metic status, rather than citizenship. But when was the status of the *metoikos* formally defined in Attika? And how closely followed were the formalities? The word *metoikos* first occurs in Aeschylus and in an Attic decree of the 460s, and there is some reason to think the status was not formally defined until after Kleisthenes, perhaps *well* after him.[8] Before the establishment of a formal status, the boundary between citizen and noncitizen must have been very permeable.[9] It is unlikely, moreover, that the archaic Greek polis could rigorously police and enforce such a distinction. Hence, in classical Athens many Athenian citizens may have descended from those who had had no good claim on Athenian citizenship.

One must also allow a considerable role for intermarriage between metics and those of pure Attic ancestry. And surely poorer agricultural workers are likely to have moved across boundary lines in times of drought or crop failure. Many of these may have found permanent work or settled on marginal land in Attika and eventually become assimilated to the local population. When the polis needed citizens for service in the army or for other reasons, there would be strong incentives to treat these immigrants as citizens.

The existence of slavery also encouraged mixture. Runaway slaves, especially homebred slaves of the second or third generation, and the offspring of unions between slaves and masters would try to pass as Athenians.[10] The progeny of foreign *hetairai* are also likely to have tried to find a place among the Athenian citizens.[11] What would stop them? Not some elaborate investigative bureaucracy, not some systematic monitoring of a citizenship list. All would depend on the efficiency of deme officials and—more importantly—the determination of a citizen to bring a case against an individual whom he believed had slipped through the system.

This picture allows for much more mobility across boundaries, both geographical and social, than is commonly admitted. It also posits that substantial numbers of offspring of non-Attic parents found their way onto the citizenship lists. This is, of course, precisely what Aristotle, in a famous passage in the *Politics,* says about Kleisthenes: "After the expulsion of the tyrants he enrolled in the tribes a number of foreigners and a number of resident aliens belonging to the slave class."[12] Some scholars doubt Aristotle's testimony, but surely it is unlikely that citizen lists had been carefully maintained during the Peisistratid period. The governments that followed had good reason to be generous and inclusive in the decisions that had to be made.

The Athenians were far from autochthonous even if the tendency for those of dubious parentage to be included among the citizens stopped at the end of the Archaic period. But despite increasingly rigorous definitions of metic status and citizenship in the classical age, the barrier between citizen and noncitizen is likely to have remained permeable. Indeed, during the great growth of Athens in the fifth century B.C., it may have become easier to find a place on the citizen lists. So it seemed to Isocrates, when he commented on the events of the century preceding his own: "They . . . filled the registers of the phratries and the *lexiarkhika grammateia* with the names of those who had no claim upon the city."[13] Earlier in the same speech, Isocrates was even more emphatic: "We glory and take great pride in being better born than the rest but we are readier to share this noble birthright with any who desire it than are the Triballians or the Leucanians who share their ignoble origin."[14]

The Periclean citizenship law of 451/0 has plausibly been seen as a reaction against this inclusiveness. To be sure, it may be an exaggeration to refer to a "sense of siege, of barricades being manned," as one author has done,[15] but one need not doubt that there was a conflict at this time between the ideology of Athenian autochthony and the social reality that Athenians saw around them.

It seems likely, then, that the Athenian citizen body in classical times

37

was more diverse than has commonly been allowed or than the Athenian panegyrists suggest. The claim of Attic autochthony is not a description of a social reality.[16] Far from it. It is a reflection of the anxiety of a people who knew that they were of very diverse origins and preferred not to look too closely at the descent lines of their fellow citizens. It was sufficient to know that *all* Athenians were autochthonous; no need, then, to trace one's ancestry back, either to a hero of the remote past or to a more recent immigrant. Autochthony *masks* divergences in status and situation. The myth of autochthony may then appear to the modern critic as "aristocratic," but it is fully consistent with Athenian democratic ideas. To suggest, as Nicole Loraux does in her stimulating book *The Invention of Athens,* that the claim of autochthony is a contradiction within Athenian democratic ideology is to overlook its anonymity. It is a claim for the Athenians as a whole, rather than for individuals, families, or extended kinship groups. It marks the city's collective excellence while deemphasizing the claims of genealogical prestige. By shifting attention from genealogy to cultural practice, from being born an Athenian to acting like an Athenian, it functions as the injunction *me phulokrinein* (*AP* 21.2) writ large and mythologized.

II.

It might still be claimed that although the Athenians were of diverse origin, they swiftly became culturally and politically homogeneous. Indeed, this is precisely what the new *Cambridge Ancient History* suggests in arguing that even in Homeric times it was believed that "the inhabitants of Attika were a homogeneous people."[17] But the need for caution is shown by the persistent affection that individual Athenians showed for their local cults, festivals, and residences. Regional differentiation and local loyalties provide an index of the degree of homogeneity in Attika. Three examples deserve special attention:

1. *The Peiraieus.* Robert Garland suggests that the Peiraieus differed from much of the rest of Attika not only in economic patterns but also in having a more democratic attitude.[18] There is some confirmation for this in the ancient sources, notably Aristotle *Politics* 1303b 12 and Xenophon *Hellenica* 2.4.10 ff. These differences in economic and political attitudes may have been reinforced by the existence of a regional cult association, the *Tetrakomoi.*

2. *Akharnai.* Aristophanes and Thucydides indicate how intense were the feelings of loyalty that bound Acharnians to their native deme and how great their potential effect was on Athenian politics, especially at the outset of the Peloponnesian War. No one would doubt their opposi-

tion to Sparta, or their affection for their own deme. Those feelings are commonly regarded as an extreme of patriotism, a hyper-Athenianism. But in practice they amounted to putting the interest of one region over that of Attika as a whole. The centrifugal tendency in Acharnian politics may, then, best be understood not simply as an attempt to urge a different strategy on the leadership of the city, but as part of regional tensions persistent within Attika even in the high classical period.

3. *Peloponnesian strategy in the early part of the Archidamian War.* Thucydides' account of the early invasions may be supplemented by several later sources that indicate that the Spartans and their allies avoided certain areas of Attika, allegedly because of cultic ties linking them to the area. The areas were:

a. The Marathonian Tetrapolis, closely linked to the Herakleidai: Istros *FGrHist* 334F30.

b. The region around the Academy, including the groves of sacred olives. Androtion *FGrHist* 324F39; Philochorus *FGrHist* 328F125; Plutarch *Theseus* 32. Legend had it that Akademas, the eponym of the site, had betrayed Helen's whereabouts to the Spartans at the time of her abduction.[19]

c. Dekeleia. Herodotus 9.73 asserts that the Spartans spared Dekeleia for a similar reason. Later in the war Dekeleia became the Spartan base in northern Attika.[20] One might suspect that there was some sympathy in the area for Sparta, even though its "inviolability" lasted only for the first year or two, as J. A. S. Evans has argued.[21]

These stories have sometimes been dismissed because they are not mentioned by Thucydides and because it has seemed implausible to many scholars that the Spartans would base their strategy on myths or legends. If, however, one recognizes that such myths could be focuses of regional identity, the stories do not appear so absurd. The propaganda of the Spartans, ever alert to religion and cult, might have stressed their ties to their "friends" in Attika, while their restraint would provide a strong incentive for these areas to argue for a speedy settlement. We should not conclude that there were secessionist movements or widely felt hostility to Athenian rule. But it is not surprising if the Spartans overinterpreted feelings of local pride and loyalty and attempted to exploit them. *They* thought there were strong centrifugal forces in Attika. Even if they overestimated these forces or underestimated the economic, social, and emotional forces that worked in the other direction, they are likely to have been better informed than scholars working at today's remove.

These cases point to the need for caution in adopting the view that Attika was culturally and politically homogeneous in the classical period.

The identity that residents of Attika felt as Athenian citizens was only one of the loyalties and ties that operated on them. Athenian civic identity was indeed problematic.

III.

Recent scholarship, not least Manville's essay in this volume, has become increasingly skeptical of the view that Athenian citizenship can best be understood through legal categories. There are many grounds for skepticism about the older view, two of which are especially relevant to our analysis. First, the distinction between citizen and noncitizen was less absolute than has sometimes been thought. For example, certain *nothoi* seem to have enjoyed some of the privileges of citizenship. Some scholars have even suggested an analogy to the French Constitution of 1791, which distinguished *citoyens actifs* from *citoyens passifs,* who were of a lower status.[22] This does not necessitate viewing citizenship among the Greeks, like slavery, as a spectrum of statuses, but it does suggest that the distinction between citizen and noncitizen was a construct that took time to develop, needed constant reinforcement, could be permeable, and was not always absolute.[23]

Second, the study of legal and constitutional institutions, while important and legitimate, is not of itself sufficient for the understanding of Athenian political life.[24] Legal definitions of citizenship could be invoked to deny citizenship to many free, adult male residents of Attika. Yet the laws themselves do not tell us how they were enforced. For example, how was the so-called citizenship law of 451/0 applied? Did each would-be Athenian from then on trudge off to the deme or the phratry and produce some proof of the citizen status of both his mother and his father?[25] Was the expectation in passing this decree that the state would shortly conduct a systematic revision of the citizen register?[26] Or was the decree designed to be applied selectively, against one class or even one individual? At the very least, it is clear that the decree itself was not the end of the story. It required interpretation and implementation. It was a political matter, constantly open to debate and discussion.

In Athens such a decree was an invitation to litigation. The arguments that followed were not accidental by-products of legal and judicial formulae, but were an expected result of those formulae. The decree anticipates, even encourages, the disputes. It annexes certain considerations into political discourse. Citizenship disputes were not an aberration or deficiency in the system, but an expected part of that system itself. The citizenship law can best be seen as an affirmation that certain issues are indeed germane to debate about citizen status. The decree, in other words, may not have had significant short-term effects on the citizenship lists, but it opened up a new chapter in democratic political discourse. This helps explain why disputes about citizenship were so frequent in Athens. We may suspect that the citizenry welcomed frequent debates, not simply out of some characteristic Athenian love of a good debate or of vitriolic personal attacks, but because such cases provided a perfect opportunity for the affirmation of democratic civic ideology. Even those whose claims on Athenian citizenship were unchallengeable in the paternal line might find themselves vulnerable to accusations about the maternal line. Their best course was to look and act like an Athenian in every possible way.[27] A trial on an issue of citizenship raised the basic questions of civic identity and demanded a defense that would affirm loyalty to the institutions and values of the city.

Each of the three parts of this argument points to a city in which civic identity was indeed problematic. Being Athenian was not the automatic result of being born into a society in which all of the members shared the same genetic and cultural inheritances. Civic identity could not be taken for granted; it had to be constructed and reconstructed in each generation by shared myths, by participation in cults, festivals, and ceremonies, and by elaborate techniques of "mixing." The construction of civic identity in ancient Athens is another, very complex story. One preliminary observation, however, arises from the material investigated in this essay. In ancient Athenian practice, diversity was to a large extent masked by language, myths, and rituals. The official civic ideology played down tensions and confronted diversity at the individual rather than the group level. Thus, while the city in many respects welcomed individual disputes and law cases concerning citizenship, discussions of conflicts among social groups, or even admissions of their existence, are relatively infrequent. We know both ends of the spectrum better than the middle— disputes about whether an individual was properly Athenian and the representation of what was involved in being one of "the Athenians." Less is known about the practices, lingering memories, and divergent loyalties that bound individuals to social and regional groups. That is itself an important fact about Athens, as well as a warning about how we can best understand what is meant to be an Athenian.

Notes

This essay is a revised version of a talk given at a conference at Brown University. I am very grateful to Adele C. Scafuro, the organizer of the conference, Philip Brook Manville, the commentator on the essay, and to other participants in the conference, especially Josh Ober, for their suggestions and criticisms. The essay was written before the publication of Manville's valuable *The Origins of Athenian Citizenship* (Princeton: Princeton University Press, 1990).

1. Davies 1977/78, 105. See also Patterson 1981, who includes a useful discussion of Davies' views.

2. See, *inter alia:* Hdt. 7.161; Thuc. 2.36.1; Lys. 2.17; Plato *Menexenus* 237b; [Dem.] 60 *Funeral Oration* 4. Ermatinger 1897 is still useful.

3. See Ober 1989, 5, summarizing Raaflaub.

4. Examples: Hdt. 5.65 on the Neleid descent of the Peisistratids; Hdt. 5.57 on the family to which Harmodios and Aristogeiton belonged, the Gephyraioi: "According to their own account, [they] came originally from Eretria" (Rawlinson). His own view was that they were originally Phoenicians (i.e., Cadmaeans) who later dwelt in Tanagra. See also Hdt. 5.66 on Isagoras' alleged Carian descent.

5. Hdt. 6.90 notes that Aeginetan supporters of Nikodromos settled in Sounion; there is not explicit testimony that they were given citizenship.

6. See Ober 1989, 271, citing Lys. 30 *Nicomachus* 2, 5 f., 27 f., 30; Aeschin. 2 *Embassy* 76 f.; Dem. 21 *Meidias* 149 f.; [Dem.] 59 *Neaera* 113.

7. Hurwit 1985, 250.

8. Whitehead 1977, 79–97 suggested that the classical metic system may have developed after 451/0. Patterson 1981, 134 notes that the "Decree of Themistokles" indicates that "there was a recognition in 480 of a class of aliens permanent enough to be registered" but that the term *metoikoi* had not yet been assigned to them. She points to the Skambonidai deme decree of ca. 460 (*IG* I² 188.52 f.) as an early indicator of an official civic status.

9. Sealey 1983 has suggested that this distinction does not antedate Solon.

10. For slaves on the Athenian citizenship rolls see Ober 1989, 271 f. See also Walters 1983, 314–36.

11. The most detailed picture of the situation of such progeny comes from a careful reading of [Dem.] 59 *Neaera*, but see also Ar. *Peace* 165 and the scholia to Plato's *Parmenides* 127c, and Patterson's essay in this volume.

12. *Politics* 3.1275b 35 ff., trans. E. Barker. The concept "resident aliens of the slave class" may be a crabbed way of alluding to the fact that Athens, unlike most other Greek cities, grouped manumitted slaves with metics: Aristotle *Politics* 1277b 22–1278a 2 and Whitehead 1984, 54.

13. Isocr. 8 *Peace* 88 (trans. Norlin, modified). Walters 1983, 325 n. 35 rejects this view.

14. Isocr. 8 *Peace* 50 (trans. Norlin). Aristotle suggests a similar pattern in his discussion of extreme democracy. He proposes as a generalization that in such democracies: "The leaders of popular parties usually follow the policy of

seeking to strengthen the populace by simply increasing its numbers to the utmost possible extent. Citizenship is given not only to the lawfully born, but also to the illegitimate; it is given to those who have only one citizen parent, whether that parent be father or mother" (*Politics* 6.1319b, trans. Barker).

15. Davies 1977–78, 110.

16. Note that the claim of autochthony coexists with the idea of an era before Athenian identity had emerged; e.g., the stories in which the Athenians had just Hellenized when the Pelasgians came to live among them: Herodotus 1.57, 2.51.

17. *CAH*². 3.3, p. 360.

18. Garland 1987.

19. Another version of the story alleges that the Spartans avoided the area because of curses that protected the sacred olives: Istros *FGrHist* 334F30.

20. I am indebted to Kenneth Walters for a useful discussion of these passages.

21. Evans 1988, 8 f.

22. See Mossé 1979 and Lotze 1981.

23. Note the entries for those who seem not to fit neatly among the citizen dead in Athenian casualty lists of the mid-fifth century: the *toxotai* in *IG* I² 929 = R. Meiggs and D. M. Lewis *GHI* 33, ll. 67 ff., and a person from Eleutherai in *IG* I² 943 = Meiggs and Lewis *GHI* 48, l. 96 f.

24. I fear this will make me seem even more of a nonconstitutionalist to those who, like Hansen (1989), have been troubled by the analysis of Athenian politics in Connor 1972. However, that book does not argue that constitutional and juridical factors are unnecessary for the understanding of ancient Athenian political life; it simply denies they are sufficient. On the issue, see Ober 1989b.

25. It is widely presumed that the decree was not retroactive, but the text does not say so. My suspicion is that those already on the citizenship rolls could be challenged if a citizen wished to bring a case.

26. This citizenship law may have resulted in the alleged purge of the citizenship rolls in 445/4 B.C., as reported in the scholia to Ar. *Wasps* 718 = *FGrHist* 328F119.

27. Cf. Ober 1989, 267 and Scafuro's essay in this volume.

Works Cited

Connor, W. Robert. 1972. *The New Politicians of Fifth-Century Athens.* Princeton: Princeton University Press.

Davies, John K. 1977–78. "Athenian Citizenship: The Descent Group and Its Alternatives." *CJ* 73:105–21.

Ermatinger, E. 1897. *Die attische Autochthonensage bis auf Euripides.* Diss. Berlin.

Evans, J. A. S. 1988. "The Medism of Pausanias." *Antichthon* 22:1–11.

Garland, Robert. 1987. *The Peiraeus from the Fifth to the First Century B.C.* Ithaca: Cornell University Press.

Hansen, Mogens H. 1989. "On the Importance of Institutions in an Analysis of Athenian Democracy." *ClMed* 40:107–13.

Hurwit, Jeffrey M. 1985. *The Art and Culture of Early Greece*. Ithaca: Cornell University Press.

Loraux, Nicole. 1986. *The Invention of Athens: The Funeral Oration in the Classical City*. Translated by Alan Sheridan. Cambridge, Mass.: Harvard University Press.

Lotze, D. 1981. "Zwischen Politen und Metöken, Passivbürger im klassischen Athen?" *Klio* 63:159–78.

Mossé, Claude. 1979. "Citoyens actifs et citoyens passifs dans les cités grecques." *REA* 81:241–49.

Ober, Josiah. 1989a. *Mass and Elite in Democratic Athens: Rhetoric, Ideology, and the Power of the People*. Princeton: Princeton University Press.

———. 1989b. Review of Mogens H. Hansen 1987, *The Athenian Assembly in the Age of Demosthenes*. "The Nature of Athenian Democracy." *CP* 84:322–34.

Patterson, Cynthia. 1981. *Pericles' Citizenship Law of 451/0*. New York: Arno Press. Reprint. Salem, N.H.: Ayer, 1987.

Sealey, Raphael. 1983. "How Citizenship and the City Began in Athens." *AJAH* 8:97–129.

Walters, Kenneth R. 1983. "Perikles' Citizenship Law." *CA* 2:314–36.

Whitehead, David. 1977. *The Ideology of the Athenian Metic*. Supplementary vol. 4 to the *Proceedings of the Cambridge Philological Society*. Cambridge: Cambridge University Press.

———. 1984. "Immigrant Communities in the Classical Polis." *L'Antiquité Classique* 53:47–59.

Aspects of Early Athenian Citizenship

FRANK J. FROST

ἔστιν τι ἕν, ἢ οὐκ ἔστιν, οὗ ἀναγκαῖον πάντας τοὺς πολίτας
μετέχειν, εἴπερ μέλλει πόλις εἶναι;
Plato *Protagoras* 324D 7–9

Plato enjoyed proposing disarmingly simple questions, as when he
had Protagoras ask: "Is there one thing, or not, which necessarily all
citizens must share, if there is to be a polis?" With only a minor change,
we can turn this into another seemingly simple question: "Is there one
thing, or not, which all citizens must share, if they are to be citizens?"[1]

One can reasonably define citizenship during the age of the orators:
it is a combination of rights and obligations, documented for political
and military purposes by the inscription of the citizen's name on the deme
register, the *lexiarkhikon grammateion*. It remained just as important to
be able to establish membership in a phratry in case one's citizenship was
challenged, or for the purpose of determining family relationships in the
event of disputed inheritance.[2] Kleisthenes instituted the recording of
citizenship status on deme registers. But it is more difficult to specify any
time period before Kleisthenes when the actual concept of citizenship
began to emerge both as a common bond among all Athenians and as a
legally defined package of rights and duties that set citizens apart from
noncitizens: *xenoi, metoikoi, douloi,* and *atimoi.* It is important to remember this distinction, for citizenship is one of those notions that becomes relevant only when it conveys a benefit that some people receive
and others do not.

A citizen is also someone who belongs. To use Aristotle's units, or

FRANK J. FROST

koinoniai, of increasing size, one belongs first to the *oikos*, then to
the association of oikoi that form the village, or *kome*, and, finally, to
the association of komai that form the mature polis (Aristotle *Politics*
1252b 9 ff.). But what Aristotle does not explain is that in an early stage
of development one's bond of loyalty to the oikos may be strong enough
to exclude a higher loyalty to kome and that later on the bond to regional
community may involve such strong economic and religious ties that the
recognition of the hegemony of a far-off *astu* may be quite obscured,
particularly in the case of a large territory like Attika. These are the
barriers to the notion of citizenship in the emerging archaic polis.

Consider, for instance, what may be thought of as citizenship in
society as described by Homer. The word *polites* simply means an inhabitant of a polis; there are no universal benefits conveyed—no "content" of
citizenship as defined by Raphael Sealey.³ The domestic scenes in the
Odyssey show a structured society on a small scale where everyone
knows everyone else and his or her station in life. There are the *aristoi* and
other landowners who have enough property to support themselves and
their oikoi. Otherwise, in this premarket economy, everyone else is dependent to a degree, from the *therapon*, or free retainer, to the lowest serving
girl. They all belong to an oikos and depend on it for sustenance and
protection. There are also a few people who do not belong to an oikos, as
far as we can tell. At the bottom end are the beggars (*Od.* 18.1) and
laborers (11.489, 18.357; cf. Hesiod *Works and Days* 602); then there are
a few more respectable individuals who support themselves by means of
their skills as craftsmen, bards, *manteis*, and doctors.⁴ The notion of
citizenship as a distinction did not exist on Ithaka because all distinctions
were imbedded in society and in kinship. For instance, Odysseus promised to reward Eumaios and Philoitios by giving them *oikia* and *ktemata*
and reckoning them as comrades and brothers of his own son: Τηλε-
μάχου ἑτάρω τε κασιγνήτω τε ἔσεσθον (21.216). This is a rare promotion
in Homeric society: from *dmos* to independent farmer and fictive kinsman of his ruler. There was no need to document status on Ithaka (although we know some literacy already existed).⁵ A strange face was
immediately noticed and remarked upon (1.405–11, 20.191–93).

Perhaps during the same century as the appearance of the Homeric
poems and their depiction of a static, structured society, a very different
kind of social organization was developing in the first Greek overseas
colonies. First, the fundamental bonds of loyalty to oikos and kome—to
home, household, and community—were broken. Second, the economic
dependency that had once bound the colonist to some landowning patron
back in the old community now no longer existed. The first and most
essential purpose of every colony was to find new land and divide it

among colonists who had joined the venture for that exact reason. This seems beyond question. Therefore, the colonist exchanged his old dependency for a bond with the entire new colonial community, a bond that included land tenure. In short, he now shared a *politeia*, he had become a polites in the real sense of assuming benefits and obligations that were shared by the whole community. His position was no longer imbedded in an archaic structure; it was a matter of written record. Because the colonists came from more than one city, they must have required written records of some kind to avoid misunderstandings. The first document that proved that someone belonged to a colony recorded not one, but two things: the name of the colonist and his title to a *kleros,* or allotment of land.[6] There is an instructive story about the ultimate folly: a Corinthian named Aithiops, on his way to help found the colony of Syracuse, traded his *kleros* for a honey cake during the journey.[7] We are left to guess what his status would have been after this loss.

The earliest extant mention of citizenship in the explicit sense of participation in a politeia is found in the foundation oath of the Theran settlers at Kyrene:[8] "If the colonists succeed in the settlement, anyone from home who later sails to Libya is to share in the politeia and 'honors'[9] and shall be allotted ownerless land." Subsequently, the oath provided that if the colony was unsuccessful after five years, "they may depart from the land with immunity to Thera to their property and be citizens."

There is obviously a significant content to citizenship at Kyrene. One shares in the politeia and is entitled to a kleros of land and other "honors." One who returned to Thera retained both citizenship there and his former property. In both cases landed property and the rights of citizenship went hand in hand. The nature of the other "honors" that went with citizenship would have been slightly different in every colony. They might include membership in the cults that had been brought to the new land, and probably in the founder cult,[10] participation in public assemblies, the right to compete for public offices, and protection in the case of homicide or other injury. The primary obligation owed by all citizens was, of course, military: to join in claiming the land first and later in protecting it. The notion of citizenship as a state of belonging that conveyed valuable distinctions thus became well defined during the first century of the colonial movement. In addition, there seems to have been an implicit principle of equality among colonists, at least below the level of *oikistes,* priests, and other aristoi.[11]

It has been necessary to define the development of the concept of citizenship outside of Athens in order to draw the contrast. At the same time that colonists were becoming accustomed to citizenship that included both political rights and property rights, the inhabitants of Attika were still mired in a rigidly structured society. Archaic Athens in the seventh century was a traditional community (or, rather, a collection of communities) more like the Ithaka of the *Odyssey*. According to Aristotle (*AP* 2.2), all the land was in the hands of a wealthy few. Everyone else was a *pelates* or a *hektemoros;* without trying to explain the meaning of these terms,[12] I believe it would be accurate to say that, as on Ithaka, the distinction to be made was not between citizen and noncitizen but between substantial landowners and those who were either completely or partly dependent on them. All positions of leadership, whether political or priestly offices, were held by the aristoi. Citizenship conveyed no benefits and had no content, and therefore it cannot be said to have existed, aside from the physical fact of being an inhabitant of Attika. It was this dependent population that would one day become the citizens of Athens, but, before such a notion was even conceivable, they would have to break the bonds of economic dependency on great landlords. Only land tenure would achieve this and allow the freeholder the luxury of perceiving a more abstract bond of community with fellow residents of Attika.[13]

Even in the seventh century there was one bond between all inhabitants of Attika: the belief that they were all at the mercy of potent divinities and that an offense against the gods by one Athenian could bring terrible retribution upon them all. The massacre of the Cylonians was thought to threaten all Athenians with the wrath of Athena Polias; the homicide law of Drakon, often assumed to be some kind of reaction to the Cylonian crisis, was a way of assuring the entire population that if a homicide occurred there would be an orderly way of avoiding the pollution.[14] So far as we know, the law of Drakon is the first extant evidence of a legal distinction between Athenians and non-Athenians.[15] The aristoi have created, or at least recorded in permanent form, a procedure for avenging homicide. Part of the orderly process that eventually allowed relatives to pursue a killer can be recovered from the inscription (as reasonably restored from Demosthenes 43.57–58 and 23.38). The individuals who may find guiltless a man responsible for involuntary homicide are named in descending order: first, the immediate family, then the cadet lines, and, finally, in the absence of surviving family, ten members of the victim's phratry, chosen from the aristoi (ll. 13–19). A later clause (l. 28, cf. Demosthenes 23.38)[16] shows that the term *Athenaios* has become the designation, if not for a citizen, at least for all members of the community who might be affected by the pollution resulting from a homicide. Before the *basileis* have decided whether a homicide had occurred, the alleged killer is protected in exile; if anyone kills an *androphonos,* "he shall be liable to the same treatment as the one who kills an *Athenaios.*" Here at last is some evidence of "content" in Athenian citizenship: all *Athenaioi* are equal before the law in at least one sense. The "state" will designate the individuals who may avenge their homicide. It is further specified that, for the purpose of determining citizenship, the group to which one belongs is the phratry.

The nature of the archaic Athenian phratry therefore deserves some discussion. As a koinonia of some kind, it seems to occupy that middle space between oikos and polis, replacing the kome in Aristotle's system. As the name suggests, the phratry was a subdivision of the Athenian people based on kinship, although most of the kinship was fictitious, having come into existence in some way during the long Athenian Dark Age to explain the relationship between great families and their retainers (on the analogy of *Od.* 21.216, cited above). The phratry was also territorial, showing that the families that settled in various areas of Attika had, by historical times, established a claim to those particular pieces of real estate by reason of ancestral graves and by the location of cult sites administered by the families that could demonstrate an ancestral relationship with the cult founder. The territoriality of the phratry can be documented both by epigraphical evidence and by the rare trustworthy literary reference.[17]

Every phratry was dominated by its aristocratic *genos* or *gene*. They were the source of all law, they held the priestly offices in all the cults, and they were also entrusted with determining who was to be admitted to the phratry, and under what terms.[18] Every phratry celebrated its own cult ceremonies several times a year, but the festival common to all Athenians (all Ionians, in fact) was the Apatouria, a three-day celebration during the month of Pyanopsion when young men who had come of age were introduced by their fathers to the general phratry membership. At some time phratry membership began to be documented in the *phraterikon grammateion,* but sworn oral testimony was always the preferred method of establishing one's phratry, which would have been equivalent to proving oneself a member of the Athenian community in the years before Kleisthenes.[19] Even in the fourth century, we can see the survival of this proof of phratry membership in the oath given by prospective officeholders; they were expected to give the location of their shrines of Apollo Patroos and Zeus Herkeios and their ancestral tombs.[20]

To summarize the nature of citizenship, such as it was, in Attika by the late seventh century, the distinction of being an Athenaios was legally recognized, and some rights had been legally extended to all Athenaioi. The most important was the right to be avenged in case of homicide, for this crime could pollute the entire community. One assumes that every Athenaios had the right to own and inherit landed property, or to acquire it as a dowry. They also had the dubious right to pledge their own persons as surety for mortgages, whatever form these might have taken (e.g., a promise to give over a proportion of a certain yield on borrowed land). On the other hand, one can list certain distinctions that Athenaioi did *not* all share. If we take *AP* 2.2 at face value, the majority did not own enough land to be economically independent. Nor was there any political content to citizenship. *Gnorimoi* could occupy such rudimentary magistracies as existed, but not all Athenaioi voted for magistrates; some did not participate in public meetings except, perhaps, as spectators. Some did not have the right to sit on juries or other judicial bodies. Not all had equal protection against legal proceedings. Solon said that some had been sold as slaves, "this one illegally, that one legally" (fr. 36.9–10 West, *AP* 12.4), seeming to show that the law of force and submission still existed in Attika. It is therefore difficult to perceive any common bond that would have been recognized as a benefit by all Athenaioi.

The group to which an inhabitant belonged in the most meaningful sense was the phratry and that part of the Attic *khora* in which the phratry was located. One should stress the parochial nature of the various rural communities to which inhabitants undoubtedly felt a deeper loyalty than they did to the distant astu. Without trying to define exactly when a meaningful *sunoikismos* can be said to have taken place,[21] one can still wonder whether a resident of Thorikos, or Anagyrous, or Myrrhinous, or Aphidna thought of himself first and foremost as Athenaios— or as *Thorikios, Anagyrasios,* and so forth. Many of these communities were a good two-day journey from Athens. They had well-established identities, their own cults, their own legends, and even public buildings, although Thucydides inexplicably said these had gone out of use at the time of Theseus.[22]

One might think that the legislation of Solon finally created an effective and credible sense of citizenship. The political content of citizenship was significantly increased by extending to all Athenians the right of participation in *ekklesia* and *dikasterion.* For Aristotle, this was the decisive step in forging a true democracy (*AP* 7.3, 9.1; *Politics* 1247a). Implicit in the act of writing down the laws for all to see is the idea that the laws apply to all equally; this might seem to enforce the notion of a common bond of citizenship, as Plutarch thought. In giving any citizen the right to bring suit on behalf of another, Solon accustomed all Athenians to think of themselves as part of one organism, as the limbs are all part of the same body (*Solon* 18.6–7). But the existence of written laws does not always reflect political reality. I have questioned elsewhere the applicability of the Solonian constitution to all of Attika.[23] Inhabitants of the Athenian astu, for instance, probably regarded themselves as superior sorts of Athenians and their city as the *axis mundi*. An early-sixth-century grave inscription urges all who pass by to grieve for the departed Tetikhos, εἴτε ἀστό]ς τις ἀνὲϱ εἴτε χσένος.[24] This certainly cannot have the same connotation as the ἀστὸς ἢ ξένος of Demosthenes (57.24), or even Theognis' Μήτε τινὰ ξείνων . . . μήτε τιν' ἐνδήμων (793–94). *Xenos* does not mean here a foreigner from outside Attika; the distinction is between an inhabitant of the city and an inhabitant of the rural demes, for the tomb was located not on a main road out of Attika, but on the road leading north toward Akharnai.[25]

If Solonian legislation did not lead to a universal notion of citizenship all over Attika, neither did it do anything to further a concept of economic equality among citizens, which had been a founding principle in at least some Greek colonies for over a century. In reality, Solon seems to have perpetuated four unequal classes of Athenians. The distinctions among them, or at least between the top three income classes and the thetes, were so great that any notion of a common Athenian bond would have been overpowered. At the bottom there must have remained a large group of Athenians who, if not totally landless, were at least dependent on landlords for the land they were allowed to sharecrop. And at the very top, it is probable that the aristoi believed that they themselves belonged more to an international aristocracy than to a group that included their own tenants—an elite like the suitors of Agariste of Sikyon.[26] Lack of any true equality is reflected in the words of Solon, when he insisted that he had *not* given an equal share of the earth to both *esthloi* and *kakoi* (fr. 34 West, *AP* 12.3). This is confirmed by evidence from Attic graves, which continue to show the domination of cemeteries by the wealthy.[27] Theoretically, all thetes may have been able to attend assemblies and sit on juries, but, because we have evidence for exactly one meeting of the Assembly and none at all for the results of any legal proceeding for almost the entire sixth century, it is impossible to say what advantage this would have conveyed.[28]

In order to end this inquiry on a more positive note, I will suggest briefly the developments that made possible the adoption of Athenian citizenship as a common bond. There is no question that the Peisistratids prepared the ground. The *political* content of citizenship made no progress between 561 and 510, but in many ways the tyrants attempted to encourage a Panathenaic ideal—the idea of a common bond among all Athenians—even if the appeal may have been mostly to the esthloi. The Panathenaic festival, if not actually founded by Peisistratos, was certainly appropriated by him and his sons.[29] I have indicated elsewhere how the Peisistratid family carefully nurtured the most potent cults of Attika by founding sites where they could be honored in the center of the astu.[30]

Again, it has long been noted that the great estates that dominated Attika at the beginning of the sixth century were in some way converted to a larger number of moderate holdings by the end of that century. There is no real evidence for how this happened, although it is often suggested that Peisistratos distributed the estates of his enemies to his own retainers and supporters.[31] Another possibility is the simple effect of almost three generations of peace and the prosperity that was promoted to some extent by the Peisistratids' foreign revenues. The average large estate may have been subdivided three or four times simply by an increase in the number of surviving sons.[32] If the latter part of the sixth century was a period of great ostentation among the aristoi, it was also a period of population growth and a corresponding decrease in the size of the average landholding. This trend, more than any political development, was vital for economic stability in the Attic countryside.

Finally, the static, stratified society of archaic Attika became more fluid with the rise of a market economy. The development of the Athenian economy lies outside the scope of this inquiry; one can show, however, by the distributive system implied by the use of currency, that a market economy had evolved and created new avenues of advancement for previously dependent classes. The agora was no longer a Homeric place of assembly but, as Kyros said, a place where people gathered to cheat one another.[33] And the aristocrats who were accustomed to make ostentatious dedications on the Akropolis were now joined by a laundress (IG I^2 473).

All these factors made it possible for Kleisthenes to "give the politeia to the demos," as Aristotle said (AP 20.1; cf. Hdt. 5.66). The registration of all Athenians by territorial deme was an immediately effective way of enfranchising all the citizens of Attika. As is commonly pointed out, deme registration obscured family connections and introduced an egalitarian element to the notion of being an Athenaios. If the history of Attika had continued to proceed as placidly as it did during the long Peisistratid years, the new tribal system might have required a decade or so to become ingrained. As it was, the average Athenian's participation in the politeia was almost immediately tested by the need to take up arms and fight off three foreign invaders—namely, the Peloponnesians, Chalcidians, and Boeotians—in 508/7 or thereabouts. To fight for one's country is one of the most meaningful acts of citizenship, as political thinkers as diverse as Livy, Machiavelli, and Jefferson have emphasized, and this was the first time all Athenians had fought together as a national army.[34] Herodotus attributed the Athenian victory to isegorie (5.78). But he may have been unaware that the new deme registers made it possible for the first time to muster efficiently a national army that would greatly outnumber the

Boeotians and Chalcidians.[35] This victory as much as anything else put the seal of success on Athenian citizenship. Both political and economic inequality would persist. *Equality* is doubted. . . . But Athenians had overcome all the psychological obstacles to the notion of equal citizenship. For the first time, the advantages of being an Athenian polites seemed just as important as economic independence.

Notes

This essay is offered in memoriam Al. N. Oikonmides.

1. The question has been posed by Sealey 1983 and Manville 1990. See also the essays by Manville and Connor in this volume.

2. Deme register, *IG* I³ 138.6: Dem. 44 *Leochares* 35, etc. Phratry membership, Isaeus 7 *Apollodorus* 15–16; Demosthenes' two speeches, 43 *Macartatus* and 57 *Eubulides,* demonstrate all the methods of establishing citizenship. For full treatment, see Scafuro's essay in this volume. The case of the infamous Pankleon (Lys. 23) illustrates how difficult it could actually be to prove someone was *not* a citizen (see Boegehold's essay in this volume).

3. Sealey 1983, 97.

4. *Od.* 17.383–85: a list of valuable *demiourgoi;* the same list of livelihoods, plus merchant and farmer, is given by Solon frag. 13.43–62 West.

5. Well-documented by Bellamy 1989.

6. That *kleroi* were recorded in some way seems implicit in the Cyrenean oath, Meiggs and Lewis 1969, no. 5; cf. Aristotle *Politics* 1266b 20 on Leukas. David Jordan brought to my attention a recent find of lead strips from fifth-century Kamarina, published by Cordano 1989, bearing the name of the citizen on one side and the number of his phratry on the other.

7. Archilochus frag. 293 West and Demetrius of Skepsis, quoted by Athenaeus 167D. Cf. Figueira 1981, 225 n. 63.

8. Meiggs and Lewis 1969, no. 5: αἱ μὲν δέ κα κατέχ[ων]τι τὰν οἰκισίαν οἱ ἄποικοι, τῶν οἰκείων τὸγ καταπλέον[τα] ὕστερον εἰς Λιβύαν καὶ πολιτήιας καὶ τιμᾶν πεδέχ[εν] καὶ γᾶς τᾶς ἀδεσπότω ἀπολαγχάνεν (ll. 30–33) . . . ἐκ τᾶς γᾶς ἀπίμ[εν] ἀδιέως Θήρανδε ἐπὶ τὰ αὐτῶγ χρήματα καὶ ἤμεμ πολιάτας (ll. 35–36).

9. I prefer the literal translation, "honors," which is also that of Graham 1983, 225, to the "offices" of Rhodes 1986, 28, and Fornara 1977, 22. "Offices" is too narrowly political.

10. On which, see Malkin 1987, chaps. 4–5.

11. Equality is doubted by Figueira 1981, 196–99, but he admits the evidence is scanty, mostly confined to the example of the *gamoroi* at Syracuse; otherwise see the Cyrenean oath, ll. 27–28; Aristotle, *Politics* 1266a 39. Graham 1982, 151 f. cites the evidence for equality but has some doubts.

12. It would be difficult to go beyond the discussion of Rhodes 1981, ad *AP* 2.2.

13. Pointed out by Finley 1980, 89 f., followed by Morris 1987, 175. In addition, there must have been a growing class of independent artisans.

14. On the law as a reaction to the Cylonian affair, see Stroud 1968, 72.

15. Text in Meiggs and Lewis 1969, no. 86; Stroud 1968, 5 f.

16. On the restoration from Demosthenes, see Stroud 1968, 53.

17. I base these brief remarks on the catalogue of Attic phratries and interpretation by Hedrick 1991; otherwise I follow the interpretation of the phratry as proposed by Andrewes 1961a, 1961b.

18. Andrewes 1961a, 8, cites the Patmian scholia to Demosthenes (Sakkelion 1877, 152) on γεννῆται . . . Φιλόχορος δὲ ἐν τῆι δ᾽ Ἀτθίδος γεννήτας καὶ ὁμογαλάκτας καλεῖ. οὗτοι δὲ τοὺς ἐγγραφομένους εἰς τοὺς φράτορας διακρίνοντες καὶ δοκιμάζοντες εἰ πολῖταί εἰσιν ἢ ξένοι ἐδέχοντο ἢ ἐπέβαλλον. The passage is a scholion to Dem. 57.23. Jacoby 1950 did not include the second sentence in his text of Philochoros 328F35, but, as Andrewes said, the explanation cannot simply be a conjecture by the scholiast and may go back to a past when *gennetai* did control entry to the phratry.

19. For the *phraterikon grammateion*, Demosthenes 44.41: IG 2² 1237.20, 98.

20. AP 55.3; Plato *Euthydemus* 302CD; Lane Fox 1985, 209 cites Aristotle's suspicion of written evidence in inheritances and comments: "Where wills were dubious there was no end to the monstrous claims which an Isaeus could plead."

21. See Whitehead 1986, 8–10; Frost 1990, 3–5.

22. Whitehead 1986; Jeffery 1976, 86; Connor's essay in this volume. The demes continued in Thucydides' own day to meet in council, to elect officials, to raise and spend money, and to erect records of their legislation in public places; these inscriptions are the proof that they did so: IG 1² 183, 186–9; SEG 10.210, etc., for the fifth century; many more in the fourth: IG 2² 1177 ff.

23. Frost 1990, 3–5; cf. Frost, 1985, 61 f.

24. IG 2² 976; Jeffery 1962, 133, no. 34; Guarducci in Richter 1961, 158 f.

25. "Sepolia and Levi, adjoining northern suburbs of modern Athens, lie just north of Kolonos hill." Jeffery 1962, 133.

26. Hdt. 6.127; see also Beringer 1985, 51.

27. Summarized by Morris 1987, 208 f.

28. Ironically, the one documented meeting was that at which Peisistratos fooled the *demos* into giving him a bodyguard; Hdt. 1.59; AP 14.1. See Aristotle *Politics* 1292b 15 ff. on the inertia of political change.

29. Discussion by Shapiro 1989, 19–20, 24; Stahl 1987, 246–55.

30. Frost 1990, for the evidence, to which add [Plato] *Hipparchus* 229A and SEG 10.345: the *horoi* set up midway between the astu and the outlying demes. Cf. Kolb 1977, 113 f.; Connor 1987, 46 f.

31. Frost 1987, 57 and n. 37. See also AP 16.2–3 with Rhodes' comments.

32. An example is the genos of the Brytidai, [Dem.] 59.61: their original land was probably in southern Attika, but sometime before Kleisthenes' reforms three members had moved to the astu and another far north to Hekale. This may be a case of a profusion of heirs. It will be recognized that it is easier

to explain how large land owners became moderate ones than to imagine any way by which a landless man could have acquired property.

33. Hdt. 1.153, used as an illustration by Starr 1982, 436.

34. Frost 1984, 283–94.

35. At Marathon the Athenians were able to muster 9,000 hoplites, according to Nepos *Miltiades* 5; Paus. 4.25.5, 10.20.2. Even a third of this would have been a formidable army in 506.

Works Cited

Andrewes, A. 1961a. "Philochoros on Phratries." *JHS* 81:1–15.

———. 1961b. "Phratries in Homer." *Hermes* 89:129–39.

Bellamy, R. 1989. "Bellerophon's Tablet." *CJ* 84:289–307.

Beringer, Walter. 1985. "Freedom, Family, and Citizenship in Early Greece." In *The Craft of the Ancient Historian: Essays In Honor of Chester G. Starr*, edited by J. Ober and J. Eadie, 41–56. Lanham, Md.: University Press of America.

Connor, W. Robert. 1987. "Tribes, Festivals, and Processions: Civic Ceremonial and Political Manipulation." *JHS* 107:40–50.

Cordano, Federica. 1989. "Primi documenti di un archivio anagrafico a Camarina." *RAL* 44:135–50.

Figueira, Thomas. 1981. *Aegina, Society and Politics*. New York: Arno Press.

Finley, Moses I. 1980. *Ancient Slavery and Modern Ideology*. London: Chatto and Windus.

Fornara, Charles. 1977. *Archaic Times to the End of the Peloponnesian War*. Baltimore: Johns Hopkins University Press.

Frost, Frank J. 1984. "The Athenian Military before Cleisthenes." *Historia* 33: 283–94.

———. 1985. "Toward a History of Peisistratid Athens." In *The Craft of the Ancient Historian: Essays in Honor of Chester G. Starr*, edited by J. Ober and J. Eadie, 57–78.

———. 1987. "Attic Literacy and the Solonian *Seisachtheia*." *Ancient World* 15:51–58.

———. 1990. "Peisistratos, the Cults, and the Unification of Attica." *Ancient World* 21:3–9.

Graham, A. J. 1982. "The Colonial Expansion of Greece." In *The Cambridge Ancient History* 3.3 2d ed., 83–162. Cambridge: Cambridge University Press.

———. 1983. *Colony and Mother City in Ancient Greece*. Chicago: Ares.

Hedrick, Charles W., Jr. 1991. "Phratry Shrines of Attica and Athens." *Hesperia* 60:241–68.

Jacoby, Felix. 1950. *Die Fragmente der Griechischen Historiker*, 3B. Leiden: E. J. Brill.

Jeffery, Lilian H. 1962. "The Inscribed Gravestones of Archaic Attica." *BSA* 57:115–53.

————. 1976. *Archaic Greece: The City States c. 700–500 B.C.* New York: St. Martin's.

Kolb, Frank. 1977. "Die Bau-, Religions-, und Kulturpolitik der Peisistratiden." *JDAI* 92:99–138.

Lane Fox, Robin. 1985. "Inheritance in the Greek World." In *Crux*, edited by P. Cartledge and F. Harvey, 208–32. London: Duckworth.

Malkin, Irad. 1987. *Religion and Colonization in Ancient Greece*. Leiden: Brill.

Manville, Philip Brook. 1990. *The Origins of Citizenship in Ancient Athens*. Princeton: Princeton University Press.

Meiggs, Russell, and David Lewis. 1969. *A Selection of Greek Historical Inscriptions*. Oxford: Clarendon Press.

Morris, Ian. 1987. *Burial and Ancient Society*. Cambridge: Cambridge University Press.

Rhodes, Peter J. 1981. *A Commentary on the Aristotelian* Athenaion Politeia. Oxford: Clarendon Press.

————. 1986. *The Greek City States*. Norman: University of Oklahoma Press.

Richter, Gisela. 1961. *Archaic Gravestones of Attica*. London: Phaidon Press.

Sakkelion, M. 1877. "Lexeis meth' historion ek ton Demosthenous logon." *BCH* 1:137–55.

Sealey, Raphael. 1983. "How Citizenship and the City Began in Athens." *AJAH* 8:97–129.

Shapiro, H. Alan. 1989. *Art and Cult under the Tyrants in Athens*. Mainz: Von Zabern.

Stahl, Michael. 1987. *Aristokraten und Tyrannen im archaischen Athen*. Stuttgart: Franz Steiner.

Starr, Chester G. 1982. "Economic and Social Conditions in the Greek World." In *The Cambridge Ancient History* 3.3. 2d ed. Cambridge: Cambridge University Press.

Stroud, Ronald S. 1968. *Drakon's Law on Homicide*. Berkeley: University of California Press.

Whitehead, David. 1986. *The Demes of Attica 508/7–ca. 250 B.C.* Princeton: Princeton University Press.

Perikles' Citizenship Law of 451/0 B.C.

𐄷𐄷𐄷𐄷𐄷𐄷𐄷𐄷𐄷𐄷𐄷𐄷𐄷

ALAN L. BOEGEHOLD

A law of 451/0 B.C. limited Athenian citizenship to τοὺς ἐκ δυεῖν Ἀθηναίων γεγονότας, "men born of two Athenians" (Plutarch *Pericles* 37.3). To put the statute in Aristotle's negative form: μὴ μετέχειν τῆς πόλεως ὃς ἂν μὴ ἐξ ἀμφοῖν ἀστῶν ἦι γεγονώς, "Whoever has not been born of parents who are both citizens has no share in the city" (Aristotle *AP* 26.4). Aristotle gives the eponymous archon's name, Antidotos, and therewith the year, and the name of the man who proposed the measure, Perikles. The reason for the statute, Aristotle volunteers elliptically, was τὸ πλῆθος τῶν πολιτῶν, "too many citizens." Plutarch cites the same law as a paradoxical antecedent to Perikles' later request that his son, Perikles, be naturalized. Son Perikles—whose mother, Aspasia, was from Miletos and for that reason not Athenian—had been barred from citizen's rights by his father's earlier legislation. The law of 451/0 as recorded by Aristotle and Plutarch does not include or allude to other provisions. Why should such a law have been passed? Aristotle says "too many citizens," and later students generally concur. But almost anyone, given no more information than the law as we have it, might advance the same explanation. The sequence is self-explanatory. Why would it be necessary to define citizenship? It must have been because there were too many citizens, that is, too many people were claiming the rights and privileges of citizenship. But shall we say, all the rights and privileges? Or just certain ones? And if certain ones, which are those that might cause a sense of crowding, if too many people claimed them?

The statute calls for further inquiry. Within the great realm of possibilities, one can imagine a single celebrated contest or crisis or trial whose outcome hinged on a definition of *citizen*. As Patterson says, "there was a need in 451/50 for a standard qualification for citizenship, for who could be considered an Athenian. . . . On a practical level, if an allied city could be fined five talents for the murder of an Athenian in its territory (*IG* I² 10–11) it was crucial to know who was an Athenian."[1] An analogous statute, one possibly as early as 510/9 B.C. (the archonship of Skamandrios), protected Athenian citizens against torture.[2] Both of these protections require a definition of the term *Athenian citizen*, and yet neither implies pressure from an excessive number of individuals claiming the rights proper to citizens. On the other hand, the requirement of Perikles' law that both parents be Athenians is obviously a real constraint, especially in a time when leading citizens had for generations been contracting marriages with prominent non-Athenian families. Let us therefore accept Aristotle's explanation that there were "too many citizens" at Athens. His explanation admittedly can be mere inference from the words of the law: what he says is not necessarily so. There were indubitably other reasons to define citizenship, but Aristotle chose to give this one because he had particular applications in mind.

Keeping in mind Patterson's observation that certain protective Athenian laws required the word *citizen* to be exactly defined, we proceed to the next questions: Why was citizenship redefined? How did a πλῆθος of citizens create pressure? What did that πλῆθος do? Who exactly was being pressed? Some answers to these questions have been offered in the recent past. They are noted here not with an aim of close analysis and polemic, but as examples and as reasons for further study. Hignett says: "The main object of the law of 451/0 was probably to preserve the racial purity of the citizen-body; hence it is possible that Pericles was not concerned to word the law in such a way as to exclude from the citizenship those born out of lawful wedlock, although they were still excluded from the ἀγχιστεία by the pre-existing Solonian law."[3] It is perhaps understandable in one who lived with the volatile issues of World War II to fix upon purity of racial stock as a basis for conjecture, but at the same time it is helpful to remember that many passionate concerns of the twentieth century are at a far remove from those of Athenians 2,400 years and more ago. Among such concerns, that for purity of racial stock may find a place. What evidence can be presented for such a concern in the fifth-century B.C.? If the evidence consists solely of the law under discussion, "concern"—indeed, the word "alarm" is used by the same authority in the same context—then turns out to be a hypothetical creation, one that has coalesced in a revery far away in time and space from the actual scene. And yet in the same pages, the writer goes on to wonder whether this concern—that is, this cloud form he has caught sight of—was shared by "conservatives" and "progressive statesmen." He concludes that this was a measure on which Kimon and Perikles could agree.[4] The cloud form has become so substantial that it can be invoked to convene leading figures of state in solemn conclave.

Walker sees in the law "the assertion of the principle of privilege in its most offensive form." He says that "the pretext of the law is stated to have been the excessive number of citizens; in other words it is alleged that the citizen body has become unmanageably large. It may be surmised, however, that the real motive of the measure was to enhance the value of the lucrative privileges attaching to the franchise, by limiting the number of those entitled to share them."[5] Our guide in this instance, although there has been no hint of subterfuge in the sources, opens up the words of the law and finds the Athenians greedy. They have gotten to heaven, and so now they want to shut the door after themselves.

Gomme infers from this law an anxiety that the citizen body might grow so rapidly as to make the constitution unworkable. Moreover, popular sentiment disapproved of intermarriage with aliens: the law was therefore an attempt to restore what many regarded as normal.[6] Humphreys sees an attempt to put a stop to aristocratic marriages with foreign women. Such unions might "obstruct rational policy both towards Athens' subjects and towards her rivals."[7] Walters hypothesizes an excessive number of instances where a female slave would bear a child fathered by her master, and the master would subsequently seek to enfranchise the child.[8] Ruschenbusch, Sealey, and Rhodes see marriage of Athenian women to metics as the threat that Perikles' law was meant to avert.[9] Jacoby interpreted the law as a political weapon, intended for possible use against Kimon (who, however, died before that weapon needed to be used).[10]

These putative motives for passage of the law are rational enough in formulation, but they lack the urgency of reality. Why, after all, are laws composed? Seldom, one might reasonably conclude, is it because a far-sighted statesman looks into the future, sees a source of trouble ahead, and devises a shield. More often new laws are formulated ad hoc as attempts to reduce pressure. And it is this consideration that tests applicability of the explanations noted above: they do not summon up known and attested pressures. None of them presents an obvious, practical response to a persistent or pervasive ill. Furthermore, the anxiety of radicals and progressive Athenians, their concern for racial purity, has the look of recent manufacture. Greed admittedly must be considered in any historical investigation as a motivating factor, but, in the present instance, a moralizing charge of selfish appetite falls short of being a sufficient explanation for the new law. The other concerns offered in explanation—namely, that for quality of the citizen body, unsuitable marriages of one sort or another, and political tactics—are each and all admittedly possible, and there is no gain in attempting to calibrate degrees of their probability. This essay attempts to present an explanation that accommodates a certain density of plausible detail.

Consider first another way of looking at the citizenship law of 451/0 B.C. To begin: What could an Athenian citizen do as a citizen that made citizenship desirable? For one thing, his identity as a citizen did confer certain protections, such as those against torture and arrest. He could also hold office and receive pay for doing so. He could represent himself in court. He could initiate court actions. He could have a share in gifts of corn to the state. He could own, inherit, and bequeath property. It is this last right that needs elaboration.

In connection with this last perquisite, Aristotle (*AP* 9.2) says that because Solon's laws were not written clearly, but were written like the law on inheritance and heiresses, many disputes arose, and these disputes, both public and private, ended up in the dikasteria to be adjudicated. And this sequence, critics said, led finally to the empowering of the people, a deplorable eventuality. The point that is important in the context of our present inquiry is Aristotle's use of the law on inheritance and heiresses as awful example. He makes it clear that at Athens in 330 B.C., about 260 years after the time of Solon, that particular law is still by reason of its ambiguities generating disputes that end in the dikasteria.

The term *inheritance* is straightforward, but it is appropriate to cite here a succinct and authoritative elucidation of the function of an Athenian ἐπίκληρος, a term that is often translated as *heiress*. She is not really an heiress. She is a woman without brothers who acts as an intermediary for an estate. "Her sons became heirs of their maternal grandfather when they came of age, thus in a way securing the continuance of the grandfather's *oikos*."[11]

Now consider the Athens of ca. 452 B.C. In the first place, wealth and position derive primarily from the land. In the second place, that land has its limits. Attika is perhaps not in its entirety thin-soiled, as Thucydides (1.2.4–5) charges, for it supported a diversity of farming possibilities.[12] But even so, the land, bounded by sea and mountains and neighboring states, cannot be divided and subdivided over many generations. In fact, given the small total amount of arable land, a modest parcel—and most Attic parcels of land were small—could hardly have continued to be sufficient if subdivided over the course of two generations or so.[13]

In this limited Attika, the number of citizens who can claim to own land is constantly increasing. How and why the number increases are matters for speculation. Modern students of Athenian history have con-

jectured that new citizens were created by Solon's legislation, by Peisistratos' plan, by Kleisthenes' reorganization of Athenian families and
tribes, or by a liberal policy of naturalization after the Persian Wars.[14]
And, indeed, any one of these explanations—and all together—is conceivable. No matter, however, where we decide to say the new citizens came
from, the Periclean law of 451/0 B.C. is an index to pressure: there were at
that time too many men at Athens with pretensions to a citizen's prerogatives. But when Aristotle says "too many citizens," he is taking it for
granted that the phrase by itself explains the pressure. What, we now ask,
is a pressure that any Athenian would understand without having to have
incident and example adduced? What physical or economic distress,
what irritation or threat, so obviously results from an excess of citizens
that Aristotle at Athens did not think to mention it? An easy and obvious
answer is, the pressure on a limited amount of land, and hence on heirs
who hope to get their living from that land. What many Greek cities did
to solve the problem of too many citizens and too little land was to send
out colonies. Populations of states all over the Greek world grew at times
to oppressive numbers and had to be thinned out, and colonization was a
frequent mode of relief. Although Athens likewise sent out a few colonies,
and in addition used klerouchies as another way of settling its citizens on
land outside of Attika, the *heliaia*, a characteristically Athenian institution, may have made a difference.

The heliaia was a particular assembly of Athenian citizens who were
heliastai (judges). It was not *the* Athenian Assembly; it was *an* assembly
of qualified men,[15] that is, citizens of thirty years of age or older who did
not owe any money to the state, and who had sworn to act as judges and
to honor in that capacity certain constraints.[16] *Heliaia* is also the word
Athenians used to denominate their whole court system. An example of
the usage would be, if on a given day one or two or three panels of
heliastai were judging, an Athenian could include the totality of their
functioning with the word *heliaia*. Furthermore, any one panel (later
called dikasterion) could likewise be called heliaia. This body of judges
was notable for its mass. Athenians at some point had determined that
500 or 1,000 or more heliastai could as a judging panel make judicial
determinations and that a judgment by such a body was in effect the city's
will and judgment. It is not necessary for the present discussion to choose
a time when this particular development occurred. Some believe it was
with Solon, in whose time the heliaia was thought to originate. Others
urge Kleisthenes, or Perikles, who by instituting pay and the secret ballot
gave the heliaia the essential form it was to have throughout the years of
the Athenian democracy.[17] By Aristophanes' time surely, and probably as

early as 452 B.C., the heliaia was one of the institutions that defined the democratic constitution. Citizens brought their disputes to the heliaia, and Athens, in its capacity of league leader, ruled that certain classes of dispute between Athens and tributary allies be judged by the heliaia. Whatever the total volume of legal business actually was, a sufficient number of citizens had recourse to court judgments for Athens to become identified in Greece generally and at home as a litigious sort of place.

Now contemplate this Athens, where recourse to the heliaia has become a popular mode of relief. It is also an Athens where the citizen population—that is, the individuals who can inherit, own, and bequeath property—has grown by the 450s beyond what a modest acreage can support. But many of these citizens had justifiable claims to plots of land in Attika, and a claim of that sort would provide one good reason not to avail oneself of the opportunities offered by klerouchies or by new Athenian colonies at Thourioi and in Thrace. If their claims were not perfectly secure, they did in any case have access to a functioning judiciary procedure and the illusion of some peaceful years ahead.[18] There was therefore no absolute need for them to emigrate, unless they knew they had no chance to establish legal ownership of the land they claimed.

If we cannot define a typical Athenian family, it may be safe to say at least that usually offspring of a single union were not numerous and that men could and did marry a second and a third time. They did as a consequence have children by more than one wife. In the sixth and fifth centuries B.C., ambitious men sought out foreign alliances in marriage, and, as a result, there were children in Athens whose parents were not both Athenians. (Such children would usually have been μητρόξενοι.) As heirs, these descendants would have a claim on land owned by their fathers. But suppose that in some instances a man had married more than once and had had male children at least once by an Athenian woman, and others by a non-Athenian woman. If there came a time when both sets of offspring were trying to establish exclusive claim to whatever land might be inherited, they might at the end find themselves addressing a heliastic court. Although not official and appointed by the state, arbitrators were important factors in the mid-fifth century, but arbitration seems never to have been enough, even in the fourth century when arbitrators were securely established as state officers.

If Solon's laws on inheritance and heiresses seemed obscurely phrased and hard to apply in the late-fourth-century B.C., and if people remarked on how often appeals to those laws had finally to be adjudicated in a dikasterion, we can imagine that in the mid-fifth-century B.C. Athenians were just beginning to explore the ramifications of these difficulties. Roughly two generations had passed since Kleisthenes' reordering of Athenian citizenship, enough time for a plenitude of disputes over bequests. It will accordingly be useful to speculate on one way an inheritance dispute might develop in court.

A male offspring of an Athenian mother and father claiming exclusive right to his father's land might need to differentiate himself from other claimants who had the same father. If the other claimants were half-brothers by reason of their foreign-born mother, he had an obvious way to differentiate himself, namely, point to the mother's foreign origin. It might then seem natural for him to argue that he had a prior right to the property, or that the half-brothers were not really citizens and therefore could not own land in Attika. Regardless of whether there was a Solonian law defining citizenship, a claimant with a sense of entitlement would attack his opponent with whatever weapons he could find or imagine. And a heliastic court had latitude in its decisions: it was an assembly composed by the instrumentality of allotment and defined by common agreement as the very city. It judged as it wanted, and there was no appeal from its decisions.

If the claimant with an Athenian mother urged that he had a prior right to inherit property in Attika, and if that particular court awarded that particular claimant the land, no legally compelling precedent was established, for each case, so far as we can determine, was argued *ab ovo* before a heliastic court. Precedents might be cited for rhetorical effect, but they had no binding, legal force. But if a tactic proved itself successful once or twice, surely hopeful litigants employed it again and again, for what went on in the courts was of interest to everyone. And after a trial, parties to the action, heliasts, onlookers—in fact, all the people in the agora—would discuss overall strategy, repeat arguments, evaluate tactics, and judge verdicts. And many of them were the litigants of the next day and the day after. Consider also the composition of an Athenian heliaia. The heliastai were apt to be men who needed the one or two obols they received for judging. Insofar as they were not among the mighty of the world, they were not contracting marriages with potent families outside of Attika.

Why would Perikles appropriate as governing principle a tactic used in court by land-hungry claimants to an inheritance? Why should he propose it as law and present it to an *ekklesia* to be ratified as *psephisma*? The answer to these questions may provide an insight into Perikles' political acuity. Imagine that on one or more occasions a heliastic panel had adjudicated claims to inheritance in a way that seemed to have been influenced by a challenge to a claimant's status as Athenian. Imagine further that on those occasions the successful claimants seemed to derive an advantage from having been able to establish birth from two Athenian parents.

A word here on procedure is appropriate. The circumstances described in Lysias 23 may give an idea of what could have happened some fifty years or so earlier, that is, in the 450s. In the Lysianic speech, one Aristodikos goes to the polemarch to indict a certain Pankleon. He chooses this particular magistrate in the belief that Pankleon is not an Athenian citizen, for the polemarch at Athens is responsible for putting cases involving *xenoi* on a court calendar. Pankleon objects, saying that the case ought not to be brought to the polemarch because he, Pankleon, is a Plataean; that is, an Athenian citizen. Aristodikos responds by producing a knowledgeable witness who asserts before the magistrate that Pankleon was not a Plataean. A statement of this sort was called *diamarturia*. Students of Greek law believe it is an archaic sort of procedure, one no longer necessary or useful by the fourth century.[19] If it is indeed a survival from an earlier time, we may justifiably envision an inheritance suit in the 450s in which proceedings are delayed or stopped altogether by such an exchange. An expert, a person certified as qualified to know, would testify for or against a single assertion on which some phase of an action at law depended. But if such a person were to testify before Perikles passed his law defining Athenian citizenship, what criteria could he use in saying yes or no? A sure way would be to say that he knew both parents were Athenians and that he knew they were because he knew their parents, and he had seen them both at ceremonies where all who took part were presumed to be *astoi*.

A keen leader of the people might see after a few such cases an opportunity to anticipate, gratify, or capitalize on a general mood of his constituency. If this was the case at Athens, Perikles' redefinition of citizenship did not arise from any large vision of population control so much as from recognition that he could implement by statute an expressed conviction of the people. The people had as heliasts expressed themselves officially as in favor of a tight definition of citizenship. For the people next as ekklesia to ratify the same stipulations was no more than a single step.

Another need for a definition of citizenship can be associated with the heliaia. Once the popular courts had been constituted solely of citizens as heliasts, and once procedures had been developed to accommodate those non-Athenians who were forced by their tributary agreements to come to Athens for certain court transactions, strict definition of citizen was again a *sine qua non*.

Perikles defined Athenian citizenship because a number of functions of citizenship required that definition, if they were to be operative. At issue were not only privileges but also the working of the state. Furthermore, Perikles made his definition rigorous because there were claims on the land, which often had to be settled or adjudicated in the heliaia, where Solonian laws had soon proved hard to interpret. It may also be that accessions of new citizens over the previous two generations increased the number of inheritance cases that went to court. In either case, it was in court that the Athenian people, by their judicial decisions in particular cases, showed that they were ready for a rather narrow definition of citizenship. In proposing the law, Perikles did not anticipate some pressing need: he could instead have been confirming a manifest consensus.

Notes

1. Patterson 1981, 104.
2. See the discussion of Hignett 1952, 304.
3. Hignett 1952, 345.
4. Hignett 1952, 347. See Patterson 1981, 97–98 and 132, for an assessment of such speculations.
5. Walker 1927, 102–3.
6. Gomme 1930, 106.
7. Humphreys 1974, 93–94.
8. Walters 1983, 332–36.
9. Ruschenbusch 1979, 83–87; Sealey 1984, 131; Rhodes 1981, 334.
10. Jacoby 1954, 477–81.
11. Wolff 1975, 404–7.
12. Cf. Manville 1990, 105–23.
13. On the size of an Athenian plot of land, see Ste. Croix 1966, 105–14.
14. See Patterson 1981, 67–71.
15. See Hansen 1981–82, 9–47. Cf. Ostwald 1986, 10.
16. Aristotle *AP* 63.1 gives qualifications for dikasts ca. 330 B.C., from which (*inter alia*) the foregoing can be postulated for an earlier time.
17. See, e.g., Hansen 1981–82, 9–47, and Ostwald 1986, 10.
18. Badian 1987, 11–12.
19. See Harrison 1971, 124–31. During the fourth century, *paragraphe* is used instead, except for—apparently—questions arising out of inheritance disputes. See MacDowell 1978, 212–19 on uses of the two procedures. For *diamarturia* and *diadikasiai*, cf. Scafuro's essay in this volume.

Works Cited

Badian, Ernst. 1987. "The Peace of Kallias." *JHS* 107:1–39.
Gomme, Arnold W. 1930. "Some Notes on Fifth-Century History." *JHS* 50:106–7. Reprinted in *Essays in Greek History and Literature* (Oxford: Oxford University Press, 1937), 87–88.

Hansen, Mogens H. 1981–82. "The Athenian Heliaia from Solon to Aristotle." *ClMed* 33:1–47.

Harrison, A. R. W. 1968. *The Law of Athens*. Vol. 1, *The Family and Property*. Oxford: Oxford University Press.

————. 1971. *The Law of Athens*. Vol. 2, *Procedure*. Oxford: Oxford University Press.

Hignett, Charles. 1952. *A History of the Athenian Constitution to the End of the Fifth-Century* B.C. Oxford: Clarendon Press.

Humphreys, Sally C. 1974. "The Nothoi of Kynosarges." *JHS* 94:88–95.

Jacoby, Felix. 1954. *Die Fragmente der Griechischen Historiker*, 3b. Leiden: E. J. Brill.

MacDowell, Douglas M. 1978. *The Law in Classical Athens*. Ithaca: Cornell University Press.

Manville, Philip Brook. 1990. *The Origins of Citizenship in Ancient Athens*. Princeton: Princeton University Press.

Ostwald, Martin. 1986. *From Popular Sovereignty to the Sovereignty of the Law: Law, Society, and Politics in Fifth-Century Athens*. Berkeley: University of California Press.

Patterson, Cynthia. 1981. *Pericles' Citizenship Law of 451/0*. New York: Arno Press. Reprint. Salem, N.H.: Ayer, 1987.

Ruschenbusch, Eberhard. 1974. *Athenische Innenpolitik im 5 Jahrhundert v. Chr.* Hamburg: Bamberg.

Ste. Croix, Geoffrey E. M. de. 1966. "The Estate of Phaenippus (Ps.-Dem. xlii)." In *Ancient Society and Institutions: Studies Presented to Victor Ehrenberg*, edited by Ernst Badian, 109–14. Oxford: Oxford University Press.

Sealey, Raphael. 1984. "On Lawful Concubinage at Athens." *CA* 3:111–13.

Walker, E. M. 1927. "The Periclean Democracy." *The Cambridge Ancient History*. Vol. 5, *Athens 478–401* B.C. Cambridge: Cambridge University Press.

Walters, Kenneth. 1983. "Perikles' Citizenship Law." *CA* 2:314–36.

Wolff, Hans Julius. 1975. "Greek Legal History—Its Functions and Potentialities." *Washington University Law Quarterly* 404–7.

Everyman's Grave

IAN MORRIS

"In our homes we find a beauty and good taste (*euprepeia*) which delight us every day and drive away our cares," says Perikles in Thucydides' funeral oration (2.38.1, trans. Saunders). Few things are so culturally specific as "good taste," and few are so revealing about their possessors' views of the structures of their world.[1] In this essay, I explore the social dimensions of one aspect of late fifth-century Athenian "good taste," the lavishness of memorials to the dead. This topic is not chosen at random. Not only did it provide the context for Thucydides' remark on good taste, but, as I shall try to show, it was a matter of serious concern and a major arena of self-definition for Athenian citizens. Around 430 B.C., the dramatic date of the Periclean oration, there was a sharp increase in the amount Athenians were prepared to spend on such display, as well as a major change in the forms of symbolism they used. This was part of a significant shift in relationships within the citizen body, as wealthier Athenians began to assert more prominent statuses for themselves than that of "citizen." This was part of a wider process affecting the whole Greek world, as a generally egalitarian fifth-century ideology began to break up.

The change in the scale of funerary commemoration has long been apparent, but its social and political implications have rarely been recognized. Our interpretation has to make sense at several levels. We need to begin by placing Athenian practices within a Panhellenic context; by doing so we discover that the Athenian increase in scale in the 420s was paralleled all over the Greek world. Any explanation must make sense of the similarities between what happens in Athens and what happens elsewhere around the Aegean. This raises large issues, which I have examined in greater detail in other publications.[2] In this essay, though, I concentrate on some of the ways in which Athens differs from the general Greek pattern, looking at how the overall movement toward greater elaboration in the late-fifth century was reinterpreted within the specifically Athenian cultural tradition. This involves asking how different social groups within Athens reacted to the new styles of burial, as well as what this meant for Athenians' perceptions of themselves.

Good Taste in Classical Athens

In writing the history of taste, we have to walk a thin line between facile generalizations and overindulgence in particular details. This is difficult enough for modern historians, who have a wealth of primary sources of many different genres;[3] but for the historian of ancient Greece, two special problems have to be faced. The first lies in the nature of the sources. In some ways, we are rather well informed about matters of taste, most strikingly in Plato's theory of mimesis (*Rep.* 10.595a–608c). However, this is not the kind of evidence I use in this essay. I make a distinction between popular taste and the philosophy of taste, on much the same lines as Dover's contrast between popular morality and moral philosophy. Dover suggests that "if we imagined that either Plato's work or Aristotle's represented an intellectual systematization of the principles which were manifested in the moral choices and judgements of the ordinary unphilosophical Greek, it is possible that we might go badly astray." This is even more true of matters of taste. Plato (*Laws* 3.700a–701c) makes his disapproval of contemporary musical tastes very clear. Instead of relying on philosophical systems, I look mainly to actual practices, judging standards of taste by what people did. To some extent the evidence for this comes from oratory, drama, and historical writing. Interpreting these texts involves problems very similar to those that Dover describes,[4] but much more evidence can be found in the archaeological record. This raises completely different source problems, which I will address later in this essay.

The second problem to face at the outset is that the study of ancient Athenian taste has itself become a central part of the history of taste in modern Western Europe. For two hundred years fifth-century Athens has been lauded as a paradigm of "noble simplicity and quiet grandeur," as Winckelmann said in 1764,[5] providing a mirror to the perceived decadence and alienation of modernity. In a series of articles, Vickers and Gill have argued that the Romantic tendencies of modern scholars of Greek art have caused them to invent an Athenian penchant for the simple and pure, and particularly to believe that Athenians valued finely painted pottery over "vulgar" ostentation in silver and gold.[6] I find much in their account of the ideology of classical scholarship persuasive, but ultimately it is more revealing about the history of archaeology than about ancient Greece.[7] The evidence is complex, but on the whole fifth-century Athenian taste *does* seem to have been remarkably restrained.[8] The modern perception of Athenian art may be a wilful misrepresentation for ideological and financial profit; but it was not created out of nothing.

To give some idea of the ambiguity of the evidence for Athenian taste about lavish displays of wealth, we might start with what ought to be one of the most revealing texts. The famous "Attic stelai"[9] record the auction of property belonging to a group of wealthy men[10] condemned for profaning the Eleusinian mysteries in 415 B.C. The inscriptions mention nothing more valuable than a single silver object and a silver coin (*IG* i[3] 427.94; 422.182), and even these might not be what they seem.[11] Pritchett concluded that "our record of the sale of confiscated furniture seems to show that there was little sense of personal luxury in Athens in the last quarter of the fifth century, even among men of wealth."[12] Any interpretation of the stelai could easily be challenged, and equally debatable counterevidence could be mustered against it (e.g., Ar. *Wealth* 808–15).

However, other sources seem to point toward a similar conclusion. Thucydides (1.6.3) says that rich clothing for men had recently gone out of fashion;[13] and although the Old Oligarch ([Xen.] *AP* 2.10) talks of the rich having houses with "gymnasia and baths and changing rooms," the archaeological record reveals little imposing private architecture. Thucydides (2.65.2) also comments that the rich had "fine and well-equipped houses in the country," and, because excavation has concentrated on urban sites, we may be missing important evidence; but the complete absence of luxurious building suggests that, at least as compared to later periods, classical Athenian tastes in housing were very restrained.[14]

There are more indications of personal display in the fourth century than in the fifth, but not many, and most of our evidence for hostility to displays of wealth comes from fourth-century legal speeches.[15] But in one type of display there was a major change in the last quarter of the fifth century, when monumental tombs began to appear all over the Attic countryside. Around 500 B.C., the mounds, statues, and stelai that had characterized Archaic Attic cemeteries disappear, and very few monuments are known until the 420s.[16] Suddenly, they reappear, growing in scale until stopped abruptly by Demetrios of Phaleron around 317 B.C.[17] We even have a few prices. In 409 one Diogeiton was asked to spend 5,000 *drakhmai* (probably enough to feed a family of four at subsistence

level for five to seven years) on his brother Diodotos' tomb. Apparently
he only spent half this and kept the rest (Lys. 32 *Diogeiton* 21). There is
no suggestion that 5,000 drakhmai was considered an excessive amount.
In 349 Apollodoros ([Dem.] 45 *Stephanus* 79) told a jury that Stephanos
spent over two talents on a tomb for another man's wife after he had
debauched her. The web of moral outrage here is complex, and the price
is no doubt exaggerated, but this general scale must have seemed credible.
In 326/5 Harpalos stole 700 talents from Alexander's treasury at Babylon
and fled to Athens, where he built such a huge tomb for his mistress
Pythionike that Diodorus mentioned it three centuries later (17.108.5; cf.
Athenaeus 13.594e). It is not just a matter of literary genre that we have
no such stories from before 425: this sort of spending would not have
been acceptable.[18] According to Plutarch, after winning the battles of the
Eurymedon around 466 B.C.[19] Kimon was allowed to set up three herms;
and

> although Kimon's name does not appear on them, his contemporaries
> regarded this memorial as a supreme mark of honor for him. Neither
> Themistokles nor Miltiades could boast of any comparable distinction;
> indeed, when the latter asked for nothing more than a crown of olive,
> Sophanes of Dekeleia rose to his feet in the Assembly and protested. His
> speech was ungracious, but it won the people's applause at the moment.
> "When you have fought and conquered the barbarians by yourself, Mil-
> tiades," he said, "then you can ask to be honoured by yourself." (*Cimon*
> 8.1, trans. Scott-Kilvert)

The actions of Diogeiton and Stephanos would have been very problematic in Kimon's day. Indeed, if we believe all of this story, they would have
provoked the wrath of the people at any point between 490 and the 460s.

Fifth-century Athenians redirected an older tradition of aristocratic
competitive display, harnessing it in the service of democracy by changing
two crucial elements. First, *philotimia* was to be demonstrated through
lavish spending on liturgies that were controlled by the polis, not through
institutions such as *xenia*.[20] Second, there was very little opportunity for
Athenian nobles to create permanent monuments to themselves. Another
story in Plutarch illustrates this. We are told that Thoukydides, son of
Melesias, orchestrated criticism of Perikles' state building program:

> Perikles appealed to the people in the Assembly to declare whether in
> their opinion he had spent too much. "Far too much," was their reply,
> whereupon Perikles retorted, "Very well then, do not let it be charged to
> the public account but to my own, and I will dedicate all the public
> buildings in my name." It may have been that the people admired such a

70

gesture in the grand style, or else that they were just as eager as Perikles to have a share in the glory of his works. At any rate they raised an uproar and told him to draw freely on the public funds and spare no expense in his outlay. (*Pericles* 14, trans. Scott-Kilvert)[21]

Until the 420s it seems that the only acceptable kind of public display of wealth was its use for the public good, and even that was defined by the *demos* through its program of liturgies and was restricted to ephemeral acts, such as funding plays or ships. This kind of spending certainly remained important in the fourth century,[22] but rich Athenians also seem to have held on to a larger proportion of their wealth than previously.[23] Their political opposition to democratic finances merged with a form of cultural subversion of democratic symbolism in the sphere of funerals. From about 500 to 425, "good taste" militated against lavish memorials, and the burials of the rich are generally indistinguishable from those of the poor. In the last quarter of the century this changed, and it became appropriate for the *plousioi* to spend in a way that distinguished them as special. There are no direct discussions of this major cultural change preserved among our literary sources, and we must begin from the burial customs themselves.

Two Problems of Method

Burial is one of the best documented cultural practices of classical Athens, but until quite recently it has played very little part in historians' attempts to understand social change. The reason for this lies in two deep-seated methodological assumptions: first, that Athenian culture can be understood in purely Athenian terms; and second, that a cultural practice has a single meaning that only needs to be decoded by the modern historian. The limitations of these assumptions need to be clarified before we can proceed to the evidence itself.

Athenocentrism. Our textual sources are, of course, almost all Athenian; and although archaeologists have worked all over Greece, the evidence from Athens is much better known than that from other regions. When historians read archaeological syntheses, they usually discover that Athenian burials are very restrained from about 500 to 425 B.C. and then grow in lavishness from 425 to 317, but are given little information about customs outside Athens. They therefore tend to view the changes in burial as a purely Athenian phenomenon, which makes it legitimate to seek explanations within the corpus of Athenian texts. Ancient authors say little about the kind of large-scale social forces which might be expected to transform artistic production across the whole Greek world, and therefore modern historians trying to use literary sources to account for these changes often turn to contingent, incidental factors.

This is strikingly true of the two most popular theories for the increase in spending on tombs in the 420s. The first builds on Thucydides' comments (2.52.3–4) that the plague that broke out in 430 caused people to neglect traditional burial customs. What Thucydides says is that the plague caused a decline in the formality of burial, with some people even going as far as to throw their dead onto others' funeral pyres. It might be possible to argue for a causal link between this behavior and the subsequent increase in funerary spending; but this remains to be demonstrated. The second theory begins from the evidence we have that sculptors came to Athens in the 440s to work on Perikles' building projects. They suggest that by 430, when the Peloponnesian War got under way and the money for statues dried up, the sculptors turned to producing gravestones; stimulated by this supply, the Athenians began to demand such markers. Once again, there is a logical problem, because most post-425 funerary monuments are not sculptural. It hardly requires talent of the kind that produced the Parthenon frieze to make dressed stone blocks for a peribolos tomb. Some art historians even combine both these theories, as when Clairmont, the leading authority, argues that "while it is essential to keep in mind the external causes—the war and the plague—that led to the rebirth of classical gravestones, the sculpture of the Parthenon, in the very broadest sense, is the preliminary *per se* for the creation of grave reliefs."[24]

A much more sophisticated approach to Athenian burial began to appear around 1980, as historians started to link funerary behavior to other kinds of rituals and to examine the changes of the 420s in more structural terms. However, the structures that they identified were generally described in purely Athenian terms, as responses to purely Athenian events. In her pathbreaking study *The Invention of Athens,* Nicole Loraux argues that restraint in fifth-century individual tombs was the mirror image of display by the state in its annual public funeral for the war dead, through which Athens as a polis appropriated the glory of death in battle to create a communal ideology.[25] The simple pit graves of the citizens, rarely marked out at all, would have contrasted sharply with the altarlike dressed stone state graves, topped with ten lists of the casualties from each tribe and (certainly in 394, and also probably earlier) with relief sculptures.[26] She speaks of the change in use of monuments in the fourth century as an "eruption of individuality" and concludes that "it is by no means certain that civic values necessarily gained by this, for the shift was already under way from the collective list to the crown rewarding an individual's acts of heroism." She explains this change as part of "the 'crisis of the fourth century,' which restored an imbalance between the public domain and private values."[27]

In another influential study, Sally C. Humphreys made a diametrically opposed interpretation:

> Commemoration in the archaic period was simply stratified: mounds and sculptured monuments, like ostentatious funerals, loudly proclaimed that the dead belonged to the elite. Paying visits to the tombs of famous ancestors was not a pious duty, but a way of reminding contemporaries of the glory of one's family. It was the state funerals for war dead which first brought the honours of heroic burial within the range of every Athenian citizen, and I would suggest that it was this significant change which stimulated the development in the late fifth and fourth centuries of monuments commemorating the domestic virtues of the ordinary citizen. Far from being gradually destroyed by the growth of the state, as Fustel thought, the idea of a visible tomb for every man and the "continuity" of all *oikoi* may have been generated by it.[28]

Although these theories are interesting and stimulating, they ignore a crucial dimension of the evidence. What happened in Athens in the 420s was but one part of a much wider geographical pattern. We find similar restraint everywhere in the Greek world from about 500 to 425. Decidedly undemocratic poleis such as Thebes and Corinth offer archaeologists no lavish tombs. The cities of Thessaly continue to use relief stelai, but these burials also are simpler than those of the sixth century; and even on the fringes of the Greek world, the great tumuli of Vergina and Trebenishte and the rock-cut tombs of Lycia all stop around 500. The Panhellenic pattern changes in the last quarter of the fifth century. Soon there are huge tombs everywhere, from the Nereid monument to the first examples of the vaulted "Macedonian" tombs. I have argued elsewhere that any explanation of the Athenian evidence which fails to take into account the wider pattern will inevitably be partial and misleading.[29]

Uniformitarianism. Cultural historians have become increasingly critical of approaches that reduce past practices to a simple coherence, assuming that all viewers (and producers) of artifacts interpret them in the same way.[30] Few would defend such a notion explicitly, but it frequently lurks behind art historical analysis as what Preziosi, borrowing from Foucault, has called "the panoptic gaze."[31] It leads to single-cause theories of cultural change, such as seeing the plague or the war as catchall explanations: it also lies behind Loraux's and Humphreys' functionalist readings. Understanding the evidence involves not only locating it within the general Greek patterns but also examining the peculiarities of how different groups within the Athenian population interpreted what they saw: as Chartier says, adopting "a definition of history primarily sensitive to inequalities in the appropriation of common materials or practices."[32]

In this essay I concentrate on the visual impact of tombs in Athens and the *meanings* they evoked in the minds of those who stood among them, either as participants in funerals or as passersby. I suggest that when Athenians thought about the glory that personal tombs might bring to their families in the early- and mid-fifth century, they did so primarily in terms of Archaic and Homeric models of *athanaton kleos,* the "deathless glory" of the hero. During the course of the fifth century, the state war funerals[33] began to create an alternative, civic, symbolic system. Far from bringing the honors of heroic burial within every citizen's grasp, as Humphreys suggested, the new symbolism took them away from everyone, even Athens' richest citizens. But in the 420s, the aristocracy muscled in on this polis iconography, abandoning the heroic symbolism of earlier times. The new private tomb styles of the late fifth century do not represent the spread of heroic honors through the citizen body. Instead, they form part of a Panhellenic movement in which the rich challenged what by then seemed like an old-fashioned and unduly narrow notion of the polis. They took back for themselves the glory of those fathers, husbands, and sons who had died in war—not now in the guise of the hero who excelled in *metis* or *bie,* always an ambiguous and threatening figure for the community,[34] but in that of the patriotic *prostates tou demou.* In the fourth century, the scale of state monuments also escalated in competition with private tombs that were using basically the same repertoire of images. The polis could always spend more on a tomb than even the richest citizen, but this was not the point: once the principle was established that individuals could honor their dead kin in the same style as that in which the polis created its communality, display took on a very different meaning. Instead of honoring themselves ritually as heroes operating above or outside the polis, fourth-century aristocrats created a ritual structure in which they absorbed that which had previously belonged to the community as a whole, and they defined themselves as its leaders in a way that had not been possible in the fifth century.

Reading Material Culture

This approach to the material remains of rituals—concentrating on the meanings evoked in the minds of ancient observers—raises still further methodological problems.[35] Much of the archaeological analysis of symbolism done in the 1980s proceeded from essentially structuralist assumptions, banishing from legitimate discourse the actors' direct interpretations of the meaningful content of their own symbolism in favor of deriving alternative, deeper forms of meaning by analyzing the inter-relations between a set of arbitrary signifiers.[36] This avoided the naïvety of earlier approaches to symbolism, but at the cost of making it all but impossible to break out of an arid, formalist universe without reintroduc-ing "meaning" as a postscript to analysis. As Tilley says, "the meaning of the structures recovered have [sic] primarily been interpreted through grafting various Marxist, hermeneutic and post-structuralist perspec-tives ... to structuralist forms of analysis ... such a structuralist ap-proach marks only the beginning of a fresh perspective on material cul-ture studies: it is something to be transcended."[37] There have been two main responses to the problem (other than that of rejecting the interest of examining such meanings).[38] Some archaeologists rejoice in the impossi-bility of reducing archaeologically recovered symbolic systems to an un-derlying "reality," moving analytical techniques (as well as interpretation) in a broadly poststructuralist direction; others seek alternative ways to make the intellectual leap into ancient meanings.[39]

The most important example of the first method is Aubrey Cannon's theory of "expressive redundancy" in mortuary symbolism. He notes that when the general level of funerary expenditure is high, it is among the wealthiest that display declines first, and that modest funerals become a symbol of "good taste," only gradually spreading down the social ladder. He says that this pattern has relatively little to do with democratic or aristocratic tendencies; rather, any style of mortuary symbolism has a point beyond which continued elaboration fails to impress anyone, and the only strategy left to someone wishing to make a point is to reduce the scale of display. It is *difference,* not the form it takes, that counts when symbols are being used to create hierarchy. In a suitably postmodern flourish, he suggests that we need to leave more room for life to imitate art: "If expressive restraint is seen as part of the same trajectory as expres-sive elaboration, then such ideological change as does occur must be considered as much the consequence as the cause of shifts in mortuary symbolism."[40] This could be used, at a very general level, to explain the changes that take place around 500 B.C. Cannon's general theory pro-poses a symbolic version of Michels' Iron Law of Oligarchy,[41] that the few always control the many, no matter how democratic appearances may be. This would have the rich cutting back on display to distance themselves from the poor, like Aristotle's "Magnanimous Man" (*EN* 4.1124b), who would never dream of sinking so low as to actually compete for honor against the riffraff. Following Cannon's model, the lower orders would continue for a while to indulge in what had been redefined as "vulgar" theatricality, before dropping into line. The change around 425 would then represent the exhaustion of the symbolic capital of restraint, with the elite quickly going back to lavishness.

The alternative is to take an empathetic plunge, exemplified by Hodder's discussion of the Neolithic village of Lepenski Vir:

> The rather dry description of symbolic oppositions that I have so far provided ignores a central component in Srejovic's text and in the displays of the Lepenski Vir material that I have seen. The site is wonderfully evocative and atmospheric. The ritual, art, and symbolism seem to reach to us and react on us not through their dry "linguistic," precise meanings, but through emotive experience. The ambiguous sculpted heads, the all-pervasive presence of death, the ordered arrays of houses, the deep gorges of the Danube all seem to appeal directly to our senses. It is as if the houses provide a setting for some drama—an ideal scene for the performance of some plot.
>
> And without drama, what would these structures be doing anyway? Who would believe them, accept them, if they were only abstract rules? It is only through emotional experience, through fear of death, joy in life, the comfort of home, the danger of the wild, that the structures have any force. Movement within the house, taking objects from front to back, burying bodies, carving and placing the stones, lighting the fire, are all enmeshed within a dramatic setting. The daily events themselves are the drama, but only because they have been "set" up as such.[42]

In what follows I draw on both methods, fortified by the greater security in inferences of meaning which comes from access to at least some texts from Athens. But no amount of literary evidence will ever remove the ambiguity that is inherent in the very act of grasping symbols, to be understood by an involuntary midact rather than reasoned discussion; uncertainty and open-endedness are a crucial part of the analysis.

Heroes and Citizens

Many historians explain the fifth-century Athenians' restrained funerary commemoration as a result of the so-called *post aliquanto* law that Cicero (*Laws* 2.64–65) placed some time between Solon (594 B.C.) and Demetrios of Phaleron (317 B.C.). Cicero says that the law curbed extravagant monuments, and, logically enough, it has been associated with the beginning of the era of restraint around 500 B.C.[43] But whether the cause behind Athenian restraint was such a law or a more complex set of social forces, there are a few monumental burials in Athens between 500 and 425. A small group of Athenian families consistently ignored restraint. Three or four sequences of monumental tombs are known, the most important of them in the Kerameikos cemetery.[44] On the southwest edge of the huge Mound G, raised around 560 B.C., we find a sequence of mounds (L–O) and mud-brick tombs (d–f) spanning the fifth century without a break. Mound G is the largest known Archaic Athenian grave marker, containing about 2,600 m³ of earth. The excavator claimed that it was the tomb of Solon;[45] whatever the case may be, it was certainly a major landmark in the fifth century, and one family line was allowed to build a series of monuments which locked directly into its spectacular heritage, within sight of the *Demosion Sema,* where the war dead were buried.[46]

These lavish burials drew on two rich veins of imagery, with their mounds and stelai continuing the aristocratic burial traditions of the sixth century and, like them, recalling the funerals of the Heroic Age.[47] There are strict limits on how far we can speculate about what "Athenians" thought when they saw mounds like those in the Kerameikos. But I find it hard to imagine that many—ordinary peasants as well as an educated elite—could have been unaware of the links between the mound/ stele combination and the Archaic/Homeric past; and still harder to imagine that the buriers who performed such funerals would have failed to make this link. We should probably assume that the users of these burial places were a small number of families, who, like the Eumolpidai or Eteoboutadai, were allowed to continue to hold special aristocratic privileges in ritual matters under the democracy.

But even if the mounds had official sanction, they evoked a golden age of aristocratic freedom in direct affront to the simplicity of others' funerals. On the one hand, they brought to mind men such as Kimon, aristocrat *par excellence* and triple Olympic chariot-race winner, thought to have been murdered by the tyrants in 528/7, whose tumulus was still visible a century later (Hdt. 6.103.3). On the other hand, they reached back still further to evoke figures like Patroklos and Hektor, as well as outward. The use of tumuli created a shared symbolic system uniting Athenian noblemen with those of other regions, but, in the fifth century, neither kind of freedom was compatible with the polis. Both were increasingly restricted to the world of *xenia,* aristocratic guest-friendship.[48] The most self-consciously Homeric burial is Kerameikos gr. C264, the final burial in the Mound G sequence, dating around 425. It consisted of the ashes of a man in an ornate bronze urn, wrapped in purple cloth and then placed in a wooden box inside a monolithic sarcophagus. The whole ensemble was covered over by mud-brick tomb e and Mound O.

The nostalgic use of sixth-century monumental styles down to 425 against a general background of restraint is closely paralleled in Thessaly, and it has looser similarities with commemoration patterns in Boiotia and the Cyclades. I have argued elsewhere that in general terms we should see this phenomenon as the resistance of an interpolis elite to a Panhellenic trend toward egalitarianism after 500 B.C.[49] But this is only part of the story: we also need to understand how these general trends were reinterpreted within the specifically Athenian context. There are a few explicit evaluations of lavish burial in our sources, but these are highly problematic. In the *Republic* Plato includes "a worthy burial when they die" in his list of reasons why the Guardians will be happier men than Olympic victors (465e)—to which Glaukon replies, " 'These are indeed great rewards.' " And to encourage the Warriors to be brave, Sokrates says, " 'We shall bury them with whatever particular ceremonies Delphi prescribes for men of such heroic mould' " (469a–b). In the *Hippias Major,* however, when Hippias of Elis includes in his definition of the good life that he who lives it is "to be buried well and magnificently (*megaloprepos*) by his own offspring" (291e), Sokrates goes on to demonstrate that this is muddle-headed. Plato's point is perhaps that recognition by the state at death is the greatest glory, a point also made by Thucydides (2.43) and Herodotus (1.30). This takes us little further forward. Plato may well have intended Hippias to represent what upper-class Greeks in general thought, but we cannot hope to build a rigorous analysis of Athenian interpretations of symbolism on the basis of this one reference.

Our most promising source is neither the texts nor the graves themselves, but paintings of visits to tombs on white-ground lekythoi.[50] The cylindrical lekythos (oil flask) and the white-ground technique were in use at Athens before 500. The white surface onto which the decoration is painted is extremely flaky, and it is likely that these pots were primarily always used as burial offerings. By the 460s nonfunerary scenes were quite common on white-ground lekythoi.[51] The first known visit-to-the-tomb scenes are attributed to the Beldam painter and conventionally dated a little before 470,[52] and by 450 such pots had become common. From then until their disappearance around 400, four main subjects were painted on them. Two of these, the *prothesis* (laying-out of the dead) and scenes of mythological death, were rather rare. The majority of the pots show either a visit to the tomb or a "mistress and maid" preparing to make such a visit.[53]

The tomb-visit scenes show a variety of grave types, but the burial is frequently marked by a stele and tumulus, like the few contemporary lavish tombs. Clairmont suggested that these pots show mourning at the state war graves,[54] but this is unlikely. The only definite exception is a fragmentary white-ground loutrophoros that seems to show a series of inscriptions, one of them beginning with the words *EN BYZAN,* which must be a state grave.[55] Some of the vase paintings that show stelai have *kalos* names, honoring living nobles, written alongside them or even on the stele; a few have names from Homer, such as Patroklos and Agamemnon; but most are plain.[56]

In the years when these scenes came into fashion, around 450 B.C., hardly any Athenians favored ostentatious display at death and the use of mounds and stelai linking the dead to a glorious heroic and aristocratic past. Yet they were clearly very interested in such images on their grave pots. In the two best-documented cemeteries at Athens, the Kerameikos and Syndagma Square, white-ground lekythoi occur in about 30 percent of the excavated graves of the late fifth century, rather more often in cremations than inhumations. They are limited primarily to graves having three or more pots placed in them as grave goods.[57] This suggests that although white-ground lekythoi were not extremely common, neither were they restricted to a narrow elite group of the kind that could actually afford to raise monumental grave mounds.[58]

Many fifth-century Athenians seem to have cherished elitist, heroizing symbolism, undermining the uniform simplicity of actual burial practices. It is not likely that their choice of pictures for funerary pots was random;[59] so what does this rejection of contemporary restraint mean? Contrasting the scenes on lekythoi with those on late-fifth-century relief tombstones, Shapiro suggests that the latter are "the public face of death, while the white lekythoi present a set of popular beliefs less shaped by official ideology."[60] These tomb scenes, where profoundly inegalitarian images are deployed in the middle of rituals that in other ways seem to conform so well to democratic ideals, present a problem of interpretation similar to that created by the use of aristocratic terminology in the state funeral orations.[61] Loraux suggests that democracy was "undermined from the inside by aristocratic values and representations." Ober argues, to the contrary, that "the 'nationalization' of the ideals of *kalokagathia* and nobility of descent does not represent a rejection of equality among citizens; rather, it demonstrates the power of popular ideology to appropriate and transvalue terms that had formerly implied the exclusivity of a few *within* the citizen group."[62]

The heroic mound-and-stele without doubt made a powerful statement. Homer continued to be read and to provide a set of aristocratic role models and images throughout classical times,[63] and when the family that used the southwest edge of the Mound G area of the Kerameikos continued to make "heroic" burials in the mid-fifth-century, it must have had a shocking effect. I would suggest that in most Athenians' eyes the people who carried out these funerals were not eccentrics to be laughed off with the kind of humor we find in Theophrastus' *Characters*. Instead, we should understand their actions in terms of the attitudes lampooned by Aristophanes in the *Wasps* in 422 B.C., where Bdelykleon's "luxurious" tastes (wanting bass and an onion) lead to charges of aiming at tyranny: "Sea bass, huh? That's real rich food—expensive, too. TOO expensive for a real Athenian democrat" (ll. 494–95, trans. Parker).

This symbolism had ineradicably aristocratic associations, but it would be naïve to assume that the symbolic force of the grand *semata* that were so crucial to the construction of the heroic persona was left uncontested in the fifth century. Like spoken language, pictorial images can be transvalued and turned against their original users, but the processes involved are often rather different. Words can be taken over on a large scale; it costs nothing to claim kalokagathia. But tombs are more problematic. It was out of the question for every Athenian to construct a monstrous tumulus. Pictures on relatively cheap pots are easier, but the critical aspect of the visit-to-the-tomb scenes is that these pictures proliferate against a background of continued restraint in the use of actual tumuli. There is nothing to suggest that more and more Athenians started to imitate Homeric funerals around 460, culminating in the collapse of restraint around 425. Real tumuli remain rare, even when big tombs do become common late in the century.

While pictures of lavish tombs may well have done something to satisfy a heroizing urge that public opinion would not allow to be realized in actual practice, they also had at least two other effects. Humphreys suggests that "families which hankered after impressive grave monuments . . . could at least flank the tomb with vases which showed what they would have liked to do."[64] However, the visitor to the graveside might be struck at least as strongly by the contrast between the heroizing scene in the paintings and the simplicity of the actual grave. The context of use made the painters' images rich and complex, undermining their own references to another age. The same applies to those present at the funerals in which white-ground lekythoi were actually buried in the grave: they were aware of the power of the tumulus, but renounced it.[65]

These remarks apply chiefly to the period when the mound scenes were introduced. From about 460 to 430 they were probably an evocative and contestable symbol: some Athenians would see them as a way to state an allegiance to nonegalitarian ideals; others, as something that had been taken over by the demos. For this latter group, visual reference to grave mounds may have said more about the power of democracy to tame elitism than about the claims of an aristocratic few to preserve heroic privileges. By the late fifth century, it seems likely that a second consequence would have come into effect. Fifty years of repeated use of the tumulus as a metaphor for the grave in otherwise non-"heroic" funerals may have debased this symbolism to the point where it became difficult to think of it as a special, subversive, and elitist statement anymore. It is certainly interesting to observe that the main period of use of these representations is the last quarter of the century, just the point at which the Athenian elite abandoned the mound as a grave marker. Kerameikos gr. C264, around 425, is the last example of the fifth-century "Homeric" tradition; the final monument in the Mound G series, around 400, is not another mound but the huge mud-brick tomb f, roughly contemporary with, and closely similar to, the first stone periboloi. I would see Cannon's model of expressive redundancy at work here. In the 420s, more and more wealthy Greeks were deciding that they wanted monumental tombs, but at Athens the traditional mound-and-stele combination had been "vulgarized" by its frequent use in the iconography of conventional funerals. An alternative set of symbols was needed.

Such symbols were readily to hand in the form of the state graves for the war dead, probably one of the most potent images in late-fifth-century Athens, lining the Demosion Sema leading out of the city. The famous cenotaph of Dexileos, killed in 394 in the Corinthian War and buried in the state grave for that year, provides a good example. The noble "knights" of Athens decided to set up their own memorial for their five fallen comrades, and its inscription (*IG* 2^2 5222) preserves Dexileos' name; but his family also built a precinct for him among their own tombs in the Kerameikos,[66] 100 meters or so from the Demosion Sema, showing him on horseback trampling down his enemies. The iconography of Dexileos' monument is virtually the same as that of a relief of the early 420s now in the Villa Albani, which probably came from a state war grave. His family was tapping into the glory of the war dead, not only by honoring him with a monument in such a symbolically strategic location but also by adopting what had previously been a polis-only form of commemoration.

Bugh and Strauss cite an unpublished paper by the late Colin Edmonson, pointing out the peculiarity of the inscription commemorating Dexileos in his precinct (*IG* 2^2 6217), which included his birth date. They suggest that this was to prove that he was too young to have been associated with the regime of the Thirty in 404/3 B.C. Bugh adds that "*IG* II^2 5222 and *IG* II^2 6217 represent an effort to refurbish the image of the Athenian cavalry";[67] that is, its members appear to be assimilating themselves to the polis rather than appropriating its symbols for their own glory. But the two strategies are not incompatible. Dexileos' family, like many other rich Athenians, were doing both things at once. Using state imagery set them above those who could not afford stone monuments and distanced them from old-fashioned heroic symbols, proclaiming them as men of the city, but also as *special* men. The changes in burial do not provide evidence for the so-called "fourth-century crisis" in the ideology of the democratic city-state.[68] Without doing anything so blatant, Athenian nobles were proclaiming that they had a grander status than that of the fifth-century concept of the citizen, turning away from the principles of *isonomia*.[69]

Dexileos' parents were by no means the only Athenians implicated in this war of style. We can trace the process back at least to the 410s, when a relief with the same iconography was set up at Khalandri, a few miles north of Athens, with an inscription proclaiming ". . . and my country (knows) how many enemies I have destroyed . . . [bear] witness how many trophies of my prowess in battle I set up" (*IG* 2² 7716). The cost of Diodotos' tomb in Lysias' speech (32 *Diogeiton* 21) takes on an extra dimension when we note that he was killed in battle at Ephesos in 409. Not only did Diodotos' family take over what had been the state's right to commemorate him, but when his sons reached maturity they even prosecuted their uncle Diogeiton, who had acted as guardian, for failing to do it grandly enough and stealing the money he should have spent; and all this was at a time when Athens was having the greatest difficulty paying for the war against Sparta.

Relatively few fourth-century reliefs have military themes, however. Unlike the sixth-century stelai, they tend to show family scenes.[70] Humphreys suggests that at the end of the fifth century we see a shift away from public themes and representations of funerals or tombs toward domestic life,[71] again perhaps part of the ritual expression of a new relationship between the elite and the polis. The graveside scenes on white-ground lekythoi perhaps belong to an intermediate stage in this development; while evoking heroizing tombs, they already look forward to the highly personalized styles of the fourth-century reliefs.[72]

The distribution of monuments also changed significantly. Throughout the fifth century, a very small group in Athens—probably as few as 1 percent of the citizens, to judge from our present sample—honored its dead with monumental mounds. Around 425 this symbolism was abandoned, and a somewhat wider group—around 10 percent—began to be buried in periboloi, drawing on the entirely different symbolic tradition of the state war graves. It is likely that a much wider group still—probably most citizens—began using inscribed tombstones around 400 B.C.[73] Everyone, it seems, was spending more. The polis as a community also joined in this escalation, building larger and larger monuments as the fourth century wore on, not only tombs but also public buildings.[74] We know little about the forms of the war graves, but the simple markers put up by the polis over the graves of Pythagoras of Selymbrias (ca. 450 B.C.)

and the Corcyraean envoys of 432/1 compare poorly with the impressive tomb for the Spartan officers killed at Athens in 403[75] or the tomb at Horos 3 (ca. 350), thought by some to be for the famous general Khabrias. The polis could always outspend the individuals within it, but there is still a sharp change from the fifth century. The Athenian polis and a man like Dionysios of the deme Kollytos, who was buried in the Kerameikos between 345 and 338,[76] were in direct competition, using more or less the same symbols. The only differences were in scale. Dionysios' family was in a very different relationship to the polis from that of the buriers in the fifth-century Mound G sequence.

Conclusion

In a book of this kind, the most important question to ask of these data is what they tell us about Athenian constructions of citizenship. The idea that there was a major change in attitudes around 430 is hardly a new one, but the archaeological evidence does provide new ways to understand it. The first conclusion is that from 500 to 430 almost all Athenians felt that lavish funerals that evoked images of an heroic and aristocratic past would be a breach of acceptable behavior. Only a few families explicitly ignored this. From about 460 onward a larger group began to use funerary vases portraying visits to elaborate tombs marked by tumuli. I have argued that the interpretation of these pictures is far from straightforward, and much about their context of use seems to undermine the obvious reading that they demonstrate an elitist hankering after just those Archaic symbols that in their open practices the Athenians had abandoned. I disputed theories that explained the Athenians' attitudes toward display in purely Athenian terms, because the archaeological record clearly shows that restraint was a Panhellenic phenomenon in the fifth century. So also was the return of monumental burial after 430. To a great extent, therefore, the rise of funerary sculpture must be explained in general Greek terms, not as a response to the plague, the war, or the Akropolis rebuilding.

In *Death-Ritual and Social Structure in Classical Antiquity*, I suggested that there was an overall shift across Greece in the last quarter of the century from a broadly egalitarian conception of the community to one which allowed far greater freedom for exceptional individuals.[77] In Athenian terms, I believe that this was manifested in the emergence of the extraordinarily complex attitudes to wealth, status, power, and equality that Dover and Ober have documented in the fourth-century legal speeches.[78] The Athenians began to want an impossible compromise in

their leaders: "an aristocrat by birth and behavior who was simultaneously a middling citizen committed to the ideal of political equality for all
Athenians."[79]

It has generally been assumed that, as the fifth century wore on,
Athenian attitudes became increasingly democratized and that displays of
any status other than that of ordinary citizen became less acceptable.
Ober, for instance, says that in the fourth century "the great displays of
the previous century might now be considered ostentatious and even
otiose."[80] However, the evidence I have reviewed in this essay leads me to
believe that this was not the case; Athenian ideology of the fifth century is
likely to have been starker than that of the fourth. The need for the rich to
win *kharis* from the demos by submitting their wealth to its service would
be greater; pre-430 rhetoric probably made much less of good birth than
our later samples; and the Athenian rich are likely to have formed even
less of a power elite than their fourth-century descendants.

There is very little literary evidence for fifth-century Athenian attitudes. Historians have generally interpreted what there is within an evolutionary framework, allowing for a few sudden breaks like Ephialtes'
reforms in 462, but otherwise taking it for granted that there was a fairly
steady growth in democratic and egalitarian sentiment between Kleisthenes' reforms and the end of the Peloponnesian War. Some have
scoured tragedy, especially that of Aeschylus, looking for evidence to
support this view.[81] But the complexities of tragedy make any such search
for direct allusions to political moods futile.[82] Obviously, when Aeschylus
staged the *Oresteia* in 458, Ephialtes' attack on the Areopagos must have
been in his mind; but while we can use what we know of Athenian social
and political ideals to understand better why Aeschylus reacted to events
as he did, we cannot use his reactions to explain the events. Rather than
imposing an evolutionary framework on the evidence, we should start
from the implications of the evidence for display, which suggests that
there was no simple linear progression from a divided, elitist society in the
sixth century to an egalitarian ethos in Perikles' day.

For example, Robert Connor has argued persuasively that there was
a major shift in politics in the third quarter of the fifth century, from using
aristocratic *philia* and kinship to get measures through the Assembly to
direct appeals to the people.[83] The implication of this seems at first to be
that Athenian society became more egalitarian after 430, but matters are
not so simple. The strongest evidence Connor found for direct appeals to
the people did not describe events in the late fifth century, but the activities of Kleisthenes in 508. According to Herodotus (5.66; cf. [Ar.] *AP*
20.1), Kleisthenes "made the people into his companions" (*ton demon*

prosetairizetai). Connor notes the similarity of this episode to the events surrounding the ostracism of Hyperbolos in 418, as well as that earlier fifth-century figures such as Kimon emulated Kleisthenes; nevertheless, he concludes that "the full realization of the power to be gained by a systematic cultivation of the *demos* . . . came only in the last third of the century."[84] The literary evidence does not compel this interpretation, and it may be more consistent with the conclusion required by the archaeological data, that egalitarianism was stronger before 430 than after.

It is widely assumed that Kimon's period of influence in the 470s and 460s was a conservative era in Athens, but this may be wrong. His pro-Spartan policies were very likely genuinely popular with those who were already adults in the Persian Wars, and historians who say that he restrained popular imperialism seem to forget that the attacks on Skyros, Lemnos, Karystos, Naxos, and Thasos all took place before 462 (Thuc. 1.98–101). According to Plutarch, Kimon put his wealth into state service with even more gusto than fourth-century politicians (*Cimon* 10, 13.6–7).[85] We will never know how Kimon talked about this in the Assembly, but the implications of fifth-century ritual behavior make it seem likely that he would have presented himself as being much more of a servant of the people than Demosthenes or Aeschines ever needed to. In narrowly political terms, Athens may have been governed by more aristocratic mechanisms than in the fourth century, but it may also have been more egalitarian in ethos.

This interpretation of Kimon's career also helps us to understand some peculiar comments in Aristotle (*Politics* 5.1304a 20–24; cf. [Ar.] *AP* 23.1). He tells us that the Areopagos council was very influential between 479 and 462, saying on the one hand that the Areopagos "seemed to have made the *politeia* more rigid" (*suntonoteran*), but on the other that the "naval mob" won *hegemonia* after 480 and made the democracy stronger. Rhodes says that "the text of the *Politics* comes dangerously close to saying that as a result of the Persian Wars the constitution changed in two directions at the same time."[86] Certainly the account in the *AP* is confused, having Themistokles helping Ephialtes in 462 even though he had certainly been in exile for several years by that time. But it is still perfectly possible for the Areopagites to have acted as *prostatai* to the state and for the democracy to have flourished alongside this if, as in the case of Kimon, the Areopagites did not sharply distinguish themselves in behavior or policy from the demos. After all, the Areopagos included Ephialtes himself, as well as Kimon.[87] The literary evidence certainly cannot prove that there was a more starkly egalitarian ideology before 430 than that which we find in the late fifth- and fourth-century texts, but

IAN MORRIS

it is at least consistent with this notion. We would do better to follow the indications of the archaeological record than to rely on evolutionary assumptions.

The fifth-century development that I see in the new cultural patterns was *not* the same as a shift from democracy to oligarchy (although this could certainly be one of its consequences); what I have in mind is more an ideological than a constitutional transformation. Egalitarian ideology continued to play a crucial part in Athenian social relations throughout the remainder of the fifth and the following century,[88] but after the 420s it was considerably easier for the elites of Athens to pronounce themselves as such than it had been in the mid-fifth century.

The precise ways in which this general trend was worked out of course varied significantly from state to state. Egalitarianism is one of the most malleable of social concepts; equality can be measured in many ways.[89] The best example of this is the Greek notion that democracy and aristocracy are based on two different kinds of equality, the arithmetic and the geometric; and that the geometric, giving power to men according to their "worth" rather than to each indiscriminately, is more truly equal than the arithmetic. The theory probably began to gain currency around 400 B.C. No elitist wanted to give up the idea that his view of society was based on *to ison,* which meant "fairness" as well as "equality"; geometric proportion allowed him to be both equal and special.[90] At Athens we see the wealthy asserting in their funerary rituals that their contributions to the community demanded a more grandiose standing than merely that of "citizen," but not in the old-fashioned way of linking themselves to an heroic past through explicitly Homeric symbols. I suggested that this was partly because of the common use of such symbols in vase painting since 460; by 430 they had lost much of their potency. Instead, rich Athenians took over for themselves the very symbols of the polis.

The appropriate symbols may have been a contributory factor in Athens' remarkable political stability in the fourth century. There is heated debate over the extent to which the reforms of 410 to 399 really changed the sociology of Athens.[91] Athenian symbolic behavior suggests to me that although the elites of the fourth-century polis were considerably freer than their fifth-century ancestors had been, they constructed their freedom in a way that wedded them strongly to their city, warts and all.[92] Carter has argued that in the late fifth century a new group of Athenians began to form, embracing well-off peasants, noble youths, and rich philosophers. They were united by their *apragmosyne,* or disinterest in public life.[93] That there were such men is beyond dispute, and "minding their own business" clearly constituted a positive elitist class pro-

86

gram;[94] but this does not seem to me to be the most important development within Athenian civic ideology. In the first two-thirds of the fifth century Greek society was dominated by a profoundly egalitarian ethic. In Athens, this was realized politically in democracy. Many noblemen resisted this ideology. Few did so openly, but when they did, it was apparently in strikingly confrontational terms. By about 430, this egalitarian social structure had begun to break up, in favor of a somewhat looser system that allowed the *kaloikagathoi* more room for maneuver, and certainly more room to assert their status.

Notes

1. See particularly Bourdieu 1984, 11–96; and Hunt, ed., 1989.
2. Morris 1991; 1992a, 108–55; and n.d.
3. E.g., Forty 1986; and Auslander 1992.
4. Dover 1974, 1–45; quotation from 1–2. See also Ober 1989a, 43–52.
5. Winckelmann's famous phrase, "ist endlich eine edle Einfalt, und eine stille Größe," was a response to the Laocoon, a highly convoluted first-century-A.D. Roman sculptural group. But he thought he was talking about a work of Pheidian times, and the expression has stuck as a Romantic catch phrase for fifth-century Athens. See Brandt 1986; and Potts 1982.
6. Vickers 1984; 1985; 1985–86; 1986; 1987; 1990 a, b, c; Francis 1990; Gill 1988a; 1991; 1993; and Gill and Vickers 1989; 1990. *Contra,* Boardman 1987; Cook 1987; and Spivey 1991.
7. Morris 1993, drawing on Vickers 1985, 122–26; 1987, 100; 1990, 105–7; and Gill and Vickers 1989, 300–301. Martin Robertson (1985; 1991) offers some valuable support to their arguments.
8. Morris 1992a, 108–55.
9. *IG* i[3] 421–30; Pritchett 1953; 1956; 1961; and Amyx 1958.
10. On their status, see Ostwald 1986, 537–50. One of the men whose property is recorded in the inscriptions may well have been Alkibiades, famous for his luxurious tastes (Thuc. 6.15.3–4; and Plut., *Alc.* 16).
11. Lewis 1966, 190 n. 37. But, as Lewis points out on p. 183, the stelai only record what was sold at auction. Any precious metals confiscated from the houses may simply have been sold off by weight, and so they would not have been entered in these records.
12. Pritchett 1956, 210.
13. Ar. *Knights* 1321–24 and *Clouds* 984–86 associates display with the generation of Marathon; and Gomme 1945, 101–3 argues that it died out by the 470s. See also Geddes 1987.
14. See Jones 1975; Jameson 1990a, 1990b; and Morris 1992a, 118–27. An unusually imposing late-fifth-century house has been found on Karyatidon Street in Athens (Stavropoullos 1964, 49).
15. Display—e.g., Dem. 3 *Olynthiac* 3.25–26; 13 *On Organization* 29; and 23 *Aristocrates* 207–8, although the archaeological evidence for housing is

somewhat ambiguous; see Hoepfner and Schwandner 1986; Schuller et al., eds., 1989. Speeches—Dover 1974, 110–12, 170–75; and Ober 1989a, 205–14.

16. The precise dates of the beginning and end of the period of restraint are disputed. Kouroi and stelai may have continued in use into the 480s (Knigge 1983; and Hölscher 1988). On the earliest inscribed gravestones, see Clairmont 1986.

17. See Möbius 1968; Garland 1982; Vedder 1985; and Scholl n.d.

18. Plutarch (*Aristides* 1 and 27) comments that Aristeides' tomb, which would have been built in the 460s, could still be seen in his day (ca. A.D. 100), on his family estates, near Phaleron. This might imply a lavish memorial, but Plutarch also comments that one story said that Aristeides died so poor that the state paid for his funeral and dowered his daughters. None of these anecdotes inspires confidence. A few other references survive for burial costs—Lys. 31 *Philon* 21 (ca. 400 B.C.), 300 dr.; [Dem.] 40 *Boeotus* 2.52 (ca. 358 B.C.), 1,000 dr.; and [Plato] *Letters* 13.361e, 1,000 dr.

19. On the date, see Unz 1986, 70–73; and Badian 1987, 4–6.

20. See Dover 1974, 292–95; Davies 1981, 92–100; Whitehead 1983; Herman 1987; Sinclair 1988, 188–90; and Ober 1989a, 333.

21. This anecdote brings into sharp focus the general problem of using Plutarch as a source for fifth-century Athens. Plutarch recounts many details of Perikles' career in the 440s and 430s which are not attested elsewhere, and many historians find his treatment of the Akropolis rebuilding particularly untrustworthy (e.g., Andrewes 1978; cf. Kallet-Marx 1989, 260–64). I have suggested in n. 18 above that his comments on the burial of Aristeides are confused; but in that case he clearly had two conflicting stories, with no way to decide between them. Hansen states that "I doubt that Plutarch, who had the political temper of the age of Trajan, could have understood the political conditions of the Greek city states in the classical period" (1983, 200; cf. 1987, 76). There is much truth in this, but the Athenian responses that he ascribes to the actions of Kimon and Perikles would have made far less sense in his own day than in fifth-century Athens. His account of Perikles' building projects constantly refers to Athenian comedy as a source, and Plutarch himself seems somewhat baffled by the incident, offering two alternative interpretations of the Assembly's response. I am inclined to see here at least a distorted representation of an account taken from a primary source (cf. Pelling 1992).

22. Davies 1967; 1981; Rhodes 1982; 1986; Brun 1983, 3–73; and Ober 1989a, 226–40.

23. The evidence for resistance to the liturgies begins during the Ionian War, with Lys. frag. 35 (Thalheim); 20 *Polystratus* 23; 21 *Bribery* 12; Isocr. 18 *Call.* 59–60; and Ar. *Frogs* 1063–68. See discussions in Ste. Croix 1953; 1981, 294–95; and Christ 1990, 152–60.

24. Clairmont 1970, 43. For examples of the two theories, see Johansen 1951, 146–47; M. Robertson 1975, 363–64; Stupperich 1977, 243–44; Neumann 1979, 45–48; and Mikalson 1984.

25. Loraux 1986, 23, 28, 31.

26. On the form of the war graves, see Clairmont 1981; 1983, 60–73,

correcting Brückner 1910, 183–200. For fifth-century state tombs, see Knigge 1972; 1980, 70–75; 1988, 159; Willemsen 1977; Ohly 1965, 314–27; Mallwitz 1980. Kaempf-Dimitriadou 1986 suggests that part of the frieze of the tomb for the Battle of Khaironeia in 338 has also been found. Generally, see Clairmont 1983, 29–45. N. Robertson 1983 and Pritchett 1985, 106–58 provide general overviews of Athenian war burial.

27. Loraux 1986, 31.

28. Humphreys 1980, 123.

29. Morris 1992a, 128–55; and n.d.

30. See esp. the debates of Chartier 1985; Bourdieu et al. 1985; and Darnton 1986.

31. Preziosi 1989, chap. 3.

32. Chartier 1985, 688.

33. The origin of the *patrios nomos* is hotly debated, but probably belongs in the early fifth century. See Clairmont 1983, 7–28; Loraux 1986, 28–30; and Thomas 1989, 207–8.

34. Redfield 1975; and Nagy 1979. Note particularly Nagy's fascinating argument (1979, chap. 5) that Akhilleus' very name symbolizes the hero's ambiguity, as "he whose *laos* has *akhos*."

35. See Morris 1992a, 17–24.

36. Miller 1985, Tilley 1990, and Hodder 1991 are the most explicit discussions. These all operate within the postprocessualist framework, but the New Archaeologists generally adopted a similar view of the arbitrary nature of the relationship between excavated signifier and ancient signified (see, e.g., Binford 1972).

37. Tilley 1990, 65–66.

38. Rejecting meaning seems to be a majority response among those working within the framework of the 1960s New Archaeology; see, e.g., Earle and Preucel 1987; and Snodgrass 1987, 33–34. There has been much heated debate and some misunderstanding over the issue; see esp. Watson and Fotiadis 1990.

39. Patterson 1989; and 1990.

40. Cannon 1989, 447.

41. Michels 1915, 50–51, 61–77, 85–128, 333–71; cf. Finley 1985, 3–12; and Ober 1989a, 15–16, 334–35.

42. Hodder 1990, 28–29.

43. E.g., Eckstein 1958; Richter 1961, 38–39; Clairmont 1970, 11; Kurtz and Boardman 1971, 89–90; and Stupperich 1977, 71–85. A legalistic approach impoverishes the potential of cultural history. Nothing has done so much to limit the use of classical Athenian burial evidence as the notion that Cicero's *post aliquanto* law "explains" the material (see Morris 1992b). The approach often results from a combination of Athenocentric and uniformitarian assumptions, and it brings with it many of the drawbacks of the constitutionalist approach to Athenian social history (see the debate in Hansen 1989; and Ober 1989b).

44. For the other examples, see Brückner and Pernice 1893, 86–100; Schilardi 1968, 44–48; Kübler 1976, 148–50; and Vierneisel 1963; 1964 a, b.

IAN MORRIS

Clairmont 1983, 263 n. 42, casts doubt on Vierneisel's dates. The radial arrangement of graves at Panepistimiou Street 11 (Alexandri 1970, fig. 33) probably indicates an early-fifth-century mound here. For the sequence Mound G to tomb f, see Kübler 1976, 5–21, 63–90. Petrakos 1976, 11–15 dates a round stone tomb at Rhamnous ca. 450, but Garland 1982, 127 puts it in the fourth century (note that this is M6 in Garland's catalogue; the references to M5 on his p. 127 are misprints). The "mound" over Tavros gr. 6 (440s B.C.; Schilardi 1975, 81–95) was just a mud-brick platform 20 cm. high.

45. Kübler 1959, 85 n. 2; 1973; and 1976, 5–21. Freytag 1975 undermines this idea. See also Knigge 1976, 10–11 n. 26; and 1988, 179 n. 88.

46. Kübler 1976, 63–90. Kübler's dating of this series (on stylistic grounds) is flatly contradicted by the stratigraphy that he publishes, and Stupperich's suggestions, 1977, 82–84, are preferable. Clairmont, 1983, 36, with references, points out that postholes found under the road through the Kerameikos, less than 100 m. from Mound G, may be from the wooden platform for the state funeral orations. See also Morris 1992a, 132–36.

47. For details, see Andronikos 1968; Kurtz and Boardman 1971; Morris 1987, 128–37, 151–54; Petropoulou 1988; and Shapiro 1991, 631–46.

48. See Herman 1987. On Homeric "freedom" and aristocratic resistance to tyrants with its slogan of *isonomia*, see Raaflaub 1985, 36–70.

49. Morris 1992a, 145–46.

50. On the difficulties involved in treating the statements of Sokrates' opponents as evidence for "typical" Greek views, see Dover 1974, 7. For general surveys of the white-ground lekythoi, see Fairbanks 1907–14; Riezler 1914; Buschor 1925; Beazley 1938; Kurtz 1975; Nakayama 1982; Wehgartner 1983; 1985; and Boardman 1989, chap. 4. On *megaloprepeia*, see Kurke 1991, 163–256.

51. It is, of course, impossible to date pots to specific decades; the calendar dates used here should be treated as conventional points allowing us to fix archaeological deposits relative to one another. The years given are probably roughly correct, and we can correlate archaeological dates with those derived from texts as long as we bear in mind a likely margin of error. This is another factor militating against explaining changes in tomb styles through events such as the plague or the outbreak of the Peloponnesian War; we cannot be certain that the changes begin in the 420s rather than, say, in the late 430s. The best discussion of the margin of error in fifth-century archaeology is in Tölle-Kastenbein 1983, arguing for fifteen years either way. Francis, Vickers, and Gill have argued for a much lower chronology. They are right to draw attention to the weaknesses of the traditional system, but their own construction is if anything less persuasive. See the rebuttal in Cook 1989, with full bibliography.

52. Kurtz, 133.

53. The iconography is summarized in Fairbanks 1907–14, 2:216–41; Beazley 1938, 7–11; and Shapiro 1991, 649–55. Reilly 1989 has argued from a study of 109 white-ground and red-figure lekythoi that the mistress-and-maid scenes show a bride preparing for her wedding and have no funerary meaning; but see Kurtz 1988.

54. Clairmont 1983, 62. Other interpretations of what the painters intended to represent have been made: Humphreys 1980, 102 sees in these scenes wooden stelai that have perished; Rupp 1980 sees altars; and Schilardi 1984 sees sarcophagi. Shapiro 1991, 655 points out that some of the monuments have "fantastic shapes," but it remains most likely that genuine tumuli and stone stelai were intended.

55. Amsterdam 2455, illustrated in Clairmont 1983, pl. 3c, with p. 62. Loutrophoros Athens NM 450 (Haspels 1936, 229 no. 59) has an inscription on its funerary mound, but its restoration is disputed.

56. See Lissarrague 1988. On fifth-century stelai and their relationship to Archaic examples, see Bazant 1987; and Baldassarre 1988.

57. Morris 1992a, 111–16.

58. Shapiro's 1991, 649 statement that "in the Kerameikos surprisingly few white lekythoi have been found" could create a misleading impression.

59. See Hoffmann 1977; 1986; 1988; 1989; and 1993, and the discussion in Bazant 1986.

60. Shapiro 1991, 652.

61. I argue for a continuity between rhetoric and treatment of the dead in Morris 1991, 161–62.

62. Loraux 1986, 217, with similar ideas in Adkins 1972, 119–26; and Ober 1989a, 291, partly anticipated (as he points out) by Seager 1982.

63. Donlan 1980, 1–2, 155–80; and Herman 1987, 156–61.

64. Humphreys 1980, 112; cf. Bazant 1986.

65. The vast majority of the lekythoi in collections of course come from grave offerings rather than from pots left outside the grave. However, the vase paintings themselves make it clear that lekythoi were often used in this way. The Kerameikos excavations have produced many stray finds of white-ground lekythoi (Felten 1976). Some come from destroyed graves, but others probably stood above ground.

66. Clairmont 1983, 209–14; and Ensoli 1987. IG 2^2 6226–27 and 6230, found within the precinct, commemorate six family members; both 2^2 7257 and 7263, also from the Kerameikos, name another dozen kin, active down to the end of the fourth century.

67. Strauss 1986, 124; and Bugh 1982, 28–29; 1988, 139. I thank Michael Jameson for pointing out to me the importance of this evidence.

68. First developed by Rostovtzeff 1953, 90–125 (= 1928), and elaborated by Mossé 1962. The evidence is discussed most fully in Weiskopf, ed., 1974.

69. On the history of *isonomia* in the fifth century, see Ostwald 1969, 149–58; Frei 1981; and Raaflaub 1985.

70. Clairmont 1970, 55–71; Neumann 1979, 35–55; Schmaltz 1983, 189–223; and Vedder 1985; 1988.

71. Humphreys 1980, 113; cf. 1977–78.

72. See Nakayama 1982; Wehgartner 1985; Kurtz 1988; and Baldassarre 1988.

73. Morris 1992a, 135–38; and Nielsen et al. 1989. It is impossible to compare the use of periboloi and tombstones statistically because so many of

our tombstones were found detached from their original context, and they are far more likely to be discovered by archaeologists if reused in buildings than blocks of stone from periboloi would be.

74. For the building program after 338, see [Plut.] *Mor.* 841D; Mitchel 1965, 199–200; 1970, 33–36; Will 1983, 79–93; and Burke 1985, 254–55.

75. The tomb of the Spartans was, of course, a special case (see Lys. 2 *Funeral Oration* 63; and Xen. *Hell.* 2.4.29–38), but because it forms part of a general pattern of increasing scale, there seems to be no reason to ignore it.

76. Knigge 1988, 123–26.

77. Morris 1992a, 149–55.

78. Dover 1974, 109–12, 144–50, 170–95, 226–43, 273–316; and Ober 1989a.

79. Ober 1989a, 289.

80. Ober 1989a, 231.

81. E.g., the long discussion in Meier 1990, 82–139.

82. See Macleod 1982; Euben, ed., 1986; and Winkler and Zeitlin, eds., 1990.

83. Connor 1971.

84. Connor 1971, 91.

85. See the good discussion in Connor 1971, 18–22.

86. Rhodes 1976, 147.

87. On these texts, see Wallace 1989, 77–87.

88. See, esp., Ober 1989a, 187–205, 320–21.

89. See the discussion in Phelps Brown 1988, 1–11.

90. Harvey 1965 argues that Arkhytas of Taras started the theory and passed it on to Plato.

91. E.g., Ostwald 1986, 497–524; Ober 1989b, 95–103; Hansen 1989; 1991.

92. The most sophisticated example is Plato's *Crito;* as Kraut explains, the *Crito* is "an attempt to strike a fair balance between the needs of citizens and the needs of their city" (1984, 6). I remain unconvinced by Kraut's interpretation of Plato's attitude to democracy (1984, 194–309), but his treatment of the *Crito* is masterful.

93. Carter 1986; cf. Ehrenberg 1947. See the rebuttal of Carter by Podlecki 1991.

94. See Adkins 1976.

Works Cited

Adkins, Arthur. 1972. *Moral Values and Political Behaviour in Ancient Greece.* London: Chatto and Windus.
———. 1976. "*Polypragmosyne* and Minding One's Own Business: A Study in Greek Social and Political Values." *CP* 71:301–27.
Alcock, Susan. 1991. "Tomb Cult and the Post-Classical Polis." *AJA* 95:447–67.
Alexandri, Olga. 1970. "3e ephoreia klassikon arkhaiotiton." *AD* 25.2:40–91.

Amyx, Darryl. 1958. "The Attic Stelai, Part III." *Hesperia* 27:163–254.

Andrewes, Anthony. 1978. "The Opposition to Perikles." *JHS* 98:1–8.

Andronikos, Manolis. 1968. *Totenkult*. Göttingen: *Archaeologia Homerica* Band O.

Auslander, Leora. 1992. "Perceptions of Beauty and the Problem of Consciousness: Parisian Furniture Makers." In *The New French Labor History*, edited by Lenard Berlanstein. Chicago: University of Illinois Press.

Badian, Ernst. 1987. "The Peace of Callias." *JHS* 107:1–39.

Baldassarre, Ida. 1988. "Tomba e stele nelle lekythoi a fondo bianco." *AnnNap* 10:107–15.

Bazant, Jan. 1986. "Entre le croyance et l'expérience: Le mort sur les lécythes à fond blanc." In *Iconographie classique et identités régionales*, 34–44. Paris: Boccard. *BCH* supp. vol. 14.

———. 1987. "Les vases athéniennes et les réformes démocratiques." In *Image et société en Grèce ancienne*, edited by Claude Bérard, 33–41. Lausanne: Bron.

Beazley, John. 1938. *Attic White Lekythoi*. London: Macmillan.

Binford, Lewis R. 1972. *An Archaeological Perspective*. New York: Academic Press.

Boardman, John. 1987. "Silver Is White." *RA:* 279–95.

———. 1989. *Athenian Red Figure Vases: The Classical Period*. London: Thames and Hudson.

Bourdieu, Pierre. 1984. *Distinction*. Berkeley: University of California Press.

Bourdieu, Pierre, Roger Chartier, and Robert Darnton. 1985. "Dialogue à propos de l'histoire culturelle." *Actes de la recherche en sciences sociales* 59:86–93.

Brandt, R. 1986. ". . . ist endlich eine edle Einfalt, und eine stille Größe." In *Johann Joachim Winckelmann 1717–1768*, edited by T. W. Gaehtegens, 41–53. Hamburg.

Brückner, Alfred. 1910. "Kerameikos-Studien." *AM* 35:183–234.

Brückner, Alfred, and E. Pernice. 1893. "Ein attischer Friedhof." *AM* 18:73–191.

Brun, Patrice. 1983. *Eisphora—Syntaxis—Stratiotika*. Paris: Annales littéraires de l'université de Besançon 284.

Bugh, Glenn. 1982. "Introduction of the *katalogeis* of the Athenian Cavalry." *TAPA* 112:23–32.

———. 1988. *The Horsemen of Athens*. Princeton: Princeton University Press.

Burke, Edward. 1985. "Lycurgan Finances." *GRBS* 26:251–64.

Buschor, Ernst. 1925. "Attische Lekythen der Parthenonzeit." *Münchener Jahrbuch*, n.s. 2:167–99.

Cannon, Aubrey. 1989. "The Historical Dimension in Mortuary Expressions of Status and Sentiment." *Current Anthropology* 30:437–58.

Carter, L. B. 1986. *The Quiet Athenian*. Oxford: Oxford University Press.

Chartier, Roger. 1985. "Texts, Symbols, and Frenchness." *Journal of Modern History* 57:682–95.

Christ, Matthew. 1990. "Liturgy Avoidance and *Antidosis* in Classical Athens." *TAPA* 120:147–69.

Clairmont, Christoph. 1970. *Gravestone and Epigram*. Mainz: Philipp von Zabern.

———. 1981. "New Evidence for a Polyandrion in the *Demosion Sema* of Athens?" *JHS* 101:132–34.

———. 1983. *Patrios Nomos: Public Burial at Athens during the Fifth and Fourth Centuries B.C.* 2 vols. Oxford: *British Archaeological Reports*. International Series 161.

———. 1986. "Some Reflections on the Earliest Classical Gravestones." *Boreas* 9:27–50.

Connor, W. Robert. 1971. *The New Politicians of Fifth-Century Athens*. Princeton: Princeton University Press.

Cook, Robert M. 1987. "Artful Crafts: A Commentary." *JHS* 107:169–71.

———. 1989. "The Francis-Vickers Chronology." *JHS* 109:164–70.

Darnton, Robert. 1986. "The Symbolic Element in History." *Journal of Modern History* 58:218–34.

Davies, John K. 1967. "Demosthenes on Liturgies: A Note." *JHS* 87:33–40.

———. 1981. *Wealth and the Power of Wealth in Classical Athens*. New York: Arno Press.

Donlan, Walter. 1980. *The Aristocratic Ideal in Ancient Greece*. Lawrence: University of Kansas Press.

Dover, Kenneth J. 1974. *Greek Popular Morality in the Time of Plato and Aristotle*. Berkeley: University of California Press.

Earle, Timothy, and Richard Preucel. 1987. "Processual Archaeology and the Radical Critique." *Current Anthropology* 28:501–38.

Eckstein, F. 1958. "Die attische Grabmälergesetze." *JdI* 73:18–29.

Ehrenberg, Victor. 1947. "*Polypragmosyne:* A Study in Greek Politics." *JHS* 67:46–67.

Ensoli, S. 1987. *L'Heróon di Dexileos nel Ceramico di Atene*. Rome: Atti della Accademia Nazionale dei Lincei. Memorie 7.29.2.

Euben, Peter, ed. 1986. *Greek Tragedy and Political Theory*. Berkeley: University of California Press.

Fairbanks, A. 1907–14. *Athenian White Lekythoi*. 2 vols. New York: Macmillan.

Felten, F. 1976. "Weissgrundige Lekythen aus der Athener Kerameikos." *AM* 91:77–146.

Finley, Moses I. 1981. *Economy and Society in Ancient Greece*. Edited by Brent D. Shaw and Richard P. Saller. London: Chatto and Windus.

———. 1985. *Democracy Ancient and Modern*. 2d ed. London: Hogarth Press.

Forty, Adrian. 1986. *Objects of Desire: Design and Society from Wedgewood to IBM*. New York: Pantheon.

Francis, E. D. 1990. *Image and Idea in Fifth-Century Athens*. London: Routledge and Kegan Paul.

Francis, E. D., and Michael Vickers. 1981. "Leagros *kalos.*" *PCPS* 207:97–136.
———. 1983. "Signa priscae artis: Eretria and Siphnos." *JHS* 103:49–67.
———. 1988. "The Agora Revisited: Athenian Chronology *c.* 500–450 B.C." *BSA* 83:143–67.
Frei, P. 1981. "*Isonomia:* Politik im Spiegel griechischer Wortbildungslehre." *MH* 38:205–19.
Freytag gen. Löringhoff, Bettina von. 1975. "Neue frühattische Funde aus dem Kerameikos." *AM* 90:49–81.
Garland, Robert. 1982. "A First Catalogue of Attic Peribolos Tombs." *BSA* 77:125–76.
Geddes, A. G. 1987. "Rags and Riches: The Costume of Athenian Men in the Fifth Century." *CQ* 37:307–31.
Gill, David. 1988a. "Expressions of Wealth: Greek Art and Society." *Antiquity* 62:735–43.
———. 1988b. "The Temple of Aphaia on Aegina: The Date of the Reconstruction." *BSA* 83:169–77.
Gill, David, and Michael Vickers. 1989. "Pots and Kettles." *RA:* 297–303.
———. 1990. "Reflected Glory: Pottery and Precious Metal in Classical Greece." *JdI* 105:1–30.
Gomme, Arnold. 1945. *An Historical Commentary on Thucydides.* Vol 1. Oxford: Clarendon Press.
Hansen, Mogens H. 1983. *The Athenian Ecclesia.* Copenhagen: Museum Tusculanum.
———. 1987. *The Athenian Assembly in the Age of Demosthenes.* Oxford: Basil Blackwell.
———. 1989. "Demos, Ekklesia and Dikasterion: A Reply to Martin Ostwald and Josiah Ober." *ClMed* 40:101–6.
———. 1991. *The Athenian Democracy in the Age of Demosthenes: Structures, Principles, and Ideology.* Oxford: Basil Blackwell.
Harvey, F. David. 1965. "Two Kinds of Equality." *ClMed* 26:101–46.
Haspels, E. 1936. *Attic Black-Figured Lekythoi.* Oxford: Oxford University Press.
Herman, Gabriel. 1987. *Ritualised Friendship and the Greek City.* Cambridge: Cambridge University Press.
Himmelmann-Wildschütz, N. 1956. *Studien zum Ilissos-Relief.* Munich: Steiner.
Hodder, Ian. 1990. *The Domestication of Europe.* Oxford: Basil Blackwell.
———. 1991. *Reading the Past.* 2d ed. Cambridge: Cambridge University Press.
Hoepfner, W. 1973. "Das Grabmonument des Pythagoras aus Selymbria." *AM* 88:145–63.
Hoepfner, W., and E.-L. Schwandner. 1986. *Haus und Stadt im klassischen Griechenland.* Munich: Zabern.
Hoffmann, Herbert. 1977. *Sexual and Asexual Pursuit.* London: Royal Anthropological Institute of Great Britain and Ireland, Occasional Paper 34.

————. 1986. "From Charos to Charon: Some Notes on the Human Encounter with Death in Attic Red-Figured Vase Painting." *Visible Religion* 4/5: 173–94.

————. 1988. "Why Did the Greeks Need Imagery? An Anthropological Approach to the Study of Greek Vase Painting." *Hephaistos* 9:143–62.

————. 1989. "*Aletheia:* The Iconography of Death/Rebirth in Three Cups by the Sotades Painter." *Res* 17/18:69–88.

————. 1993. "The Riddle of the Sphinx." In *Classical Greece: Ancient Histories and Modern Archaeologies,* edited by Ian Morris, 71–80. Cambridge: Cambridge University Press.

Hölscher, T. 1988. "Eine frühe zweifigurige Grabstele." In *KANON: Festschrift Ernst Berger,* 160–69. Basel: *Antike Kunst* Beiheft 15.

Humphreys, Sally C. 1977–78. "Public and Private Interests in Classical Athens." *CJ* 73:97–104.

————. 1978. *Anthropology and the Greeks.* London: Routledge and Kegan Paul.

————. 1980. "Family Tombs and Tomb Cult in Ancient Athens: Tradition or Traditionalism?" *JHS* 100:96–126. Reprinted in S. C. Humphreys, *The Family, Women and Death,* 90–120. London: Routledge and Kegan Paul, 1983; 2d ed., 1993.

Hunt, Linda, ed. 1989. *The New Cultural History.* Berkeley: University of California Press.

Jameson, Michael H. 1990a. "Private Space and the Greek City." In *The Greek City from Homer to Alexander,* edited by Oswyn Murray and Simon Price, 169–93. Oxford: Oxford University Press.

————. 1990b. "Domestic Space in the Greek City-State." In *Domestic Architecture and the Use of Space,* edited by Susan Kent, 92–113. Cambridge: Cambridge University Press.

Johansen, Keith Friis. 1951. *The Attic Grave-Reliefs of the Classical Period.* Copenhagen: Mundsgaard.

Jones, J. Ellis. 1975. "Town and Country Houses of Attica in Classical Times." *MIGRA* 1:63–144.

Kaempf-Dimitriadou, S. 1986. "Ein attischer Staatsgrabmal des 4. Jhs. v. Chr." *AntK* 29:23–36.

Kallet-Marx, Lisa. 1989. "Did Tribute Fund the Parthenon?" *Classical Antiquity* 8:252–66.

Knigge, Ursula. 1972. "Untersuchungen bei den Gestandtenstelen im Kerameikos zu Athen." *AA:* 584–629.

————. 1976. *Kerameikos 9: Die Südhügel.* Berlin: de Gruyter.

————. 1980. *Kerameikos 12: Rundbauten.* Berlin: de Gruyter.

————. 1983. "Ein Jünglingskopf vom Heiligen Tor in Athen." *AM* 108:45–56.

————. 1988. *Der Kerameikos von Athen.* Athens: Krene Verlag.

Kraut, Richard. 1984. *Socrates and the State.* Princeton: Princeton University Press.

Kübler, Karl. 1959. *Kerameikos 6.1.* 2 vols. Berlin: de Gruyter.

————. 1973. "Eine archaische Grabanlage vor dem Heilige Tor und ihre Deutung." *AA:* 172–93.

————. 1976. *Kerameikos* 7.1. 2 vols. Berlin: de Gruyter.

Kurke, Leslie. 1991. *The Traffic in Praise: Pindar and the Poetics of Social Economy.* Ithaca: Cornell University Press.

Kurtz, Donna. 1975. *Athenian White Lekythoi.* Oxford: Clarendon Press.

————. 1984. "Vases for the Dead, an Attic Selection, 750–400 B.C." In *Ancient Greek and Related Pottery,* edited by H. A. G. Brijder, 314–28. Amsterdam: Allard Pierson Series.

————. 1988. "Mistress and Maid." *AnnNap* 10:141–49.

Kurtz, Donna, and John Boardman. 1971. *Greek Burial Customs.* London: Thames and Hudson.

Lauffer, Siegfried. 1974. "Die Liturgien in der Krisenperiode Athens." In *Hellenische Poleis,* edited by Elizabeth Welskopf, 1:147–59. Berlin: Steiner.

Lewis, David. 1966. "After the Profanation of the Mysteries." In *Ancient Society and Institutions,* edited by Ernst Badian, 177–91. Oxford: Oxford University Press.

Lissarrague, François. 1988. "La stèle avant la lettre." *AnnNap* 10:97–105.

Loraux, Nicole. 1982. "Mourir devant Troie, tomber pour Athènes: De la gloire du héros à l'idée de la cité." In *La mort, les morts, dans les sociétés anciennes,* edited by G. Gnoli and J-P. Vernant, 27–43. Cambridge: Cambridge University Press.

————. 1986. *The Invention of Athens: The Funeral Oration in the Classical City.* Translated by Alan Sheridan. Cambridge, Mass.: Harvard University Press.

Macleod, Colin. 1982. "Politics and the *Oresteia.*" *JHS* 102:123–33.

Mallwitz, Alfred. 1980. "Das Staatsgrab am 3. Horos." In Knigge 1980, 99–125.

Meier, Christian. 1990. *The Greek Discovery of Politics.* Cambridge, Mass.: Harvard University Press.

Michels, Robert. 1915. *Political Parties: A Sociological Study of the Oligarchical Tendencies of Modern Democracy.* Glencoe, Ill.: Free Press. Reprint. New York: Collier Books, 1962.

Mikalson, Jon. 1984. "Religion and the Plague in Athens." In *Studies Presented to Sterling Dow.* Greek, Roman, and Byzantine Monograph 10:217–25. Edited by Kent J. Rigsby. Durham: Duke University.

Miller, Daniel. 1985. *Artefacts as Categories.* Cambridge: Cambridge University Press.

Mitchel, F. 1965. "Athens in the Age of Alexander." *G&R* 12:189–204.

————. 1970. *Lykourgan Athens, 338–322 B.C.* Cincinnati: University of Cincinnati Press.

Möbius, Hans. 1968. *Die Ornamente der griechischen Grabstelen, klassischer und nachklassischer Zeit.* 2d ed. Berlin: W. Fink.

Morris, Ian. 1987. *Burial and Ancient Society: The Rise of the Greek City-State.* Cambridge: Cambridge University Press.

————. 1988. "Tomb Cult and the 'Greek Renaissance.'" *Antiquity* 62:750–61.

————. 1991. "The Archaeology of Ancestors: The Saxe/Goldstein Hypothesis Revisited." *Cambridge Archaeological Journal* 1:147–69.

————. 1992a. *Death-Ritual and Social Structure in Classical Antiquity.* Cambridge: Cambridge University Press.

————. 1992b. "Law, Culture, and Funerary Art in Athens, 600–300 B.C." *Hephaistos* 12.

————. 1993. "Archaeologies of Greece." In *Classical Greece: Ancient Histories and Modern Archaeologies,* edited by Ian Morris, 8–47. Cambridge: Cambridge University Press.

————. n.d. *The Archaeology of Democracy.* Oxford: Basil Blackwell. Forthcoming.

Mossé, Claude. 1962. *La fin de la démocratie athénienne.* Paris: Presses universitaires de France.

Nagy, Gregory. 1979. *The Best of the Achaeans: Concepts of the Hero in Archaic Greek Poetry.* Baltimore: Johns Hopkins University Press.

Nakayama, N. 1982. *Untersuchung der weissgrundigen Lekythen dargestellten Grabmäler.* Ph.D. thesis. Freiburg: Albert Ludwigs Universität.

Neumann, G. 1979. *Probleme des griechischen Weihreliefs.* Tübingen: Wissenschaftliche Buchgesellschaft.

Nielsen, T. H., L. Bjerstrup, M. H. Hansen, L. Rubinstein, and T. Vestergard. 1989. "Athenian Grave Monuments and Social Class." *GRBS* 30:411–20.

Ober, Josiah. 1989a. *Mass and Elite in Democratic Athens: Rhetoric, Ideology, and the Power of the People.* Princeton: Princeton University Press.

————. 1989b. "The Nature of Athenian Democracy." *CP* 84:322–34.

Ohly, Dieter. 1965. "Kerameikos-Grabung. Tätigkeitsbericht 1956–1961." *AA:* 277–375.

Ostwald, Martin. 1969. *Nomos and the Beginnings of Athenian Democracy.* Oxford: Oxford University Press.

————. 1986. *From Popular Sovereignty to the Sovereignty of Law: Law, Society, and Politics in Fifth-Century Athens.* Berkeley: University of California Press.

Patterson, Timothy C. 1989. "History and the Post-processual Archaeologies." *Man* 24:555–66.

————. 1990. "Some Theoretical Tensions within and between the Processual and the Postprocessual Archaeologies." *Journal of Anthropological Archaeology* 9:189–200.

Pelling, Christopher. 1992. "Plutarch and Thucydides." In *Plutarch and the Historical Tradition,* edited by Philip Stadter, 10–40. London: Routledge.

Petrakos, Vassili. 1976. "Anaskaphi Rhamnoundos." *Praktika:* 5–60.

Petropoulou, A. 1988. "The Interment of Patroklos (*Iliad* 23.252–57)." *AJP* 109:482–95.

Phelps Brown, Henry. 1988. *Egalitarianism and the Generation of Inequality.* Oxford: Clarendon Press.

Podlecki, Anthony. 1991. "*Apragmosyne.*" *Ancient History Bulletin* 5:81–87.

Potts, A. 1982. "Winckelmann's Construction of History." *Art History* 5:377–407.

Preziosi, Donald. 1989. *Rethinking Art History: Meditations on a Coy Science.* New Haven: Yale University Press.

Pritchett, W. Kendrick. 1953. "The Attic Stelai, Part I." *Hesperia* 22:225–99.

———. 1956. "The Attic Stelai, Part II." *Hesperia* 25:178–328.

———. 1961. "Five New Fragments of the Attic Stelai." *Hesperia* 30:23–29.

———. 1985. *The Greek State at War: Part 4.* Berkeley: University of California Press.

Raaflaub, Kurt. 1985. *Die Entdeckung der Freiheit.* Munich: *Vestigia.* Vol. 37. Munich: C. H. Beck'sche Verlagsbuchhandlung.

Redfield, James M. 1975. *Nature and Culture in the "Iliad": The Tragedy of Hector.* Chicago: University of Chicago Press.

Reilly, J. 1989. "Many Brides: Mistress and Maid on Athenian Lekythoi." *Hesperia* 58:411–44.

Rhodes, Peter J. 1976. *"Athenaion Politeia* 23–8." *LCM* 1:147–54.

———. 1982. "Problems in Athenian *Eisphora* and Liturgies." *AJAH* 7:1–19.

———. 1986. "Political Activity in Classical Athens." *JHS* 106:132–44.

———. 1991. "The Athenian Code of Laws, 410–399 B.C." *JHS* 111:87–100.

Richter, Gisela. 1961. *The Archaic Gravestones of Attica.* London: Phaethon.

Robertson, Martin. 1975. *A History of Greek Art.* 2 vols. Oxford: Oxford University Press.

———. 1985. "Beazley and Attic Vase Painting." In *Beazley and Oxford,* edited by Donna Kurtz, 19–30. Oxford: Oxford University Press.

———. 1991. "Adopting an Approach." In *Looking at Greek Vases,* edited by Tom Rasmussen and Nigel Spivey, 1–12. Cambridge: Cambridge University Press.

Robertson, Noel. 1983. "The Collective Burial of Fallen Soldiers at Athens, Sparta and Elsewhere." *EMC/CV* 27:78–92.

Rostovtzeff, Mikhail I. 1953. *Social and Economic History of the Hellenistic World.* 2d ed. Oxford: Oxford University Press.

Rupp, David. 1980. "Altars as Funerary Monuments on Attic White Lekythoi." *AJA* 84:524–27.

Ste. Croix, Geoffrey de. 1953. "Demosthenes' *Timema* and the Athenian *Eisphora* in the Fourth Century B.C." *ClMed* 14:30–70.

———. 1981. *The Class Struggle in the Ancient Greek World.* London: Duckworth.

Schilardi, Demetrius U. 1968. "Anaskaphai para tis Irias Pylas kai topographika provlimata tis periokhis." *AE* chronika: 8–52.

———. 1975. "Anaskaphai para ta Makra Teikhi kai i oinokhoi tou Tavrou." *AE:* 66–149.

———. 1984. "Representations of Free-standing Sarcophagi on Attic, White-ground Lekythoi." In *Ancient Greek and Related Pottery,* edited by H. A. G. Brijder, 264–70. Amsterdam: Allard Pierson Series.

Schmaltz, Bernard. 1983. *Griechische Grabreliefs.* Darmstadt: Wissenschaftliche Buchgesellschaft.

Scholl, Andreas. n.d. *Die attischen Bildfeldstelen des 4. Jhs. v. Chr. Untersuchungen zu den kleinformatigen Grabreliefs im spätklassischen Athen.* Beiheft to *Athenische Mitteilungen.* Forthcoming.

Schuller, W., W. Hoepfner, and E.-L. Schwandner, eds. 1989. *Demokratie und Architektur: Der hippodamische Städtebau und die Entstehung der Demokratie.* Munich: Steiner.

Seager, Robin. 1982. Review of Loraux 1986. In *JHS* 102:267–68.

Shapiro, H. Alan. 1991. "The Iconography of Mourning in Athenian Art." *AJA* 95:629–56.

Sinclair, R. K. 1988. *Democracy and Participation in Athens.* Cambridge: Cambridge University Press.

Snodgrass, Anthony M. 1987. *An Archaeology of Greece.* Berkeley: University of California Press.

Spivey, Nigel. 1991. "Greek Vases in Etruria." In *Looking at Greek Vases,* edited by Tom Rasmussen and Nigel Spivey, 131–50. Cambridge: Cambridge University Press.

Stavropoullos, Phoibos. 1964. "3e ephoreia klassikon arkhaiotiton." *Arkhaiologikon Deltion* 19.2.

Strauss, Barry. 1986. *Athens after the Peloponnesian War.* Ithaca: Cornell University Press.

Stupperich, Reinhart. 1977. "Staatsbegräbnis und Privatgrabmal im klassischen Athen." Ph.D. thesis. Münster: Westfälischen Wilhelms-Universität.

Thomas, Rosalind. 1989. *Oral Tradition and Written Record in Classical Athens.* Cambridge: Cambridge University Press.

Tilley, Chris. 1990. "Claude Lévi-Strauss: Structuralism and Beyond." In *Reading Material Culture,* edited by Chris Tilley, 3–81. Oxford: Basil Blackwell.

Tölle-Kastenbein, Renate. 1983. "Bemerkungen zur absoluten Chronologie spätarchaischer und frühklassischer Denkmäler Athens." *AA:* 573–84.

Unz, Ron. 1986. "The Chronology of the Pentekontaetia." *CQ* 36:68–85.

Vedder, Ursula. 1985. *Untersuchungen zur plastischen Ausstattung attischer Grabanlagen des 4. Jhs. v. Chr.* Frankfurt am Main: H. Lang.

———. 1988. "Frauentod-Kriegertod im Spiegel der attischen Grabkunst des 4. Jhs. v. Chr." *AM* 103:161–91.

Vickers, Michael J. 1984. "The Influence of Exotic Materials on Attic Whiteground Pottery." In *Ancient Greek and Related Pottery,* edited by H. A. G. Brijder, 88–97. Amsterdam: Allard Pierson Series.

———. 1985. "Artful Crafts: The Influence of Metalwork on Athenian Painted Pottery." *JHS* 105:108–28.

———. 1985–86. "Imaginary Etruscans: Changing Perceptions of Etruria since the Fifteenth Century." *Hephaistos* 7/8:153–68.

———. 1986. "Silver, Copper and Ceramics in Ancient Athens." In *Pots and Pans,* edited by Michael Vickers, 137–51. Oxford: *Studies in Islamic Art* 3.

———. 1987. "Value and Simplicity: Eighteenth-Century Taste and the Study of Greek Vases." *Past and Present* 116:98–137.

———. 1990a. "Attic Symposia after the Persian Wars." In *Sympotica,* edited by Oswyn Murray, 105–21. Oxford: Oxford University Press.

————. 1990b. "Golden Greece: Relative Values, Minae, and Temple Inventories." *AJA* 94:613–25.

————. 1990c. "Impoverishment of the Past: The Case of Classical Greece." *Antiquity* 64:455–63.

Vierneisel, Karl. 1963. "Kerameikos-Grabung." *AD* 18.2:27–30.

————. 1964a. "Die Ausgrabungen im Kerameikos 1963." *AD* 19.2:38–42.

————. 1964b. "Die Grabung in der Nekropole 1962." *AA:* 420–62.

Wallace, Robert. 1989. *The Areopagus Council, to 307 B.C.* Baltimore: Johns Hopkins University Press.

Watson, Patty Jo, and Mihalis Fotiadis. 1990. "The Razor's Edge: Symbolic-Structuralist Archaeology and the Expansion of Archaeological Inference." *American Anthropologist* 92:613–29.

Wehgartner, I. 1983. *Attisch weissgrundige Keramik.* Berlin: Philipp von Zabern.

————. 1985. *Ein Grabbild des Achilleusmalers.* Berlin: Philipp von Zabern.

Welskopf, Elizabeth, ed. 1974. *Hellenische Poleis.* 4 vols. Berlin: Akademie Verlag.

Whitehead, David. 1983. "Competitive Outlay and Community Profit: *Philotimia* in Democratic Athens." *ClMed* 34:55–74.

Will, W. 1983. *Athen und Alexander: Untersuchungen zur Geschichte der Stadt von 338 bis 322 v. Chr.* Munich: Steiner.

Willemsen, F. 1977. "Zu den Lakerdämoniergrab im Kerameikos." *AM* 92: 117–57.

Civic Ideology and Counterhegemonic Discourse: Thucydides on the Sicilian Debate

[decorative rule]

JOSIAH OBER

For a number of scholars (myself included), the subjects of Athenian citizenship and political identity seem to lead almost inevitably to an investigation of civic ideology. And, as this volume itself demonstrates, civic ideology is a deeply fascinating, if sometimes disquieting subject. I have argued elsewhere that in fifth- and fourth-century Athens the political identity of the citizen was enunciated in a civic ideology that was in turn defined by public discourse. This discourse was hegemonic and thus was the source of genuine political power for the ordinary citizens.[1] But civic identity and ideology are only one half of the equation. As several critical discussions of the work of Michel Foucault have shown, the study of discourse-as-power draws attention to the equally problematic issue of discourse-as-resistance.[2]

Civic ideology thus points to its own dialogical opposite: counter-ideology and critical discourse. With these considerations in mind, I offer here a preliminary reading of how a familiar text, Thucydides' *History of the Peloponnesian War*, resists the hegemonic tendencies of Athens' democratic civic ideology and criticizes the apparatuses through which that ideology was formulated and maintained. In brief, I hope to show that if Athenian civic ideology constructed the identity of the citizen by promulgating a specifically democratic way of learning about and acting in the public realm, then Thucydides' history offered its reader a technique for constructing an oppositional identity through mastery of a very different, although equally political, sort of knowledge.

The investigation of counterideologies seems particularly important because (among other reasons) the argument I have made for linking democracy and ideological hegemony might be mistaken as an attempt to demonstrate that democracy is no better—indeed, perhaps much worse—than other forms of government.[3] This was not my intention, nor do I believe that it is correct to draw the inference "hegemonic discourse makes for bad politics" from the historical Athenian experience with democracy. One way to challenge the validity of such a position is to investigate the form and substance of political criticism written under the democratic regime. The limits of hegemonic political discourse can be defined by the ability and willingness of a society's members openly to challenge the central premises of civic ideology. Moreover, I believe that reading classical Athenian texts against the context of ideological hegemony can deepen our appreciation of the achievement of the texts themselves and can further our understanding of the relationship between criticism as expressed in literature and acts of political resistance.

A contextual reading of the sort I am proposing requires a brief description of what is meant by ideology, hegemony, resistance, and discourse.[4] Athenian political ideology was formulated through, maintained by, and revealed by public speech, especially the formal rhetoric of Assembly and law-court debates. This ideology held (*inter alia*) that (1) political equality was both fundamentally important and compatible with social inequality, (2) consensus among citizens and liberty of citizens (esp. freedom of public speech) were simultaneously desirable, (3) collective decisions of the citizenry were inherently wise, and (4) educated and wealthy individuals were both a threat to democracy and indispensable agents in furthering the political process that permitted public-policy decisions to be made and implemented. Athens' cohesive, if internally contradictory, civic ideology mediated between the reality of social inequality and the goal of political equality, and so it helped to diffuse the class tensions that elsewhere in Greece led to bloody *staseis*.[5]

Athenian civic ideology was founded neither on a formal constitution nor on a set of epistemological certainties, but rather on a socially and politically constructed truth regime that I call "democratic knowledge." The practical functioning of democratic knowledge depended on the implicit willingness of the citizen-participants to accept the truths they lived by as political artifacts, rather than as absolutes denoted by a transcendent natural order. Democratic knowledge was grounded, in the language of J. L. Austin's speech-act theory, in the "conventional effects of conventional procedures," rather than in objective reality. It was created and re-created through the collective processes of public discussion, rather than being given from above by a metaphysical authority or discovered through intellectual efforts.[6]

Athenian political culture was thus based explicitly on opinion rather than on scientific certainty—in Platonic terms, on *doxa* rather than on *episteme.* The enactment formula of the Assembly, *edoxe toi demoi,* "it appeared right to the citizenry," defines the relationship between democratic knowledge and political action. The Athenian sociopolitical order was relatively stable because popular ideology provided a basis for collective decision-making. On the other hand, democratic knowledge remained flexible and dialectical because the frequent meetings of Assembly and People's Courts allowed contrasting views to be publicly aired. Through the process of open debate, public meanings evolved in response to changing external circumstances.

By responding to elite speakers in the Assembly and courtroom, the Athenian citizenry controlled the language employed in political deliberations. The resulting hegemony of the discourse of ordinary citizens was the real foundation of Athens' political order: Athens was a democracy because the ordinary citizen was a participant in maintaining a value system that constituted him as the political equal of his elite neighbor. This was a boon for the Athenian citizen masses, but a problem for some elite citizens, who saw enforced equality as oppression. Because revolutionary activism was discredited by the deplorable conduct of the ephemeral oligarchic governments of 411 and 404, the most visible (to us) resistance to civic ideology in late fifth- and fourth-century Athens was the creation of a literature critical of the failings of democratic knowledge. Because the educated elites of Athens were subject to, and searched for ways to resist, the hegemony of popular civic ideology, classical Athens generated many texts that struggled against the operations of what Foucault called the regime of truth.[7]

Thucydides begins his text by stating that he began his work right at the beginning of the war because at the time he believed (*elpisas*) that it would be great and worthy of record and because he saw (*horon*) that the rest of the Greek world was either allied to, or inclining toward, one side or the other (1.1.1).[8] The text, its subject, and the author's work have in this opening sentence a common point of origin, and from the very start Thucydides hints that there is simultaneously a connection and a distinction between inference (what he believed) and observation (what he saw). He was correct in his initial prediction, as we are told in the next sentence: the disturbance (*kinesis*) caused by the war engulfed almost the whole of mankind (1.1.2). The only emendation of Thucydides' original (prewar) assessment suggested by his second (explicitly postwar) sentence is that the conflict involved barbarians as well as Greeks.

In these opening sentences, the reader is alerted to the greatness of the events, the perspicacity of the historian, and the importance of the text. Thucydides *foresaw* great events, accurately assessed their importance, and studied them as they happened. Our author is no mere chronicler of past facts, but is possessed of a mantic gift for seeing the general direction of future developments. Having established his *bona fides*, Thucydides underlines the significance of the events he has recorded, by comparing the Peloponnesian War with previous conflicts. Despite the lack of fully reliable information about these early events, Thucydides used inference and probability (*ek tekmerion*) to show his readers that the wars and other affairs of the past were really not very great after all (1.1.3).

Having run through a brief précis of the more distant Greek past, Thucydides returns to the issue of the reliability of historical knowledge, launching (1.20.1) an attack on those who believe whatever they happen to hear about the past, including things about their own country, without subjecting the accounts to rigorous testing (*abasanistos*). His case in point is the belief, held by "the majority (*to plethos*) of the Athenians," that Hipparkhos, who was killed by Harmodios and Aristogeiton, had been the tyrant of Athens. This is no casual example: many Athenians assumed that the assassination of Hipparkhos set into motion the chain of events that led to the establishment of the democratic government.[9] By showing that Hipparkhos was a minor figure, Thucydides undermines a foundation myth of the democracy and so robs popular rule of a "usable" aspect of the polis' past history. The word Thucydides uses for the ignorant Athenians who supposed Hipparkhos to have been tyrant—*to plethos*—refers to the mass of ordinary citizens.[10] Thus, we are alerted to the text's critical project: it will present facts that have been "tested" and so are more reliable than the hodgepodge of erroneous beliefs that constitute democratic knowledge and underlie Athens' civic ideology.

Thucydides implies that the general (and specifically popular Athenian) unwillingness to test the truth is bad enough when it has to do with the distant past. But he goes on to show that "the many" are equally credulous when it comes to affairs unobscured by the passage of time. Thucydides cites as examples two errors regarding Sparta.[11] He then sums up: "Such is the degree of carelessness among *hoi polloi* in the search for truth (*aletheia*) and their preference for ready-made accounts" (1.20.3).[12]

Having chastised the many for their ignorance and laziness in regard to truth, Thucydides (1.21.1) proclaims the trustworthiness of his own history of the distant past: the reader will not go too far wrong in believing Thucydides' account, which is based on the clearest possible sources of evidence (*epiphanestaton semeion*). His compressed history is, he says, more reliable than the accounts of poets or *logographoi*. The former try to make the events of which they sing seem greater than they actually were. The latter are more concerned with persuading listeners than with hewing close to the truth. The events they relate are too distant in time to be checked (*anexelegkta*) and, indeed, "have won their way into the realm

of the fabulous" (*epi to muthodes eknenikekota*). This last phrase introduces the idea of a contest. Thucydides locates the quasi-historical accounts of poets and (other) writers of *logoi* in the context of a tourna-
ment of words; the victor's reward is public acclaim and the easy belief of
the gullible many.

Of course Thucydides himself has introduced a competition between
the "greatness" of the Peloponnesian War and all previous events. But he
informs us that this contest will not be judged by popular acclaim. Although (1.21.2) it is human nature (*kaiper ton anthropon*) for men to
overrate the war they are engaged in while they are fighting it, and then to
fall back into naïve wonderment at the glories of the distant past, *this* war
will demonstrate to anyone who is willing to pay attention to the actual
facts (*ho polemos houtos . . . ap' auton ton ergon skopousi delosei*) that
it was the greatest of all. Here Thucydides introduces a conception that is
central to his critical project: the superior importance and the self-evident
significance for the interpreter of the past of what actually happened, of
the brute facts about what was really done (*ta erga*). It is the *war* that
demonstrates, by the *facts* themselves, its own greatness.[13] The historian
has disappeared: historical truth is no longer a matter of words, of verbal
persuasion or interpretation, but a self-evident matter of seeing.

Facts (*erga*) occupy a privileged place in Thucydides' narrative in
relation to speech (*logos*). Words (especially those spoken in public by
politicians) and facts often collide in his text. As we shall see, individual
men and states (i.e., men acting collectively) who attempt to impose their
own speech-dependent meanings on brute facts come to bad ends. This
pattern in the text is significant from the perspective of criticism of democracy. As Thucydides has explained, most Athenians believe silly
things about their own past and about the institutions of their opponents.
They came to believe these errors through listening to pleasing poetry and
equally pleasing speeches.[14] Assemblymen whose understanding of the
past and present derives only from poets and public speakers—whose aim
was not correspondence with "facts," but rather the pleasure and acclaim
of the audience—cannot possibly decide rightly in regard to the future. If
sustained by the empirical evidence of an objective historical narrative
(which Thucydides' text is often taken to be), this chain of reasoning
would be a devastating criticism of democracy.[15]

Athenian Assembly speakers based their arguments on democratic
knowledge, which took for granted both a citizenry with a good grasp of
past and present political practices and the validity of public opinion.[16]
When Thucydides removed facts from the realm of affairs that could
properly be understood through listening to public speakers, or by reference to examples drawn from the ordinary citizens' knowledge of the

distant past, or by surface appearance and collective opinion, he also removed facts from the realm of things that could be adequately understood (and hence dealt with) by the existing procedures of the Athenian Assembly. Thucydides' version of historical knowledge is thus (according to its own internal logic) shown to be incompatible with, and indeed superior to, democratic knowledge.

Thucydides is not a simple sort of critic, and he recognized that the problem of perspective presented a challenge to his goal of understanding and presenting to his readers the objective facts about the past.[17] He complicates the reading of facts as objective entities that can exist in a pure realm beyond perspective: "My investigation proved very laborious, because the witnesses to each of the things that actually happened (*tois ergois*) did not relate the same things about these things, but rather [each spoke] according to his individual preference (*eunoia*) for one side or the other, or according to individual memory" (1.22.3). In his prior discussion on how he treated speeches and events (1.22.1–2), Thucydides had established a hierarchical relationship between logoi and erga. There he stated that, while speeches neither could be nor need be reported exactly, he subjected all reports of events (as well as his own perceptions) to the most rigorous scrutiny. But here he reminds the reader that his own knowledge of the facts about the war was largely a product of listening to things others said about what had actually happened in the war—that is, Thucydides' account of the erga is built up from logoi recounted by multiple witnesses who had imposed their own ideological perspectives on their narratives, and whose memories were imperfect.

We are now set for the grand revelation: Just how did Thucydides extract objective truth (*aletheia*) about the erga from multiperspectival logoi? The hoped-for revelation never comes. In its place we get a digression on the probable reception of Thucydides' text: "When people listen to (*kai es . . . akroasin*) my account, the very lack of fables (*muthodes*) will probably make it appear rather unpleasant" (1.22.4). Here the wording draws an explicit contrast between Thucydides' history and the accounts of the logographoi, which were composed with an eye toward aural reception and which may win their way into the realm of fable. We have now been warned: investigating the facts of the war was not easy, the author does not intend to reveal the alchemical secret of extracting objective historical truth from subjective accounts, and we should not expect to enjoy his narrative. Why should we (the members of his intended audience) bother to read it? The answer comes in the next sentence: "But as many as wish genuinely to understand (*to saphes skopein*) that which happened in the past and that which will happen in the future—a future which over time, in accordance with human nature (*kata to anthropi-*

non), will be much the same as the past, or at least similar—if they judge this account useful, that is quite enough [for me]. It is as a possession for all time rather than as an entry into the contest (*agonisma*) for current listening pleasure that I wrote" (1.22.4).[18]

This is a heady claim: those who do the hard work of reading this text will be rewarded with genuine understanding of both the past and (in its general lines) the future. Thus, Thucydides' readers may hope to achieve a position similar to that which the author claimed for himself in the text's opening sentence: they will have learned how to recognize the significance of great things in the offing. Confronted with the objective account of great political events, they will come to an empirical understanding of complex phenomena that conspire to create future tendencies.[19] The text's claim to teach an understanding of both past and future demonstrates that, despite his initial statement that the war was "most worthy of recording," Thucydides' account is hardly "history for its own sake." It is intended as a thoroughly tested, trustworthy, useful, empirically derived critical theory of political power in the form of a precise chronological prose narrative. This critical theory is in turn based on specific understandings of power and human nature.

In the so-called "Archaeology," Thucydides uses examples from earlier phases of Greek society to show that power is both restless and destructive. The reader concludes from these examples that once a state has become powerful it has only two choices. Either it will extend its power and thereby destroy the freedom of others, or the internal inequalities generated by undeployed power will lead to the self-destructive trauma of *stasis*.[20] The conceptualization of power as unstable and destructive in its effects is significant for reading Thucydides as a critic of popular rule. The two commonest terms for power in fifth-century Athens were *dunamis* (national financial or military strength relative to other states) and *kratos*. For most ordinary Athenians, kratos, at least in the political context defined by *demokratia,* had the positive sense of "legitimate authority." The *demos' kratos,* the people's political power, was regarded as a natural political good. But in Thucydides' much darker vision, kratos is the violent flip side of dunamis: either raw military might, or the forceful measures by which control over others is gained.[21] The Athenian demos was powerful because the common people were many and were well aware of their collective strength. If the kratos of the demos is a sort of power, and power destroys freedom and produces civil strife, the implication must be that, for Thucydides, *demokratia* is the power of the demos to destroy the freedom of others and, unless controlled by some external force, demokratia will embody a tendency toward the horrors of stasis. This reading is strengthened by a consideration of the other leg on which Thucydides' critical theory stands: his view of human nature.

Thucydides assumes throughout that human beings will, by nature, act according to perceived self-interest. But this does not *necessarily* mean narrowly selfish personal or individual interest.[22] He seems to regard circumstances in which each individual acts to further his narrow, personal interests as a pathological extreme. For example, despite their power, the tyrants of archaic Greece never accomplished much of note because each was interested only in his private household (*idion oikon*, 1.17). In plague-stricken Athens the ordinary bonds of family, community, and friendship were shattered by a force beyond human ability to control or comprehend. Thucydides' description of the hedonistic behavior of individual Athenians who had contracted the plague might be read as an explanation of how human "nature" (*phusis*) asserted itself in a condition free of the artificial bonds of social "custom" (*nomos*). But Thucydides claims that the effects of the plague were "beyond the capacity of human nature (*ten anthropeian phusin*) to endure" (2.50.1). Thus, we are to suppose that the plague overcame humanity and the behavior of the plague-stricken went beyond the realm of acting according to human nature. The plague narrative describes the ghastly end point of a continuum of behavior whose middle range is, for Thucydides, "human nature." For Thucydides, the selves that naturally act to further their perceived interests are collectivities: poleis or groups within the polis.[23] The stress of horrible circumstances has the *potential* to fragment society so individuals act only to further individual self-interest, but life under those conditions is not truly "human."

The demotic Athenian view of human nature was probably not so different from that of Thucydides, but Athenian civic ideology tended to put a great deal of emphasis on the Demos as a whole as the "self" that naturally acted to further human interests. The Athenian political ideal was for all of the citizens to decide and to act collectively in the interests of the polis as a whole.[24] In Athens the discontinuity between actual political actors (those who attended the Assembly, made proposals, served as jurors, implemented decisions, etc.) and the corporate whole (*hoi Athenaioi*) was deeply concealed behind the elaborate ideological structure that was maintained in turn by the hegemonic language of democratic politics. The functioning of the democracy was dependent on maintaining the illusion that the part of the citizen body that made policy in the Assembly stood in the place of the whole polis. For the Athenians, the enactment of a decree in the Assembly represented the collective will of the (imagined entity) Demos. Imagined Demos, identified with the state, naturally (in Athenian ideology) acted in the interest of the state.[25]

Thucydides' text attempts to expose this construct as a fragile political myth by demonstrating the existence and function of much narrower interests that were concealed by the language of Athenian politics. His text suggests that under the stress of war the myth of Demos often broke down and that, in light of the majoritarian decision-making mechanisms of the democratic state, this had serious consequences: Athenian political life after the death of Perikles is depicted as tending toward the selfish extreme typified by poleis beset by tyrants or plague. Alternately, the myth of unity was from time to time revived during the war, and Thucydides suggests that the consequences of this revival were, if anything, even more destructive to the polis.

For an ordinary Athenian, the term *demokratia* meant something like "the monopoly over legitimate public authority is held by the whole of the citizenry." For Thucydides, the same term denoted something like "the lower classes possess the raw power that gives them the means to constrain the rest of us." Thucydides does sometimes use the term *demos* to refer to the abstraction *citizenry*, but his primary use of the term is to denote a large, sociologically defined, and self-interested political faction within the state. *Demos* in this narrower sense means "the mass of the poor" and is equated with *to plethos* and *hoi polloi*.[26] If *demos* means "the masses as an interest group or faction," then demokratia is reenvisioned as an unstable system likely to promote the spread of destructive, narrowly defined self-interest, and this instability will unleash the great destructive potential innate in the *dunameis* of both Athens and Sparta. The only way around this reenvisioning is for two conditions to be met. First, the demos of Athens must be not only "the many" imagining themselves as Demos but also "the many and the few united in fact." Second, that unified demos must have an accurate understanding of the effect of its present decisions and actions on the future. This second condition requires that public decisions be grounded in objective facts. Thucydides depicts the Athenian process of linking (or failing to link) facts with speech in a number of passages of the *History*, notably in the Funeral Oration scene, and the three debate scenes (debates over Corcyraean alliance, the fate of Mytilene, and the Sicilian expedition) in which sets of speeches are delivered in the Athenian Assembly. These passages lead the reader to form certain judgments about the failure of the Athenians to fulfill either of the conditions noted above. Here I will touch on only the final scene, the Sicilian Debate.[27]

Book 6 begins: "In that . . . winter the Athenians decided . . . to sail against Sicily and, if possible, conquer it," although "hoi polloi were ignorant (*apeiroi*) of the great size of the island, of the numerousness of its Greek and barbarian population, and that they were undertaking a war not much smaller than that against the Peloponnesians" (6.1.1). Thucydides then describes the island's size, population, and early history (6.1.2–6.5) in order to demonstrate that "it was against such an island that the Athenians were eager (*hormento*) to make war." They intended, we are told, to rule the entire island, although they wanted to make it appear that they were offering aid to allies and kinsmen (6.6.1). Thucydides' sober and detailed description of Sicily contrasts sharply with the transparent duplicity and pathetic ignorance he attributes to the Athenian masses. In the three speeches by Nikias and Alkibiades that follow, as in other Assembly speech scenes, Thucydides establishes a contest between his historical way of knowing and democratic knowledge, between his text and public speeches, between his readers and Athenian assemblymen.

The scene is set: Sicilian Segesta has asked for Athenian military aid; the Athenians dispatched a fact-finding mission (6.6.1–2) that returned with accounts of Sicilian resources "both encouraging and untrue" (*ouk alethe*, 6.8.2). On the basis of this misinformation, which they evidently believed, the Assembly voted to send a force of sixty ships to Sicily (6.8.2–3). Five days later, a second Assembly was held, to vote on any additional material the generals felt would be necessary (6.8.2–3). As the debate opens Nikias, who had been designated a leader of the expedition, has come to feel that the slight and specious pretext of the alliance is inadequate to the monumental reality (*megalou ergou*) of attempting to conquer the entire island of Sicily (6.8.3–4). He hopes to persuade the Athenians to rescind the decree authorizing the expedition, in effect to "undo" the speech act performed at the previous meeting of the Assembly (6.9.1). This is a tall order. Nikias admits that his logos is unlikely to prevail against the Athenian character (*tropoi*) and that it will be difficult to dissuade his audience from taking risks in regard to "the still-obscure future." But he nonetheless tries to teach (*didaxo*) his audience that it will not be easy to accomplish that which they are eager to do (*hormesthe*, 6.9.3). Nikias' language recalls Perikles' comments on speech and action in the Funeral Oration, but Nikias hopes that, "instructed by speech," the Athenians will be willing *not* to act.[28]

Nikias establishes his political credentials with a claim never to have spoken in public "against his own opinion" (*para gnomen*, 6.9.2). He points out that he has no *personal* interest in blocking the expedition (6.9.2), thus setting up a contrast to Alkibiades' great personal interest in having the expedition sail. But ever-moderate Nikias qualifies his statement: I do, however, believe that a good citizen takes forethought for his own body and goods because this man will sincerely wish that the affairs of the polis should prosper so that his own will (6.9.2). Like other Athenian public speakers, Nikias hopes to show that there is no *necessary* gap between personal and public interests. But his comment undercuts the contrast between himself and Alkibiades and leaves his opponent with a deadly rhetorical counter.[29]

Nikias attempts to show the Athenians that the expedition is dangerous in light of the continued antagonism of the Spartans. The plots of certain Athenians and our enemies have made the peace treaty into "merely a name" (*onoma*). He correctly predicts that the treaty will not stop the Peloponnesians from attacking should Athens suffer a defeat abroad. But, like other Assembly speakers in Thucydides' history, Nikias also resorts to dubious arguments from probability and vague maxims.[30] He also appeals to Athenian fear of antidemocratic conspiracies.[31] Thucydides' forthcoming description of Athenian hysteria over the affair of the Herm-smashers will show his readers how very dangerous this last line of argument could be.

Like other public speakers, Nikias emphasizes the need to concentrate on national interests.[32] He points out the Segestans' national interests lie in telling plausible untruths; they have nothing to contribute but *logoi* (6.12.1). This leads to his attack on Alkibiades' narrowly *personal* and *selfish* motivation (*to heautou monon skopon*): Alkibiades hopes to profit from the command, but the Athenians must not endanger the polis in order that Alkibiades may appear brilliant in his private life (*idiai*). Nikias claims to fear Alkibiades' supporters; he calls upon older citizens to counter their claim that voting against the expedition is a sign of cowardice (6.13.1). Nikias appeals again and again to polis and *patris* (6.13.1–6.14), and in a key passage he argues that forethought (*pronoia*) is the best thing for the state, intense desire (*epithumia*) the worst (6.13.1).

Alkibiades is epithumia personified.[33] Grabbing the thread of Nikias' linking of private and public interest, he unravels his opponent's argument by evoking an Athens in which the successful risk-taker is freed from the constraints of egalitarian mores. Alkibiades trumpets the propaganda effect of his recent triple chariot-racing victory at Olympia: as a result of my victory the other Greeks have come to believe our dunamis is great. The reference to Olympia underlines the agonistic nature of the current speech competition in the Assembly, and Alkibiades confronts Nikias' charge of self-interest head on: "It is a useful sort of folly if, by expending private means, someone profits not only himself, but also the polis" (6.16.3).

Alkibiades admits that because of his desire for great personal fame he has been criticized in regard to his private affairs (*ta idia*), but he asks the Athenians to look around and see if there is anyone better than himself at public administration (*ta demosia*).[34] The proof? I brought about a useful anti-Spartan alliance in the Peloponnesos which "entailed no significant danger or expense for you" (aneu . . . kindunou kai dapanes, 6.16.6). This sounds good, but is it true? Alkibiades' "alliance" is the "plot" that Nikias claims rendered the peace treaty a mere name and too insubstantial to restrain Spartan aggression. Readers may remember the Corcyraeans' confident and erroneous prediction that their alliance would make Athens stronger "without dangers or expense" (aneu kindunon kai dapanes, 1.33.2). Thucydides' readers should by now have extracted from his historical examples (e.g., Epidamnos and Corcyra) the rule that every alliance is a potential source of danger and expense, for every alliance redirects the flow of power.

Readers will be even more dubious when they come to Alkibiades' follow-up: it was by means of appropriate logoi that I found a way of dealing with the dunamis of the Peloponnesians, and by stirring up passion (orge) I won their trust (6.17.1). Alkibiades' naïve confidence that logoi could tame dunamis is unlikely to persuade the reader who has got this far in Thucydides' narrative, and who has learned Thucydides' core lesson: the all-important difference between mere words and brute fact. The blithe expectation that orge could be the basis for a sound policy smacks of Kleon's demagogic appeals to righteous anger in the Mytilenian Debate (3.40.7).

Alkibiades then argues, "on the basis of what I hear from my informants" (ex hon akoei aisthanomai, 6.17.6), that the Sicilians are lightweights who will not put up much resistance.[35] This is patently false, but Alkibiades' ignorant listeners accept the speaker's words as an adequate representation of the men they will soon be fighting. Alkibiades concludes his portrayal of Sicilians by suggesting that it is hardly likely (ouk eikos) that such a mob (homilos), unable to listen to a logos as if with a single mind (mia gnome), will be able to engage in communal erga (6.17.4). By implication, if the Athenians do listen to him with "a single mind," if they ignore or forbid opposition, they will be able to initiate a great project in common. The danger of this line of argument will soon become apparent.

Alkibiades brushes aside the charge that the expedition will be risky, offering a specious historical analogy with the Persian Wars (6.17.7), and then he fires off a string of highly questionable maxims, predictions, and arguments from history and probability.[36] He concludes with appeals to national unity and to Athens' innate nature: a polis active by nature will ruin itself if it becomes passive, so it is better to stick to our active ways, even if they are imperfect (6.18.7). The sentiment, the context, and the vocabulary all recall Kleon.[37] Thucydides' readers have by now learned that one must be skeptical of this sort of oration. Not so the Athenian assemblymen. Having heard Alkibiades' speech, they were much more eager (*homento*) than before for the expedition (6.19.1). Nikias now made a momentous decision: because his previous argument had failed to deter the assemblymen, he would attempt to alter their resolution by grossly overestimating the size of the force that would be needed (6.19.2, cf. 6.24.1).

Nikias begins his second speech by acknowledging that it is the will of the Assembly to sail, and he claims that he will now inform them of what is needed (6.20.1). Thucydides' readers know that this acknowledgment is insincere and that Nikias is drifting perilously close to saying one thing in public while believing another—a form of political dishonesty that he proudly renounced in his previous speech. He contradicts Alkibiades' overconfident assessment of the Sicilian situation: "According to what *I* hear from *my* informants" (*hos ego akoei aisthanomai*), we will be going against poleis, many of them Greek, which are large, not at odds with one another, not likely to want a new government, or willing to give up their freedom in order to be ruled by us" (6.20.2). By mimicking his opponent's words, Nikias initiates a contest of facts: Alkibiades' information about Sicily versus his own. Nikias supposes that he can win this contest and thereby deflate Athenian enthusiasm. Much of the speech (6.20.2–23.3) details the tactical difficulties the Athenian expeditionary force will encounter, an assessment that Thucydides' subsequent narrative confirms as factually correct.[38] So far, this fact-oriented presentation of realia seems a model speech by Thucydidean standards. But then, at the end of the speech comes the rhetorical kicker that Thucydides' prior discussion of Nikias' intentions had prepared us for: the invading forces will have to be immense, but if [only if!] we do all this, I believe that there will be maximum security (*bebaiotata*) for the polis, and safety (*soteria*) for our soldiers (6.23.3).

Nikias' seemingly clever rhetorical plan, to deter enthusiasm by means of hyperbole, backfired badly: the assemblymen's desire (*to epithumoun*) for sailing was in no way dampened by the greatness of the necessary preparations; the Athenians, now convinced that the expedition would be completely safe if they voted for all that Nikias demanded, became even more eager (*polu de mallon hormento*: 6.24.2). And so "a passionate lust (*eros*) to sail burst upon everyone equally" (6.24.3).[39] In the feverish atmosphere opposition was impossible: because of the intense desire (*epithumia*) of the great majority, those few who still harbored doubts dared not speak out against the expedition lest they appear traitors to the polis, and so they kept quiet (6.24.4). Born of selfish and factional interests, midwifed by clever public rhetoric and ignorance, the myth of perfect unity possessed the Athenians.

The results of this erotic possession are, by turns, magnificent and horrific. The huge expedition was duly voted (6.25). The preparations completed, the entire population of Athens went down to Peiraieus to witness the launching (6.30.2). There was a moment of fear, when the true riskiness of what they were doing impressed itself upon the throng, but unease gave way to confidence as the Athenians feasted their eyes upon the sight of the huge fleet (6.31.1).[40] Thucydides lavishes superlatives on the expeditionary force (6.31.1–32.2). Yet he also points out that to the other Hellenes it seemed more a display (*epideixis*) of dunamis than a military expedition (6.31.4) and that on it rested all the hopes of the polis (6.31.6). The eventual outcome, the utter destruction of the Athenian naval and land forces in Sicily in 413 B.C., was equally great: "This accomplishment [*ergon* = the Syracusan defeat of Athens] was the greatest of the war, indeed, in my opinion the greatest in the known history of the Greeks" (7.87.5).[41]

If the destruction of the expedition is the greatest ergon of the war, then the decree that launched it, enacted by a collectivity possessed and artificially unified by desire, was commensurately wrong-headed.[42] Who was to blame? Not just naughty, sexy Alkibiades. Thucydides makes it clear that Nikias *himself* was responsible for much of the general lust. The verb that traces the upward spiral of Athenian enthusiasm is *hormao*, "to be eager to initiate an affair."[43] The Athenians do not seem especially mad for the expedition before the speech-contest of the second Assembly, a meeting that was called simply to iron out the administrative details of sending out a moderate-sized sixty-ship mission. It is Nikias who rekindled the general debate (6.14). In his first speech, Nikias describes the Athenians as "eager to initiate" (6.9.3) the expedition; after his second speech they are "even more eager" (6.24.2). By his violent personal attack on Alkibiades, Nikias ensured (6.15.2) that his opponent would make the reply that made the assemblymen "much more eager than before" (6.19.1). Rather than cutting his losses after the success of his opponent's speech, Nikias decided to act against both the general will and his own character, by challenging his enemy directly in a rhetorical contest. In his second speech Nikias abandons "his own genuine opinion" in favor of an overclever rhetorical strategy that feeds the flames of popular enthusiasm.

The construction of the scene suggests that Nikias, an excellent and moral man (as Thucydides is at pains to tell us, 7.86), was tricked by the agonistic context of the democratic decision-making process into the self-betrayal that will destroy both himself and Athens' power. Nikias' strategy in his second speech was based on the assumption that the assemblymen recognized a distinction between words and facts. His rhetorical bluff required that his own words invoke an external reality of expensive material necessities. He imagined that the Athenians would be sobered by a confrontation with the facts (huge expense, tactical difficulties) to which his words referred. But he forgot that in the context of the Assembly language was less referential than performative: the Assembly was a battleground of speech in which words were, through felicitous speech performances (i.e., the enactment of decrees), transmuted into social and political realities.[44] The Funeral Oration ideal, which elides the difficulty of moving from political speech in a democracy to effective action, here reaches its telos: speech becomes more than a spur to action; with the enactment of the decree authorizing the great expedition, speech is isomorphic with action. The distinction between words and facts melts away with predictably (in Thucydides' realm) bad results.

Thucydides' explanation of why Nikias' hyperbole fanned the fires of public desire is implicit in his depiction of how the Assembly "processed" the knowledge presented in verbal arguments. In the debates over Corcyra and Mytilene, the assemblymen were forced to choose between two positions. Thucydides' text suggests that in neither case was the final choice completely rational, because the assemblymen had no independent means of judging or testing the accuracy of each speaker's factual statements. But Thucydides also showed that even self-interested speeches might contain some truth, and so the decisions made by the Assembly did not *necessarily* result in bad outcomes.[45] The Sicilian Debate might have followed the same scenario. Nikias tries to refute Alkibiades' facts with his own better facts, but the Athenians refuse to choose between the two competing descriptions of external reality. They solve the political/epistemological dilemma posed by Thucydides—democratic decision-making as typically based on misinformation because of the agonistic nature of Assembly debate—by rejecting contradiction and combining Alkibiades' argument that there must be an expedition with Nikias' argument that it must be almost impossibly huge. As Thucydides told us at the beginning of the scene, they are still ignorant of the realities of Sicily, but, through their speech act, they have created an imaginary Sicily as an opponent for the imagined Demos. This imaginary Sicily cannot be strong enough to hurt the great dunamis that the assemblymen have called into being by the authorizing decree. And thus, in Alkibiades' dangerously optimistic and exclusionary formulation, the only outcomes they can foresee are the conquest of Hellas, or helping their friends and hurting their enemies.

The result of this "solution" is that the Athenians become (in Alkibiades' words) a being with a single mind (*mia gnome*) and a single purpose, a being that embodies the ideological dream of an end to all the complex contradictions, distinctions, and uncertainties that led to political friction. The idealizing discourse of Perikles' Funeral Oration is ac-tualized: the *agon* of politics becomes a love feast where "everybody wins."[46] Individual self-interest and desire to excel unites with the public good. Social unequals and political equals, the many and the few, old and young, dissolve into an ideological "all." The future is no longer unknown because the huge dunamis called into existence by the Assembly's decree has transmuted uncertainty into a sure thing. Justice and expediency go hand in hand because Athens will help its Sicilian allies through the self-serving act of conquering Sicily. The demos, freed from the braking ten-dency of sociopolitical friction, driven by desire, impatient with delay, is angered by any hint that contradictions or impediments remain. This unity is of course false. But it is highly dangerous to oppose the consensus in public, and so all critics of unanimity are gagged. Political criticism of the political myth becomes impossible in the face of the hegemonic will of the mass.

The tragic outcome is practically foreordained. The expedition, a product of false words and personal interests, crashes into the complex and harsh realities of war in the real world, and sinks; fragile unity de-volves into stasis.[47] Books 6 and 7, with their detailed and vivid descrip-tions of the initial successes, subsequent crumbling, and final collapse of the Athenian expeditionary force in Sicily, present Thucydides' strongest case for the priority of erga over logoi and for the instability of democ-racy when it is reenvisioned as government by competing speeches.

Thucydides' summation of why Athens lost the Peloponnesian War (2.65) begins with the statement that under Perikles' leadership Athens was a democracy only in logos (2.65.9). The implied inverse is that, after Perikles' death, demokratia existed as an ergon and that this led to disas-ter. Real demokratia meant that democratic knowledge was the epistemic authority undergirding decisions about actions the state would under-take. As a result, decisions were predicated on speech-contests rather than on fact and foresight. Speech-contests were the result of, and in turn exacerbated, selfishness and factionalism. As the contests became fiercer, there was a growing tendency for speaker and audience to confuse politi-cal enactment with reality. In Thucydides' text, the public performance of a speech act in the democratic polity does not felicitously call into being sociopolitical realities, it evokes a false and fragile vision of reality that is shattered by its inevitable collision with brute fact. Perikles' inferior suc-cessors competed through public speech for the "leadership" of the de-mos—a leadership that the text now reveals as the spurious privilege of using lies in order to persuade the demos to enact fictions. These fictions were dangerous first because the contests reflected and inflamed the self-ish ambitions of individuals and sociopolitical factions, and second because they involved a mighty dunamis and the communal kratos wielded by a numerous and increasingly willful demos, a demos that tended to confuse ideology with truth and political speech with reality. When this kratos was unleashed by unrestrained speech-contests, Athens' dunamis was misdirected and lost in Sicily, and Athens fell into the stasis of 411/10.

Here, with the apparent demise of demokratia, Thucydides' text abruptly ends. His critical argument, if not his historical narrative of the twenty-seven-year (5.26.1) war, is complete. The text as we have it empirically demonstrates the validity of his historical counterepistemology, by showing how and why the linkage between democratic knowledge and democratic political power led to the destruction of both democratic Athenian political life and Athenian dunamis. It is, however, worth noting that Thucydides' critical project, compelling (if chilling) as a logos, was not fully sustained by the erga. Demokratia bounced back after 410, Athens rebuilt its military power, and the conflict with Sparta lasted a good deal longer than twenty-seven years.[48]

Because of its vulnerability to falsification on the empirical basis of observable "realities," a political theory that claimed to explain the probable future on the basis of accurate knowledge about the recent past was perhaps, in the long run at least, a flawed vehicle for literary resistance to Athenian civic ideology. We certainly need not accept Thucydides' pessimistic conclusions about public speech and collective action. But the fact that Thucydides could conceive, execute, and find an audience for such a profound and sustained criticism of Athenian democracy should help us to define the limits of the hegemonic tendencies of democratic discourse.

Notes

This essay is adapted from parts of two chapters of a book-in-progress, tentatively entitled "Athenian Critics of Popular Rule." I wrote drafts of the chapters while I was a Junior Fellow of the Center for Hellenic Studies. I thank the Director and Fellows (both Senior and Junior) of the center for the year 1989–90. Along with the administration of Montana State University (who helped support my stay at the center), they made it possible for this study to be undertaken in the pleasantest of circumstances.

1. Civic ideology, democratic discourse, and hegemony: Ober 1989a.

2. Power-as-discourse: Foucault 1980, 78–133. Although Foucault refers briefly to the possibility of resistance (e.g., 1980, 82–83, 108, 134–45), several of Foucault's critics have pointed out that his theory fails to give an adequate account of the phenomenon of resistance (including the resistance to power-as-discourse implicit in his own writings); see essays by Taylor and Said in Hoy 1986, 69–102, 149–55.

3. See, for example, Bloom 1987, who argues that the supposed hegemony of democratic egalitarianism is among the evils of modern American society.

4. Importance of context: Skinner in Skinner et al. 1988, 56–63. The notion that these two analytic modes are compatible is important to my argument. Although Skinner and Foucault may seem far apart on (esp.) the issue of intention, the sharpness of the contrast can be overdrawn. Cf. Skinner 231–88 (esp. 271–73), where the hermeneutic scope he allots to authorial intentionality is considerably scaled back.

5. This is among the central arguments of Ober 1989a; see esp. 293–339.

6. Austin 1975. Austin's argument is usefully extended and reworked to better explain political speech, esp. in revolutionary situations, by Petrey 1988. Conventional effect quote: Petrey 1988, 77, slightly rephrasing Austin's "rule A.1."

7. Foucault's theory of power: n. 2 above. Democratic hegemony: Ober 1989a, 332–39. I adapt the concept of ideological hegemony from A. Gramsci; for a useful discussion, see Femia 1981, 1–129. The issue of textual resistance to ideological authority is also important to Skinner: Skinner et al. 1988, 276, 286–88.

8. On historical knowledge and discourse-as-resistance, cf. Petrey 1988, 193: "A verbal form alien to dominant discourse takes legitimacy from its appeal to a different historical moment producing different rules for what words can do."

Thucydides' political viewpoint is far from transparent. The *loci classici* are 2.65 (praise of Perikles, see below) and 8.97: praise of the broad-based oligarchy of the Five Thousand. Modern readings have had Thucydides all over the political map, e.g., Finley 1942, 237: Thucydides was by nature a democrat incapable of conceiving a great progressive city except as a democracy. Woodhead 1970, 34–35: Thucydides did not approve of democracy. De Romilly 1976, 93–105: Thucydides was an advocate of a "mixed constitution." Connor 1984, 237–42 (with review of literature): Thucydides was neither a simple antidemocrat nor a proponent of oligarchy. Pope 1988, 276–96: Thucydides was not esp. antidemocratic but regarded both democrats and oligarchs as contributing to the breakdown of community during the Peloponnesian War.

My argument looks at the text as a whole and offers no contribution to the "Thucydidean question" of composition. For this long, largely sterile, debate, see Rawlings 1981, 250–54.

9. The Athenian ignorance of the facts regarding the tyrants has tragic political consequences during the affair of the Herms (6.60.1); see Rawlings 1981, 256–59; cf. Euben 1986, 361: the tyrannicide story "reveals human beings as creators of meaning in the context of political struggle."

10. *Plethos* as a term for the mass of ordinary citizens: Ruzé 1984, 259–63. Note that *plethos* could, in the mid-fifth century, be used in official documents as a synonym for *demos:* ML 40 (= *IG* i^3 14: Erythrai decree).

11. The suppositions that each Spartan king had two votes in council and that there was a Spartan battalion called the Pitanes.

12. This criticism has (at least) two targets: Herodotus, whose *Histories*

JOSIAH OBER

contain these two errors, and the Athenian masses, who are implied by the term *hoi polloi*. Herodotus and the errors on Spartan kings and Pitanes: Gomme in *HCT* 1, ad loc. *Hoi polloi* as term for citizen masses: Ober 1989a, 11. Hornblower 1987, 155–90, points out Thucydides' authorial self-certainty and the rarity of this stance in ancient historiography.

13. In translating *ergon* as "fact," I am following the lead of Parry 1981, 13, 76–89, and esp. 92–93: *ergon* can mean anything wrought or done, or deeds of war, or the whole business of war. "But then there is a slightly different direction in the meaning of *ergon*, whereby it stands for *fact*, or *reality*, the thing that was *actually* done. It is this side of the word that makes it appropriate for the *logos/ergon* antithesis." As Parry points out, the two meanings of *ergon* as fact and as deed are quite close and are often conjoined in Thucydides. Thus, *ergon* in the antithesis "means *external reality*, but then it also means the *deeds of war*, and so *war;* and by insisting on this, Thucydides presents war as *the* reality, *the* complex of external forces within which the human intellect strives and operates."

14. The ranks of the *logographoi* must include the political orators of Athens. *Logographos* is not used again in Thucydides' text; for the translation here, cf. Connor 1984, 28. *Logographos* as a term for speech-writer in later Greek rhetoric: Lavency 1964. As Aristotle points out (*Rhet.* 1418a 21–29), speeches presented in Assembly deal with the affairs of the future, and speeches were the basis of decision-making in the democracy.

15. True historical objectivity, if defined as the absence of perspective, the "view from nowhere," is, of course, simply impossible; see Novick 1988. Yet it is important to keep in mind that Thucydides' motive for claiming to be "objective" was not the same as that of the "scientific" historians of late-nineteenth and twentieth centuries who attempted (and attempt) to follow von Ranke's dictum that it was the historian's duty to relate history "wie es eigentlich gewesen war." Thucydides was not writing within the confines of an established discipline, or for a disciplinary audience. Thus it seems relatively meaningless to criticize him for not being "truly" objective by Rankean standards (cf. n. 18 below). Objectivity is a rhetorical stance for Thucydides, one that offered him a needed *point d'appui* for his critical project.

16. Rhetorical appeals to the validity of public opinion and to historical examples: Ober 1989a, 156–70, 177–82.

17. Cf. Parry 1981, 48, 83–88.

18. For this much-discussed claim that history should be useful, see, e.g., Rawlings 1981, 254–63; and Connor 1984, 243–48. Gomme in *HCT* 1.149–50, argues "the future things" are future still to Thucydides, but assumed to be past to the reader. Thus, Thucydides does not suggest that his work will be of any help to one who hopes to understand what is still in his own future; and therefore Thucydides is not to be taken as giving practical advice for political agents. Gomme's argument strains the sense of the passage and is predicated on seeing Thucydides as a historian, with a modern historian's interests. The other side of the "modernist Thucydides" coin is the view of him as a dishonest

historian, who knew that historians should be objective, but willfully decided not to be: e.g., Wallace 1964; and Hunter 1973, esp. 177–84. Cf. Rawlings 1981, 263–72: no meaningful line can be drawn between the historian as reporter of events and historian as artist; Connor 1984, esp. 235–36: the text is complex and forces the reader to challenge positions the text itself seems to establish.

19. On the text's didactic tendencies, cf. Hunter 1973, 179–83; Cogan 1981, xvii; Rawlings 1981, 261–62; and Connor 1984.

20. See esp. 1.2.4, 1.7.1, 1.8.2–3. Population, capital, and navy as the main elements of Thucydides' definition of power: 1.4, 1.7.1, 1.8.2–3, 1.9.2, 1.9.3, 1.11.1–5, 1.13.1–1.14.3, 1.15.1. Cf. Connor 1984, 20–32, 246–48. For Thucydides on power, see also Woodhead 1970; Immerwahr 1973; Allison 1989; and the essays collected in Lebow and Strauss 1991.

21. *Kratos* as domination: 1.143.4, 4.98.2, 8.46, 8.76.4; the strength to carry out a war: 3.13.7; violent means used to take a city: 1.64.3, 1.118.3. For other examples, see Bétant 1843, s.v.

22. See, e.g., Pouncey 1980, xi: Thucydides' "assumption is that human nature remains relatively constant." But contrast Farrar 1988, 135–37, 139, who claims that Thucydides' view of human nature is not static; Flory 1988, 43–56: Thucydides' view of human nature is neither rigid nor strict.

23. Plague and individual selfishness: 2.53. Contrast 2.51: examples of self-less care of others. Late-fifth-century Athenian political writers were very interested in the issue of what is "natural" (*phusis*) and what is a product of human society (*nomos*); see Ostwald 1986, 260–73. Because I do not accept the postulates of methodological individualism as universally valid, I cannot agree with Pouncey 1980, xii, that Thucydides' view is that in times of crisis (e.g., *stasis*) human nature is "tracked to its proper ground in the human individual." On Thucydides' emphasis on groups rather than individuals, see Pope 1988.

24. Athenian ideal of consensus (*homonoia*): Ober 1989a, 295–99.

25. Imagined Demos: Ober 1989b, 329–32. The citizens in the Assembly were not, of course, in any formal sense "representatives" of their fellow citizens, for every Athenian citizen had the right to attend any Assembly. For a review of Athenian governmental procedure, see Ober 1989a, 53–155.

26. Ober 1989a, 4 with n. 2 for bibliography on this distinction. Sealey 1973, 283–90, unsuccessfully attempts to show that *demos* in Thucydides has no class meaning.

27. The three sets of speeches: 1.31–44 (Corcyraean Debate), 3.36–49.1 (Mytilenean Debate), and 6.8–26 (Sicilian Debate). I exclude Assembly scenes in which speeches are given in indirect discourse, and those in which only one speech is presented. Bibliography on speeches in Thucydides (to 1970): West III in Stadter 1973, 124–61. Useful discussions of the Sicilian Debate include Tompkins 1972; Stahl 1973; and Connor 1984, 162–68, 237.

28. By referring to the revoking of a decree as "undoing a performed speech act," I am consciously casting the political process of the Assembly in terms of Austin's theory; see above. The relationship between persuasive public speech

and collective action is of key importance in Perikles' Funeral Oration (2.40.2–3) and in the Mytilene Debate (3.38.1–4, 3.42.2).

29. For comments of other Athenian speakers on the issue of personal and public interests, cf. 2.37.1–3 (Funeral Oration) and 3.38.2–3, 3.40.3, 3.42.3–6 (Mytilenean Debate).

30. We should not fear the creation of a Syracusan empire, for it is hardly likely (*ouk eikos*) that an empire would attack another empire (6.11.3); it will impress our enemies more if we do not sail because "we all know" that people are most impressed by that which is most distant and least testable (6.11.4). Examples of other Assembly speakers' maxims: Corcyraeans (1.33.4, 1.34.3, 1.35.5), Corinthians (1.41.2–3, 1.42.2, 1.42.4), Kleon (3.37.2, 3.39.2, 3.39.5, 3.40.1), and Diodotos (3.45.3–6).

31. If we are soberly realistic (*sophronoumen*), we will realize that the contest (*agon*) is not against the barbarous Sicilians, but against Spartan plots to impose an oligarchy upon Athens (6.11.7).

32. Other Assembly speakers on the priority of Athenian interests: Corcyraeans (1.32.1), Kleon (3.40.4), and Diodotos (3.44).

33. In Thucydides' one-paragraph introduction (6.15), Alkibiades is first called "most-ardent" (*prothumotata*) for the expedition, and desirous (*epithumon*, 15.2) of the generalship. His desires were greater (*epithumiais meizosin*, 15.3) than his means, and eventually the demos came to believe that he lusted after (*epithumounti*, 15.4) tyranny. Cf. Hunter 1973, 180 on Alkibiades; she seems to go too far (8–9) in arguing that "Thucydides' characters . . . are not real people at all but *mere* [my emphasis] personifications of one quality or another."

34. This claim is supported by Thucydides' narrative comments on Alkibiades: 6.15.4.

35. The Athenians will not be facing a big dunamis in Sicily (6.17.1); like all Greeks, the Sicilians falsify their numerical strength (6.17.5). Each Sicilian is just out to get what he can for himself by making clever speeches, or by stirring up a stasis so that he can take from the common store; if unsuccessful, he will simply move to some other land (6.17.3). This last does *not* accurately describe the real Sicilians whom the Athenians will encounter in the invasion, but it could be taken as a succinct (if hostile) posteventum description of Alkibiades' own career: he is just now making a clever speech, he will soon defect to Sparta, and he will benefit by the Athenian stasis of 411/0. Thucydides' readers will learn all this in due course.

36. All empires were gained by helping those in need; inactivity is more risky than action; if we do not expand we risk being conquered ourselves (6.18.2–3). Don't worry about the Peloponnesians, our sailing to Sicily will befuddle them. Anyway, the expedition can have only two possible outcomes: either we conquer Hellas, or we'll hurt Syracuse and help our allies (6.18.4). Don't be fooled by Nikias' attempt to create social unrest (*diastasis*) by appealing to the elders; let's do as our fathers did and stand united, young and old. Keep in mind that, like all things, a polis can wear out if it is inactive, but if it

engages in contests (*agonizomenen*) it will gain experience and will be able to defend itself, not just in speech (*logoi*) but in fact (*ergoi*, 6.18.6).

37. Vocabulary: Alkibiades: *gignosko . . . nomois . . . kheiro.* Kleon (3.37.3): *gnosometha . . . kheirosi nomois.*

38. Sicilian cavalry will be a big factor; the Athenians cannot expect to recruit cavalry in Sicily; they might need to send home for more supplies; the money promised by the Segestans exists only in logos; if we don't conquer the whole island quickly, we'll be surrounded by enemies.

39. The old men thought such a great dunamis was likely to succeed or at least to be invulnerable; the young hoped to see wonders and felt they could do so safely; the mob (*homilos*) looked forward to military pay.

40. *Dia to plethos hekaston hon heoron, tei opsei anetharsoun.* This example of the masses' false confidence resulting from *seeing* demonstrates that visual perception can be just as misleading as verbal persuasion. Cf. Stahl 1973, 73–74; Brittan, "History, Testimony, and Two Kinds of Scepticism," in Chakrabarti, ed., *Testimony* (n.d.). The inability of visual perception alone to overcome the illusions of speech within the context of the democratic regime is an important issue for the Athenian antidemocratic "critical enterprise"; it recurs in Aristophanes (*Ecclesiazusae*) and, of course, in Plato's epistemology.

41. The location of this *edokei moi*–type construction in the sentence fits the methodological scheme Thucydides laid out in the proemium. According to Thucydides' categories, it was a demonstrable *fact* that the defeat was the greatest *ergon* of the war. But because ancient history is knowable only by inference, it can only be his (informed) *opinion* that this was the greatest *ergon* of all Greek history.

42. However, cf. 6.47–50 (victory in Sicily seems possible); 2.65.11: Thucydides here claims that the error was not so much ignorance about what to expect in Sicily (*ou tosouton gnomes harmatema en pros hous epeisan*), as a failure by those at home in Athens to support the expedition. This claim is contradicted by Thucydides' narrative; see Gomme in *HCT* 2. ad loc.

43. See above: 6.6.1, 6.9.3, 6.19.1, 6.24.2. The chronological context of 6.6.1 (*hoi Athenaioi strateuein hormento*) seems to be after the second Assembly, but before the launching of the expedition.

44. Felicity (successfulness) of speech performances (as judged by the subsequent behavior of the relevant parties): Austin 1975, 14–24, 116–17; and Petrey 1988, 32–48.

45. Truth, that is, as judged by conformity to the erga, or to Thucydides' own interpretation: e.g., the Corcyraeans predict the coming war and identify Spartan fear (*phobos*) of Athenian power as the prime cause (1.33.3); Corinthians predict that Athens' allies will revolt (1.40.6).

46. Athenian ideal of consensus: above n. 24. *Mia gnome*, vel sim. in (later) Athenian rhetoric: Dem. 19.298; Din. 1.99; And. 2.1; Lys. 2.12, 17, 24; and Aeschines 3.208. Idealizing discourse of the Funeral Oration (Perikles' and others): Loraux 1986.

47. Cf. Eco 1976, 66: death, once it has occurred, is the one thing that cannot be semioticized.

48. The last years of the twenty-seven-year war, and the ongoing conflict between Sparta and Athens in the 390s and 380s, are recounted by Xenophon, *Hellenica;* cf. Strauss 1986. On the question of whether Thucydides survived into the 390s, see the contrasting views of Pouilloux and Salviat 1985; and Cartledge 1984.

Works Cited

Allison, June. 1989. *Power and Preparedness in Thucydides.* Baltimore: Johns Hopkins University Press.

Austin, J. L. 1975. *Philosophical Papers.* Edited by J. O. Urmson and G. J. Warnock. 2d ed. Oxford: Oxford University Press.

Bétant, E.-A. 1843. *Lexicon Thucydideum.* 2 vols. Geneva. Reprint. Hildesheim: Georg Olms Verlag, 1961.

Bloom, Allan. 1987. *The Closing of the American Mind.* New York: Simon and Schuster.

Brittan, Gordon. n.d. "History, Testimony, and Two Kinds of Scepticism." In *Testimony,* edited by Arindam Chakrabarti. Dordrecht: Synthese Library Series, Kluwer Academic Publishers. Forthcoming.

Cartledge, Paul. 1984. "A New Lease on Life for Lichas, Son of Arkesilas?" *LCM* 9:98–102.

Cogan, Marc. 1981. *The Human Thing: The Speeches and Principles of Thucydides' History.* Chicago: University of Chicago Press.

Connor, W. Robert. 1984. *Thucydides.* Princeton: Princeton University Press.

de Romilly, J. 1976. "Alcibiade et la mélange entre jeune et vieux: Politique et médecine." *WS* 10:93–105.

Eco, Umberto. 1976. *A Theory of Semiotics.* Advances in Semiotics. Bloomington: Indiana University Press.

Euben, Peter. 1986. "The Battle of Salamis and the Origins of Political Theory." *Political Theory* 14:359–90.

Farrar, Cynthia. 1988. *The Origins of Democratic Thinking: The Invention of Politics in Classical Athens.* Cambridge: Cambridge University Press.

Femia, Joseph V. 1981. *Gramsci's Political Thought: Hegemony, Consciousness, and the Revolutionary Process.* Oxford: Oxford University Press.

Finley, John. 1942. *Thucydides.* Cambridge, Mass.: Harvard University Press.

Flory, S. 1988. "Thucydides' Hypotheses about the Peloponnesian War." *TAPA* 11:43–56.

Foucault, Michel. 1980. *Power/Knowledge: Selected Writings and Other Interviews 1972–1977.* Edited by Colin Gordon and translated by Colin Gordon, Leo Marshal, John Mepham, and Kate Soper. New York: Pantheon.

Hornblower, S. 1987. *Thucydides.* Baltimore: Johns Hopkins University Press.

Hoy, David Couzens, ed. 1986. *Foucault: A Critical Reader.* Oxford: Basil Blackwell.

Hunter, Virginia. 1973. *Thucydides: The Artful Reporter.* Toronto: Hakkert.

Immerwahr, H. I. 1973. "Pathology of Power and the Speeches of Thucydides." In *The Speeches in Thucydides*, edited by P. A. Stadter, 16–31. Chapel Hill: University of North Carolina Press.

Lavency, M. 1964. *Aspects de la logographie judiciaire attique.* Louvain: Louvain Nauwelaerts.

Lebow, N., and B. S. Strauss, eds. 1991. *Hegemonic Rivalry: From Thucydides to the Nuclear Age.* Boulder: Westview Press.

Loraux, Nicole. 1986. *The Invention of Athens: The Funeral Oration in the Classical City.* Translated by Alan Sheridan. Cambridge, Mass.: Harvard University Press.

Novick, Peter. 1988. *That Noble Dream: The "Objectivity Question" and the American Historical Profession.* Ideas in Context. Cambridge: Cambridge University Press.

Ober, Josiah. 1989a. *Mass and Elite in Democratic Athens: Rhetoric, Ideology, and the Power of the People.* Princeton: Princeton University Press.

———. 1989b. Review of Mogens H. Hansen 1987, *The Athenian Assembly in the Age of Demosthenes.* "The Nature of Athenian Democracy." *CP* 84:322–34.

Ostwald, Martin. 1986. *From Popular Sovereignty to the Sovereignty of Law: Law, Society, and Politics in Fifth-Century Athens.* Berkeley: University of California Press.

Parry, Adam. 1981. *"Logos" and "Ergon" in Thucydides.* New York: Arno Press. Reprint. Salem, N.H.: Ayer (Ph.D. thesis, Harvard University, 1957).

Petrey, Sandy. 1988. *Realism and Revolution: Balzac, Stendahl, Zola and the Performances of History.* Ithaca: Cornell University Press.

Pope, M. 1988. "Thucydides and Democracy." *Historia* 37:276–96.

Pouilloux, J., and F. Salviat. 1985. "Thucydide après l'exil et la composition de son histoire." *RP* 59:13–20.

Pouncey, P. R. 1980. *The Necessities of War: A Study of Thucydides' Pessimism.* New York: Columbia University Press.

Rawlings, Hunter R., III. 1981. *The Structure of Thucydides' History.* Princeton: Princeton University Press.

Ruzé, F. 1984. "*Plethos:* Aux origines de la majorité politique." In *Aux origines de l'hellénisme: Hommage à H. van Effenterre,* 259–63. Paris: Sorbonne.

Sealey, Raphael. 1973. "The Origins of *Demokratia.*" *California Studies in Classical Antiquity* 6:253–95.

Skinner, Quentin, et al. 1988. *Meaning and Context: Quentin Skinner and His Critics.* Edited by James Tully. Princeton: Princeton University Press.

Stadter, P. A., ed. 1973. *Speeches in Thucydides.* Chapel Hill: University of North Carolina Press.

Stahl, H.-P. 1973. "Speeches and Course of Events in Books Six and Seven of Thucydides." In *Speeches in Thucydides,* edited by P. A. Stadter, 60–77. Chapel Hill: University of North Carolina Press.

Strauss, Barry S. 1986. *Athens after the Peloponnesian War.* Ithaca: Cornell University Press.

Tompkins, Daniel P. 1972. "Stylistic Characterization in Thucydides: Nicias and Alcibiades." *YCS* 22:181–214.

Wallace, W. P. 1964. "Thucydides." *Phoenix* 18:251–61.

Woodhead, A. G. 1970. *Thucydides on the Nature of Power*. Cambridge, Mass.: Harvard University Press.

Private Lives and Public Enemies: Freedom of Thought in Classical Athens

ROBERT W. WALLACE

Personal freedom—"to live as you wish" (*zen hos bouletai tis*), "to say what you wish" (*parrhesiazesthai*)—is cited by many ancient sources as an outstanding quality of the Athenian democracy. At a moment of crisis outside Syracuse in 413, Thucydides' Nikias sought to encourage his soldiers by reminding them that their country was "the most free of all states" (*eleutherotate*) and that "all who lived there had the liberty to live their own lives in their own way" (7.69.2, trans. Warner). Both Plato and the Old Oligarch complain that in Athens even animals or slaves do just as they please.[1] Most famously of all, in the Funeral Oration Thucydides' Perikles remarks that "just as our political life is free and open, so is our day-to-day life in our relations with each other. We do not get into a state with our next-door neighbor if he enjoys himself in his own way, nor do we give him the kind of black looks which, though they do no real harm, still do hurt people's feelings. We are free and tolerant in our private lives, but in public affairs we keep to the law" (2.37.3, trans. Warner). Thus, perhaps as a consequence of the history of fifth-century Athens, personal freedom has come to be associated with the democratic form of government.[2]

As traditionally conceived, however, there are at least two outstanding categories of exceptions to this principle of personal freedom, first for those citizens who took part in city government, and second in the area of the freedom of thought, especially in connection with prominent intellectuals and in religious matters. Among many examples in the first of these categories were the official state examinations into the personal conduct of Athenians who were selected to hold public office. These examinations concerned issues such as whether they treated their parents badly. Candidates who failed these examinations were excluded from office, but usually, it seems, not otherwise punished. The personal behavior of Areopagites was also subject to control: Areopagites were, for example, forbidden to write comedies or even (we are told) to eat in taverns, both of which were of course permitted to private citizens. The case of Timarkhos, the subject of Aeschines' first oration, is especially illuminating in this respect. Timarkhos was accused of having once been a male prostitute. Accordingly, the law barred him from speaking in the Assembly or otherwise serving in government. The Athenians did not make it illegal to be a male prostitute; indeed, they collected a part of a prostitute's profits by means of a tax. However, they restricted the rights of such men to govern the state.[3] These are examples of behavior that was perfectly legal for private individuals, but restricted if they wished to play a leading role in the democracy.

As for the second type of exception, many extant reports attest the harassment and judicial prosecution of intellectuals at Athens during the fifth century.[4] Sokrates was condemned by a public court on a charge of corrupting the young and of not believing in the gods that the city believed in, but in other, new spiritual beings. The physicist and cosmologist Anaxagoras was tried for impiety, we are told, and imprisoned, fined, condemned to death, or rescued by Perikles' intervention: the sources differ on his fate. Another friend of Perikles, Aspasia, a woman whom ancient philosophical sources describe as a brilliant intellectual,[5] was also prosecuted for impiety and also, we are told, for procuring women for Perikles. She was acquitted only after Perikles burst into tears in court and begged for her release. So, too, according to Plutarch, Damon, son of Damonides, was ostracized for being too intelligent, a consummate sophist who concealed his cleverness by the study of music, and who in secret trained Perikles, "rubbing him down like a political athlete." The atheist Diagoras of Melos, we are told, was outlawed for impiety. Euripides also was prosecuted for impiety, by the politician Kleon, according to the Alexandrian biographer Satyros. The natural scientist Diogenes of Apollonia, who argued for the primacy of air among the different elements, "came within an ace of danger" (*mikrou kinduneusai*), the late-fourth-century philosopher Demetrios of Phaleron reported. Demetrios also stated that the atomist Demokritos of Abdera "did not even go to Athens." According to Plutarch, an oracle monger named Diopeithes sponsored a decree providing for the prosecution "of those who do not accept what has to do with the gods or teach theories about what is up in the sky." According to the *Souda,* the sophist Prodikos was executed by hemlock for having corrupted the young. Finally, according to Cicero and Diogenes Laertius (whom I quote), the Athenians "burned the books of

Protagoras in the marketplace, to the accompaniment of public procla-
mation, collecting them from their individual possessors."
    If all of this is true, the evidence is certainly sufficient to show that
what is commonly regarded as the great age of Greek enlightenment was
marked—in the words of E. R. Dodds—by the "banishment of scholars,
blinkering of thought, and even (if we can believe the tradition about
Protagoras) burning of books."[6] For Momigliano, this material suggested
that the Athenians were more concerned with political freedoms than
with the freedom of thought.[7] But is all this true? And to the extent that
the Athenians did harass certain intellectuals, why did they do so?
    Before looking more closely at specific cases, some general remarks
are in order. Intellectual persecution, of course, is also very much a modern topic, and modern discussions of this phenomenon at Athens are
often conditioned by special and contemporary factors. Thus, along with
everyone else classical scholars have witnessed, in Eastern Europe and
elsewhere, attempts by totalitarian regimes to control intellectual activity.
By contrast, the political traditions of at least certain western democracies are informed by the notion of the primacy of the individual over the
state, and the paramount importance of protecting individual liberties as
guaranteed, for example, by a bill of rights. The struggle against religious
intolerance has been continuous in the West since the time of the Roman
empire. Finally, largely as a consequence of Plato, the figure of Sokrates
has been of enduring fascination. As a result of these and other factors,
first, scholars and others have come to focus on the fate of a few philosophers and friends of Perikles without fully understanding the complexities of these cases within their specific historical contexts, and without
fitting them within the wider context of fifth-century intellectual or personal freedoms, and fifth-century values and ideologies. Second, we also
take the side of the intellectuals. That is to say, we have been preoccupied
with, and react in horror to, a few famous cases of intellectual persecution because of their parallels with and consequences for later history,
without adequately evaluating these in Athenian terms. The problem is a
familiar one. Sophocles' *Antigone* may stand in the twentieth century
quite validly as a compelling document of feminism and the martyrdom
of the individual for a higher ideal, against the authority of government.
But the play was probably not these things for at least a majority of its
fifth-century audience.
    As part of a larger attempt to fit intellectual freedom at Athens
within its historical and ideological contexts, in this essay I mention three
points. First, it is important to establish where (generally speaking) Athenian law drew the line between activities of public as opposed to private
concern. We in the United States regulate, for example, drinking, pros-

titution, and gambling. What behavior did the Athenians punish, what did they ignore, and how are actual cases of intellectual sanctions to be judged when viewed in this broader context? Second, as I have stated, intellectual sanctions must be set in a general context of Athenian values and ideologies. Thus, for example, while prior loyalty to the polis, as opposed to either the family or the *hetaireia,* was certainly a topic of debate during the fifth century,[8] it is a topos of Attic literature that the polis must take precedence over individual rights. "When the whole state is on the right course it is a better thing for each separate individual than when private interests are satisfied but the state as a whole is going downhill," remarks Thucydides' Perikles (2.60.2, trans. Warner).[9] As an argument against the Sicilian expedition, Thucydides' Nikias condemns Alkibiades for "endangering the state in order to lead a brilliant life of his own" (6.12.2). Andocides, also, in the speech *On His Return,* contends that when the state is prospering, each Athenian is better off individually, but "those who do not identify their interests as individuals with yours as a community can only be hostile to the city" (2.2–3).[10] To the extent that this ideology obtained in Athens generally, it must affect our conception of the prosecutions of intellectuals. Third, another basic difference between modern and Athenian perspectives on these issues concerns the nature of jurisprudence. Our legal tradition is based on a code of highly precise laws, whereas the Athenian conception of what constituted impiety, *asebeia,* or other offenses, was generally less fixed. Athenian jurors had by necessity to reach verdicts on rather more impressionistic bases than is technically possible today. The oath that jurors swore at the start of their year of service included the provision "and in those areas where there are no laws, I shall decide as seems most just to me."[11]

The evidence for the various cases of intellectual persecution in fifth-century Athens raises at least two questions: first, the relevance of the events reported to the issue of intellectual intolerance; and second, the credibility of the sources attesting these cases. On the question of credibility, ever since the nineteenth century a number of scholars have been unhappy with the attestations of at least some of the cases which I have mentioned. In many respects this scepticism reached its furthest point in an article by K. J. Dover, published in *Talanta* in 1976.[12] Thus, for example, beginning as early as Welcker in 1833, many scholars have doubted whether Prodikos *was* executed by hemlock for corrupting the young. In their view, the *Souda*'s report is a fabrication modeled on Sokrates.[13] This hypothesis is supported by the silence of other, often detailed sources for Prodikos in respect to the *Souda*'s tradition, despite the obvious parallel to Sokrates and the usefulness of a further example of Athenian intellectual intolerance to the many authors of Socratic *apologiai.* Furthermore, the phenomenon of fabricating historical parallels to Sokrates is well attested. Thus, for example, although Aristotle's death at age sixty-two of a disease of the digestive organs is well documented, Diogenes Laertius (5.6) reports that "according to Eumelos in the fifth book of his *Histories*, [he died] by drinking hemlock at the age of 70."[14] For a second parallel, the scholiast to Aristophanes *Frogs* 320 calls Diagoras of Melos "an atheist poet who also introduced *daimonia kaina* like Sokrates." Finally, Dover has observed that Aristotle's reported reason for fleeing Athens, lest the city sin *twice* against philosophy, implies that among philosophers only Sokrates had been executed.[15] Accordingly it would be difficult to defend the execution of Prodikos as historically accurate.

The prosecution of Aspasia by the comic poet Hermippos (Plutarch *Pericles* 32.1, 5) for impiety and procuring has also frequently been challenged, both on the grounds of attestation and in terms of its significance for the question of intellectual tolerance. The issue of sources is raised by Hermippos' mention as prosecutor: Might this tradition be based on an illegitimate deduction from remarks in a *play* by Hermippos?[16] The phenomenon of Hellenistic and even fourth- and fifth-century scholars taking literally remarks in ancient comedies can be readily documented. Thus, most famously, for his biography of Euripides Satyros accepted as a historical event the plot of Aristophanes' *Thesmophoriazusae*.[17] (This same sentence is our single source for Kleon's prosecution of Euripides.)[18] A similar tendency to use comic evidence can be demonstrated for Ephoros.[19] In addition, a willingness to take comedy seriously lies at the heart of Plato's argument concerning Sokrates in the *Apology*. As for the story that Aspasia was *prosecuted* by a comic poet, when we combine this anecdote's sexual slander against Perikles and Aspasia (for procuring), first with the comic picture of the notoriously aloof Perikles shedding tears in court for his mistress, second with Perikles' status as a favorite target in Hermippos' plays especially for his erotic insatiability,[20] and third with the motivation for the Peloponnesian War adduced in the immediate context (in Plutarch), namely, that Perikles wished to divert attention from Aspasia and his other friends (compare this with the *Acharnians*), many scholars have found it hard to avoid the conclusion that here, too, Plutarch's source has taken drama as fact, and therefore Aspasia's prosecution for impiety was just a comic fantasy.

Despite Dover's arguments, however, several scholars have subsequently defended the historicity of Aspasia's trial.[21] Accordingly, the case for doubt on the basis of attestation may be reinforced by several points. First, Plutarch identifies his immediate source for this story as Aiskhines of Sphettos, the fourth-century Socratic.[22] Only one type of literature is attributed to Aiskhines: the philosophical dialogue. (In particular, his work the *Aspasia* is called a dialogue.)[23] Now, accepting philosophical dialogues as valid sources for the anecdotal material that they contain must always be done with prudence and circumspection. The case of Aiskhines gives cause for special concern. I note that Aiskhines' *Aspasia* is our single source for the view that Aspasia instructed not only Perikles in political rhetoric but also the "sheep-seller" Lysikles, whom she married after Perikles' death, and who thereby (Aiskhines says) was transformed from a low-born and humble condition into Athens' leading politician (FF 23, 26 Dittmar = Plutarch *Pericles* 24). The slanderous epithet "sheep-seller" in particular suggests that Aiskhines made use of comic sources; compare, for example, Aristophanes' calling Euripides' mother a vegetable seller.[24] Aiskhines also liked to write about people bursting into tears. In his *Alcibiades,* Sokrates remarked that Alkibiades once burst into tears from a sense of inferiority toward Themistokles (FF 9–10, cf. 6, 7 Dittmar). Furthermore, as a devoted follower of Sokrates,[25] Aiskhines might have had an uncommon interest both in possible historical parallels to his master such as the story about Aspasia provided and in examples of disgraceful conduct by Athens' democracy and its leaders. Finally, Athenaeus (220a) remarks that "most philosophers are by nature even more abusive than the comic poets." He cites Aiskhines as his first example of this, and, in summing up Aiskhines' characteristics, he remarks that he condemned everyone except his beloved Sokrates (220c–d). This then is our source for Aspasia's prosecution for impiety, which, I agree, on the basis of unacceptable attestation we should reject as a fantasy.

In addition to the problems of attestation, the case of Aspasia raises a second problem, noted by both Ostwald (1986, 195) and Stadter (1989, 297–98). As Stadter writes, if the accusation of *asebeia* brought against Aspasia is vague and uncertain, "the additional charge of procuring free women suggests that Aspasia was accused of entering sanctuaries or participating in sacred rites although as a prostitute or procuress she was excluded (cf. [Dem.] 59. 113–14). There is no reason to think she was prosecuted for intellectual activity or for holding the 'atheistic' views of which Anaxagoras was accused." Although I prefer to believe that the real explanation to the puzzle of Hermippos' alleged prosecution lies in Aiskhines' pernicious combination of old comedy and philosophical invective, the issue raised by Stadter and Ostwald is substantive. If they are right, it eliminates the case of Aspasia as an example of Athenian intellectual intolerance.

As for Diagoras of Melos, Jacoby and others have pointed out that at least two fourth- or early third-century sources state clearly that the accusation raised against him was that of divulging the Eleusinian Mysteries and ridiculing them so as to dissuade people from seeking initiation.[26]

Revealing the Mysteries was a specific crime—there was a law against this. So again, at least on the basis of Diagoras' flight from Athens, the Athenians cannot be accused of anti-intellectualism. We should also note that this event quite possibly occurred at the time of the profanation of the Mysteries in 415[27] and that Diagoras came from Melos, destroyed by Athens in 416.

In addition to these cases, Dover has discredited on equally cogent grounds the evidence for the intellectual harassment of Demokritos (who "did not even go to Athens") and Diogenes of Apollonia (who "came within an inch of danger"), both examples of intolerance which our single source, Demetrios of Phaleron, mentions not as actual occurrences but merely future possibilities.[28] Demetrios was, of course, a Peripatetic philosopher set up by Macedon as Athens' oligarchic governor between 317 and 307 B.C. He despised the democracy that subsequently expelled him.

So far, I think, the case for scepticism is justified. This is reinforced by the point that almost all of those alleged to have been persecuted for their intellectual views were not Athenians. Presumably, as in the case of Diagoras, at the onset of difficulties nothing would have prevented them simply from leaving Athens. Four general explanations for the distortions by our sources are the usefulness of comic evidence for polemical attacks written during the fifth and fourth centuries; the hostility of philosophers among themselves; the powerful influence of the figure of Sokrates and the antidemocratic bias of many ancient philosophers, which led them sometimes to think the worst about Athens in this regard; and the need in a later age of biography to flesh out inadequate records by means of sources that we would regard as unacceptable evidence.[29]

On the other hand, many scholars continue to think that something happened to Protagoras and Anaxagoras, and I think that more can be said about Damon and the decree of Diopeithes. So I shall address in greater detail the evidence for these four. Concerning Protagoras, I have mentioned the statement in Cicero (*De Natura Deorum* 1.63) and Diogenes Laertius (9.52) that the Athenians publicly burned his books.[30] We have various other reports of things happening, or almost happening, to him, much of which is or has seemed inconsistent or self-contradictory. As for the reports of book-burning, these must be set against two statements, first a remark by Timon of Phleious in the third century B.C., that the Athenians *wished* to burn the books of Protagoras.[31] (Momigliano suggested that this tradition may have been based on a statement by the late fourth-century Aristotelian Aristoxenos [F131 Wehrli] that Plato *wished* to burn the writings of Demokritos.)[32] Second, in Plato's *Meno* (91e) Sokrates argues that it would be odd if the sophists did harm to their pupils but still could attract them as students. In this context he remarks:

"It looks as if no one in the whole Greek world noticed for a good 40 years that Protagoras corrupted those who associated with him—I think he was about 70 when he died, and 40 years in his profession—and in all that time, up to today, he's never ceased to enjoy a high reputation"— εὐδοκιμῶν οὐδὲν πέπαυται. In the light of Timon and Plato, it would be difficult to defend the statements of Cicero and Diogenes Laertius about actual book-burning as historically accurate.[33]

Plato's statement in *Meno* 91e certainly suggests that nothing very serious happened to Protagoras. On the other hand, against this passage we must juxtapose two others. First, Athenaeus quotes several lines of the *Flatterers* by Eupolis—a play that both he and the hypothesis to Aristophanes' *Peace* date to 421—in which Protagoras is said to be in Athens and is referred to as an ἀλιτήριος περὶ τῶν μετεώρων, "a sinner in regard to celestial matters."[34] Second, in Plato's *Theaetetus* (171d) Sokrates remarks to Theodoros that if Protagoras could come hear the present discussion he would rebuke them and then go, sinking down (*katadus*) and running away (*apotrekhon*). Since these comments are unrelated to anything in their immediate contexts or in the dialogue as a whole, we may infer that they allude to some well-known biographical facts about Protagoras. In addition to these two texts, the early third-century Atthidographer Philochoros said that Protagoras died at sea (*FGrHist* 328 F217). Finally, scholars generally agree that the chronological data supplied for Protagoras in Plato's *Protagoras* suggest dates for him of about 490 to about 420,[35] although of course Plato's dialogues are not free of chronological inconsistencies.[36]

If we put together the information from Eupolis, Philochoros, and Plato (provided for the moment we accept Plato's testimony), Protagoras was born about 490, he was about seventy when he died, and—in particular—both Eupolis and Plato (in one of the *Protagoras* passages) imply that he was alive in 421. That is, Protagoras died shortly after the time of Eupolis' play, and Plato suggests that he ran away from Athens, *apotrekhon*. Eupolis' remark about "sinners," in a comedy, certainly suggests that some kind of negative public perception of Protagoras for his philosophical views was then current in Athens. So if we put this together with Plato's *apotrekhon*, we *may* conclude that as a result of this public perception, whatever it was, Protagoras left Athens and died shortly thereafter. (It is possible, as, e.g., Derenne pointed out, that Plato's *katadus*, sinking down, supports the tradition from Philochoros that Protagoras died at sea, since *kataduno* is usually used of sinking into the sea.[37] But the watery deaths of philosophers at sea is a biographical topos: Hippasos, Empedokles, and Diagoras of Melos are also said to have died at sea, presumably as a punishment for impious speculation.)[38] Alternatively, if we disallow any chronology supplied by a philosophical dialogue, Eupolis' remark about sinners, Plato's phrase *apotrekhon,* and the comment of Plato's Sokrates in *Meno* 91e, while insufficient to reconstruct Protagoras' dates, show at least that some public comment arose against him for his philosophical views; that he "ran away" from Athens presumably as a result of this; but that these comments were not sufficient or serious enough permanently to affect his reputation. None of this evidence provides any basis for supposing that the Athenians took any form of legal action against him.[39] The later sources for Protagoras are not inconsistent with this reconstruction. Thus Plutarch in the *Life of Nicias* (23) says that the Athenians were suspicious of natural science and therefore drove Protagoras out of the city. Josephus remarked that had Protagoras not promptly fled from Athens, he *would have been* arrested and put to death for his religious opinions (*Contra Apionem* 2.266). According to Sextus Empiricus (*Adversus Mathematicos* 9.55–56), Protagoras was attacked for his beliefs, left Athens, and drowned on his way to Sicily.

There are two final aspects of this affair, the first of which is politics. According to Diogenes Laertius, Protagoras' accuser was a certain Pythodoros, who was a member of the Four Hundred and later archon under the Thirty.[40] Protagoras was, of course, a friend of Perikles, he was a democratic theorist—the only one known to us—and he wrote the constitution for Thourioi.[41] If Pythodoros was Protagoras' main opponent, the contrasting political perspectives of these two men suggest in part a political motivation for the accusations made against him. Second, Eupolis' play, produced in 421, should be set in the context of other dramas that were produced near that date. Aristophanes' *Clouds,* also (and violently) against new philosophy, was initially produced in 423. Ameipsias' *Konnos,* with its chorus of intellectuals (*phrontistai*) and criticism of Sokrates (Konnos was Sokrates' music teacher), was staged that same year. Euripides' *Suppliants,* a play marked by conventional piety and the absence of theological speculation, was produced between 424 and 421.[42] And Aristophanes rewrote *Clouds* between 420 and 417.[43] The production of these particular dramas within the circumscribed period of the closing years of the Archidamian War suggests that this period was characterized by a suspicion of intellectual or religious speculation, a suspicion that was expressed at least in public by some of Athens' intellectuals. This in turn may have produced, or responded to, an element of popular discontent. It is worth noting that political leadership in this period is associated with Nikias, who was known for his traditional piety, and also with Kleon, who at least in Thucydides (3.38) attacked sophistic rhetoric, admittedly while practicing it.

There are a remarkable number of conflicting traditions about Anaxagoras. Of sources extant from the third and early second centuries B.C.,[44] for example, Sotion claimed that Kleon brought a charge of impiety against Anaxagoras because he called the sun a "red-hot mass of ore." Anaxagoras was defended by Perikles, given a five-talent fine, and exiled. By contrast, Satyros claimed that Thoukydides, son of Melesias, brought against him a charge of impiety and also treason in the interest of Persia. Anaxagoras was condemned to death, but he had already fled Athens.[45] In contrast with this, Hermippos claimed that Anaxagoras was condemned to death and imprisoned, but obtained his release through Perikles' intervention. In shame, however, he committed suicide. Finally, according to Hieronymos of Rhodes, during Anaxagoras' trial Perikles led his teacher into court in so debilitated a state that the jury acquitted him out of pity.

The two traditional approaches in dealing with the many variants of this story are either to pick out one version, or else to pick and choose details from among several.[46] The methodological problems inherent in both approaches are clear. In the first case, all the stories may be erroneous; or if one is right, how can we determine which? All of them are equally plausible internally, and each is consistent with the general facts of fifth-century history. The second case runs the risk of violating the integrity of every source in accordance with subjective criteria, yielding an account that agrees with nothing.

Yet we need not despair. For as Gershenson has demonstrated, virtually all our stories about Anaxagoras have one, and only one, point in common: that he was accused and brought to trial.[47] Every discrepancy in our sources can be explained as a scholarly elaboration from that point, based on calculations of historical probability. That is, given the trial, each source had to figure out the nature of the charge, why it was brought, and what happened afterward. Anaxagoras' remark that the sun was a red-hot stone was famous; so in most accounts that becomes the charge. Anaxagoras was known as a friend of Perikles; accordingly, the deeper motivation for his trial was hostility to Perikles, either by Thoukydides, son of Melesias (if the writer followed the early chronology for Anaxagoras), or by Kleon (if he followed the later); and hence the confusion about Anaxagoras' fate.

Now, why did our sources think that Anaxagoras had been brought to trial? In a conversation with his accuser Meletos in Plato's *Apology,* Sokrates provokes Meletos into accusing him of believing in no gods at all, and then ridicules him for this accusation. "Do you imagine that you are prosecuting Anaxagoras, my dear Meletos? Have you so poor an opinion of these gentlemen [i.e., the jurors], and do you assume them to

be so illiterate as not to know that the writings of Anaxagoras of Klazo-
menai are full of theories like these?" Sokrates here alludes to the availability of Anaxagoras' writings in the agora for one drakhma (*Apology*
26c–d). Gershenson suggests that on the basis of this passage ancient
writers concluded that Anaxagoras had been tried. We ourselves have
noticed examples of the ancient scholarly technique of mining philosophical works for historical "information."[48] Indeed, this passage is still adduced against the view that nothing happened to Anaxagoras.[49] But Gershenson is right. This passage does not at all presuppose that Anaxagoras
had been tried, and may well exclude it. For had Anaxagoras been tried
for his intellectual views, Sokrates should have referred an Athenian jury
to that trial, and not to Anaxagoras' books, as their source of knowledge
for his religious views. When Sokrates discusses his earlier interest in
Anaxagoras in *Phaedo* 97–98, he makes no reference to any public rejection or condemnation of Anaxagoras by the Athenians.[50] If these arguments are justified, we have eliminated the evidence that anything at all
happened to Anaxagoras, who, in addition, had probably not been in
Athens since about 450.[51]

The decree of Diopeithes, which provided for the *eisangelia* of "those
who do not accept what has to do with divine matters or teach theories
about what is up in the sky," and which (we are told) was directed against
Anaxagoras (Plutarch *Pericles* 32.2), might at first sight seem more difficult to discredit, because for once we seem to have a public document. Yet
the authenticity of reported decrees is not absolute, as the controversial
Kallias decree most obviously demonstrates.[52] Questions about the authenticity of Diopeithes' measure may be raised on five points. First,
although arguments from silence cannot be decisive, Dover and Stone list
an impressive series of texts where Diopeithes' decree might naturally
have been mentioned, but it is not. Dover (1976, 39 = 1988, 146) cites
what may be Ephoros' account (Diodorus 12.39.2) of the attacks of Perikles' enemies against Anaxagoras for his religious views, but which does
not mention Diopeithes. Dover also cites the scholia on Aristophanes
Birds 988, *Knights* 1085, and *Wasps* 380, each discussing Diopeithes'
fanatical religiosity without reference to the *psephisma*. Stone (1988b,
241–42) points out that at *Memorabilia* 4.7.6 Xenophon attributes to
Sokrates the same reactionary views on astronomical speculation as those
attributed to Diopeithes, and quotes Sokrates to the effect that anyone
who thinks about these matters "runs the risk of losing his sanity as
completely as Anaxagoras did." However, Xenophon makes no reference
to any legal or public action by Diopeithes against that philosopher. Our
single source for Diopeithes' decree is the passage in Plutarch's *Pericles*.

The express connection between Diopeithes' decree and the attacks on Anaxagoras is, of course, a second problem, if indeed Anaxagoras had not been in Athens since about 450. For the decree is clearly dated by Plutarch sometime during the 430s.

Third, the term *metarsios* for "celestial matters" is not used in the fifth century. So at a minimum the report of Diopeithes' decree has been modernized.

Fourth, no cases are known in which anyone was brought to trial under the terms of Diopeithes' decree, by means of an eisangelia. In particular, as Dover points out (1976, 40–41 = 1988, 147), the common view that Sokrates was prosecuted by Diopeithes' measure is inconsistent with Plato's statement (*Euthyphro* 2) that Sokrates' case was brought by means of a *graphe,* presented to the archon in the usual fashion.

Finally, fifth, so far as we can determine, foreign philosophers continued to visit and teach in Athens during the 420s, with no signs of hesitation or fear. The excitement generated in 427 by Gorgias' visit—Gorgias, of course, delighted in rejecting the existence of everything—is especially notable.

Accordingly, for these various reasons one may be permitted at least to question the authenticity of Diopeithes' decree. Yet even if the decree is genuine, we cannot rely on the connection that Plutarch makes between it and the harassment of Anaxagoras, and so cannot know the actual circumstances in which it may have been proposed. For example, Rosenberg suggested that Diopeithes' measure may have been a panic-stricken reaction to the Athenian plague.[53] The absence of any actual prosecutions known to have been brought as a result of Diopeithes' decree, as well as the absence of any other attested effects, argues that, even if it is genuine, we should probably not take that measure as an important or significant indication of Athenian attitudes.

Thus, after the very long list of persecuted intellectuals provided at the beginning of this essay, we are reduced to Sokrates and Damon—not (I think) incidentally, almost the only Athenians among that group. I need not say very much here about Sokrates. The contemporary tradition that he was prosecuted for not believing in the gods of the city is explicit; in the *Apology* (18b) Plato makes clear that attacks against him had been going on for years. There was, then, certainly an anti-intellectual motivation, connected with religion, in the Athenian jury's condemnation of Sokrates.[54] Nevertheless, collective and even individual motivations are often complex, and, in the case of Sokrates, other factors were certainly at work. First, Sokrates had many friends and former students, including Kritias, among the Thirty tyrants, who cruelly dominated Athens in 404. These associations must have been a significant issue for many members of the jury. Aeschines expressly states (1 *Timarchus* 173) that the Athenians executed Sokrates because he was "the teacher of Kritias, one of the Thirty who put down the democracy." Furthermore, Sokrates' main accuser, Anytos, is known to have been a politically engaged supporter of the democracy. A second prejudicial factor was undoubtedly Sokrates' perverse defense in court, and his perverse personality, which had irritated Athenians for many years: Plato is explicit about this (e.g., *Apology* 21b–23b). A third factor was Athens' defeat in the Peloponnesian War, for which, at least to certain members of the jury, the "impious" Sokrates may have been a scapegoat. Finally, we must remember that out of presumably a very large jury, had just thirty Athenians voted differently, Sokrates would have been acquitted.[55]

One case remains: the ostracism of Damon, the music philosopher, which I and others date to the mid-440s.[56] Because of Damon's obscurity this ostracism is almost never discussed, except to be denied. That is, to a number of scholars it has seemed sufficiently strange that a philosopher of music should be ostracized—a procedure otherwise reserved, so far as we know, for politicians—that they have tried to discredit the evidence for it.[57] This attempt, however, has proved unsuccessful. Damon's ostracism is reported by the *AP* (27.4); it is reported three separate times by Plutarch (*Pericles* 4, *Nicias* 6, *Aristides* 1), which suggests at least that Plutarch did not derive his account simply from the casual reading of a single source; it is mentioned by Libanius in his *Defense of Socrates* (*Declamationes* 1.157), which responded to Polykrates' attack against Sokrates written in the later 390s; finally, two ostraka have been found, inscribed with Damon's name.[58] No one has provided any reason why we should doubt all of these sources. But why was a philosopher of music banished from Athens?

According to the *AP*, Damon was ostracized because he was thought to have suggested to Perikles many of his initiatives. This statement is certainly unclear. Did the *demos* not like Perikles, or not like Damon's initiatives, or not like that someone was advising Perikles? In the *Aristides* Plutarch says that Damon was banished because he was "too intelligent" (*perittos phronein*). In the *Nicias* he says that the demos was always suspicious of those who were clever (*deinoi phronein*), and so they ostracized Damon. Finally, in the *Pericles*, in the passage already alluded to, he writes that Damon was "a consummate sophist, who took refuge behind the name of music in order to conceal from *hoi polloi* his cleverness (*deinotes*). He associated with Perikles, that political athlete, as it were, as rubber and trainer" but was caught out, and ostracized as *megalopragmon* and *philoturannos,* and "became the butt of the comic poets. Plato [Comicus] at any rate represented someone inquiring of him thus: 'first tell me, I ask, for you, they say, are the Kheiron who nurtured up

Perikles.'" A crucial point in this evidence is the *AP*'s vagueness. Only Plutarch directly states that Damon's ostracism was a result of his cleverness, and, sure enough, Plutarch expressly mentions that the comic poets made accusations against Damon. Once again, then, this evidence may be bad evidence. We can easily imagine that a comic poet made fun of Damon as an overly brainy intellectual, and later scholars took this joke seriously, as the reason why he was ostracized. (It is also difficult to imagine what other sources ancient scholars could have had to *explain* an ostracism in the 440s.)

Yet even if our evidence for the reasons for Damon's ostracism is bad evidence, Damon was nonetheless ostracized, and this procedure was, so far as we know, reserved for political figures. The most common explanation modern scholars offer for Damon's ostracism is factional politics: Perikles' friend Damon was ostracized either in the political struggle against Thoukydides, son of Melesias, in the 440s, or else in the next decade as a part of Perikles' troubles before the Peloponnesian War. Of course it may well be true that, for some Athenians, opposition to Perikles helped influence their vote against Damon. The example of Sokrates should encourage us to adopt a flexible approach in understanding group events. Yet whatever effect factional politics may have had, we must also consider that ostracism was a public procedure. Surely the demos would not have banished Damon simply as an indirect attack against Perikles. Just as in condemning Pheidias for theft and Sokrates for impiety, the demos must have cared about, or been convinced to care about, something that Damon himself was doing, something that affected the polis and for which ostracism, as a political tool, would have been appropriate. What aspect of Damon's activity could be regarded as a danger to the community?

Damon's teaching on music may here provide a clue. For this we have two central testimonia, both from Plato's *Republic*. (Plato must be considered our best source for Damon, because he was a contemporary, a philosopher, and both his uncle and his music teacher are cited as Damon's students.)[59] First, in a discussion of which types of rhythms imitate which sorts of life, Sokrates says to Glaukon (400b): "Well, on these matters also we shall take counsel with Damon, as to which steps (*baseis*) are appropriate to *aneleutheria* and *hubris* or *mania* and other evils, and what rhythms we must leave for their opposites. I think I have heard him obscurely naming an *enoplios* (a composite), and a dactyl and a *heroon* which he somehow arranged and made equal up and down, passing into a short and a long, and, I think, he named something an iamb and something else a trochee, and he added longs and shorts. And in some of these he censured or praised the tempo of the foot no less than the rhythms themselves, or else some combination of the two, I can't say. But let these things, as I mentioned, be postponed for Damon's consideration, for to determine the truth would require no little discourse. Or do you think otherwise?" Four points are clear from this passage. First, according to Damon as Plato represents him, certain rhythms are appropriate to certain psychological states or modes of behavior; second, Damon studied the technicalities of rhythms and meters; third, Damon was concerned to name or label various rhythms; and fourth, Plato found him obscure. A little later in the *Republic* (424c), Sokrates remarks: "Never are musical styles altered without altering the most important rules of the city. So Damon says and I believe him." This text shows that, according to Damon as Plato represents him, music had important political consequences. I also mention here a third text, the report in Ps.-Plutarch's *De Musica* (1136e) that Damon created a *harmonia* called "the relaxed Lydian," which Plato banned from his state as "soft and sympotic" (*Republic* 398e–399a).

Understanding Damon in his political and historical contexts requires an understanding of the function and role of music in Greek society. Greek music itself is a complex topic, and, whatever it sounded like, musicologists appear to agree that it would probably sound quite strange to us.[60] On the sociology of music, however, progress can be made, and the background for Damon's research can thus in part be reconstructed. Within the restricted scope of this essay, I can indicate only several general points. First, music played a central role in Greek social life. Although certainly the Greeks could sing or play musical instruments in solitude, usually musical performances were public, communal events, and they constituted an essential part of most social and ritual occurrences. Music was fundamental to education, as songs transmitted the traditional ideologies of the city. It was no less important in the military, in the preparations for battle on both land and sea, in war dances, and in marching toward the enemy. In all of these music was linked with the physical rhythms that were essential to the life and safety of the city: not only in the dance but, for example, in the communal dexterity needed for 170 men to row a trireme, or to turn in a hoplite battle line. As Alan L. Boegehold has suggested, the rhythmical abilities of the Greeks may have been born through the dance so pervasive in Greek life.[61]

Second, the power of music was very familiar to the Greeks of Damon's time: its ability to assuage the emotions is attested, for example, in the *Iliad* and the *Homeric Hymns;* its ability to enflame is mentioned by Euripides.[62] Music was also thought to have the power to cure diseases or effect spells—for example, it healed the wound of Odysseus in *Odyssey* 19. According to Theophrastus, many believed that aulos music played directly above a limb afflicted with sciatica would cure it.[63]

Finally, given the widespread perception of the power of music and its central role in society, music's capacity to change or disturb the state was frequently recognized, in anecdote, poetry, and philosophical discussion. We are told, for example, that in listening together to Terpander the Spartans "ceased their love of internal strife."[64] Pindar several times formulated the concept: thus Apollo with his lyre "brings *eunomia* without discord into the hearts of men" (*Pythian* 5.65–67). We are also told that when Timotheos brought a nine-string lyre to Sparta, one of the ephors took a knife and asked him from which side he should cut off two strings, so that his lyre not prove to be corrupting.[65] Sokrates, too, in the *Republic*, forbids any change in music, because of its deleterious social consequences (424b–e).

Thus for the Greeks music was essentially political, of direct and immediate concern to the polis. According to Plato's Sokrates, Damon himself made this connection explicit through his teaching: "Never are musical styles changed without changing the most important rules of the city. So Damon says and I believe him." Damon's direct association with Perikles (and other Athenian politicians) is well documented in fifth- and fourth-century sources: in *AP* 27.4, in the passage from Plato Comicus already discussed, and in Plato (?) *Alcibiades* 1.118c, where Alkibiades says that "even in his old age Perikles associates with Damon" in order to gain wisdom. In his commentary on the latter passage, Olympiodorus remarks: "Damon taught Perikles the songs through which Perikles harmonized the city" (*In Platonis Alcibiadem Commentaria* 138.4–11). These perspectives serve to indicate the political reason for the ostracism of Damon. Whatever the truth of the accusation, when Damon's research into the behavioral effects of music took the form of advice to Perikles, this could be represented to the demos as a secretive attempt to manipulate the city's music and thus affect the behavior of the polis. As a political phenomenon, music itself offers the bridge between Damon's political and intellectual activities. It thus may explain his ostracism.

At the beginning of this essay I noted several alternative perspectives from which to view the evidence for intellectual freedom in Athens. Upon examination, this evidence proves to consist of Sokrates' execution for impiety and for corrupting the young, Damon's ostracism for his philosophical activities, and a number of satirical or hostile references to philosophers in Attic comedy. These references, especially in comedy, show that an element of popular prejudice certainly existed, during certain periods, against these figures. In one case, that of Sokrates, these prejudices led to judicial action, and in another to ostracism. However, it is easy to overestimate the extent of this prejudice, or to magnify its religious component. Some scholars imply that as a group the Athenians might be quite superstitious, terrified of possible divine consequences if they sheltered impious philosophers, philosophical Oedipuses, in their midst. In part as a result of the influence of comparative anthropological studies, notably by E. R. Dodds, we have become attuned to the "primitive" and "irrational" in ancient Greece, especially among the lower classes (see, e.g., Dover 1976, 25 = 1988, 136). The most obvious counterbalance to this conception is provided by the Sicilian Expedition. Shortly before the expedition sailed there occurred the two greatest sacrileges ever in Athenian history, the mutilation of the herms and numerous parodies of the Mysteries. Nonetheless, the fleet sailed; even though their commander Alkibiades was directly implicated in the sacrilege, Athenian sailors did not hesitate to board the boats with him. It is also worth remembering that nothing happened to Sokrates until he was seventy years old, that Damon was not ostracized for his religious views, and that year after year the Athenians, including the lower classes, paid to hear various characters in Euripides utter the grossest blasphemy. Mostly the prejudice that existed did not lead to legal action; but when it did, imprecise legal concepts such as that of asebeia made the Athenians liable to punish in accordance with prejudice.

On the other hand, all three of our cases of intellectual harassment—Damon, Sokrates, and Protagoras—are marked by a significant political element. Damon was an associate of Perikles; Protagoras was a democratic theorist and a friend of Perikles, and he wrote a constitution for Thourioi; Sokrates was closely associated with Alkibiades and some of the Thirty tyrants. The standard modern interpretation of the attacks on Perikles' intellectual friends is that they were a means of getting at Perikles. In fact, we should reverse this: in a sense the Athenians ostracized Damon to save Perikles from him—or, put more judiciously, in order to prevent these philosophers from continuing to have an effect on the city and its leaders.

It is clear, I believe, that the Athenians only really got exercised about intellectual speculation when this activity was conducted in public and affected the polis. The proof of this is most obviously furnished by Plato. Plato's philosophy was fundamentally antidemocratic and also probably impious by normal Athenian standards: his Forms or Ideas could certainly have been represented as *hetera daimonia kaina* (cf. *Apology* 24b). Yet for more than forty years he was allowed to say what he wanted, unharmed, behind the walls of his Academy—located outside the city of

Athens. Impious talk or even impious actions, in themselves, seem generally not to have been thought especially dangerous to the city, or else Euripides' plays would not have been performed, and the Athenians would have pursued those who on numerous occasions before 415 had mutilated herms (Thucydides 6.28.1). Many other similar examples to Plato might be cited, such as Kritias and Antiphon, who were ignored by the demos until they actively entered politics.

Finally, I have alluded to various literary statements, and one from a court speech, concerning the primacy of the polis over the individual. Although John H. Finley, Jr., for example, believed that this was an "oligarchic" idea[66] and I myself once thought it was "democratic," I now believe it was simply a general attitude. In the case of ostracism, for example, all admitted that the winning candidate, Themistokles, say, or Kimon, had committed no crime: but for the good of the community it was better that he leave. A similar argument applies to the "crime" of deceiving the people, or giving them bad advice, or losing military battles; generals who lost battles, for example, were notoriously and rightly reluctant to return home. In every case, the individual may have been blameless, and in our eyes these punishments are a gross violation of individual rights. But their advice or action had harmed the city, and therefore they were punished.[67] Indeed, the Athenians' almost casual propensity to execute people in defense of the polis is a noteworthy characteristic, especially in a democracy that regarded itself as gentle, *praos*. Thus, shortly after the amnesty of 403, for example, a man who tried to prosecute an offense committed before 403 was executed. In 414 Aristophanes' joking reference to the massacre at Melos two years earlier sets my hair on end; and many of those merely denounced for parodying the Mysteries in 415 were executed. As Thucydides notes, it was impossible to say whether these executions were just, but "it was quite clear that the rest of the city benefited greatly."[68] Sokrates' execution was just one of many, done for the good of Athens. There is no reason why we should single him out for our especial horror.[69]

At the beginning of this essay I noted that in addition to restricting certain intellectual freedoms—as it turns out, under particular circumstances—the Athenians also exercised some control over the personal conduct of those who made use of their citizen's right to participate in leading the state. In the case of Timarkhos, for example, the Athenians did not restrict his right to do as he wished with his person. They did, however, decide that such people should not be allowed any significant role in guiding the polis. As Aeschines wrote (1 *Timarchus* 195), "the law scrutinizes not those who mind their own private business (*idioteuontes*), but those who are politically active (*politeuomenoi*)." Recent students of

Greek homosexuality have rightly called attention to the explicit rationale for this provision contained in the ancient sources.[70] That is, as
Aeschines remarked, "one who has sold his own body . . . would not
hesitate to sell the interests of the community as a whole" (1 *Timarchus*
29). A similar explanation is provided by Demosthenes (22 *Androtion*
30–32). Solon established a law, he says,

> which forbids persons guilty of prostitution to make speeches or propose
> measures. For he saw that most of you do not make use of your right to
> speak, so he thought the prohibition no great burden, and he could have
> set down many harsher penalties if his object had been to punish these
> offenders. But that was not his aim: he forbade these things in the inter-
> est of you and of the state. For he knew—I repeat he knew—that of all
> states, that state which is most antagonistic to those who live disgrace-
> fully is the one in which everyone can talk about their disgraces. And
> what state is that? A democracy. He thought it would be dangerous if
> there ever happened to coexist a considerable number of men who were
> bold and clever speakers, but full of such disgraceful wickedness. For the
> people could be led astray by them to make many mistakes. In addition,
> such men could attempt either to overthrow the democracy completely
> (for in oligarchies . . . no one may speak ill of government officials) or
> else to debauch the people, so they might be as nearly as possible like
> themselves. He therefore absolutely forbade such men to have any share
> in the counsels of state (*metekhein tou sumbouleuein*), lest the people
> should be deluded into some error.

As Winkler notes (1990, 60), "the crucial point seems to be not sexual behavior in itself but rather some notion of preserving the political
order by restrictions placed on its directors at the top." However, it is
important to observe that provisions of this type were not restricted to the
sphere of sexual activity. A similar argument is advanced by the speaker
of [Demosthenes] 26 *Aristogeiton* 2.1–2, 4, in connection with indebted-
ness to the state:

> It has been conclusively proved, men of Athens, that this man Aris-
> togeiton is a state debtor and is not in possession of citizen rights, and
> that the laws expressly forbid such a man to address the assembly. It is
> your duty to restrain and check all law-breakers, but especially those
> who hold public office and those who take part in public affairs (*hoi
> politeuomenoi*). For such men tend naturally to harm the community if
> they are evil, or to confer the greatest benefit on it if they are honest and
> willing to abide by the laws. . . . (4) That was why Solon ordained that
> the penalties for private citizens should be slow but for magistrates and

political leaders swift, supposing that from the former one can obtain justice even after some delay, but that for the latter one cannot wait. For no possibility of punishment will remain if the *politeia* is destroyed.

It is the thesis of this essay that the principle directly stated to underlie Athenian legal restrictions of male prostitutes and state debtors applied more generally, not only in government (e.g., in the case of the Areopagos Council) but also in the area of intellectual freedom. Individual behavior that directly harmed the polis was subject to legal control. Individual behavior that affected only the individual was not. This demonstration in turn is part of a wider argument, that a similar generalization both in law and (typically, if less categorically) in the less formal sphere of social censure, obtained also in the areas of freedom of expression and freedom of action.[71] In the case of legal restrictions on intellectual freedom, the only sustained exception to this principle appears in the oligarchic movement of 404, which excited Plato's enthusiasm when it came to power, vowing to make the city "pure" (*katharos:* Lys. 12 *Eratosthenes* 5, see also Plato *Letters* 7.324d). Kritias himself proposed a measure banning the teaching of how to write speeches (Xenophon *Memorabilia* 1.2.31). As Momigliano has written, it remains a permanent scandal that later, in the *Laws,* Plato himself theorized and legislated the concept of intellectual persecution.[72]

At the beginning of this essay I asked the question: Where, under the democracy, did Athenian law draw the line between personal conduct that was subject to public sanction and conduct that was not restricted? In Thucydides' Funeral Oration Perikles remarked: "We are free and tolerant in our private lives, but in public affairs we keep to the law." This assessment of Athenian democratic principles is thus in essence correct. The Athenians punished those who were judged to have harmed the polis, its public enemies, but they left private citizens alone.

Notes

Versions of this essay were presented at the Institut für alte Geschichte, Munich, at Loyola College (Maryland), and at Brown, Harvard, and Rutgers Universities. I have profited from comments and suggestions on these various occasions. I am also grateful to Philip Stadter and Mary Lefkowitz for observations on written drafts of this essay, and to my invaluable research assistant, David Berkey.

　　1. See esp. Plato *Republic* 562a–563d and Ps.-Xenophon *Athenaion Politeia* 1.10.

　　2. See Momigliano 1971c, 515–17.

　　3. For restrictions on Areopagites, see Plutarch *De Gloria Atheniensium*

348b–c and Athenaeus 566f. On Timarkhos and Athenian provisions concerning male prostitution and the right to participate in government, see Dover 1978, 19–109; Cohen 1984; Winkler 1990, 54–64; Halperin 1990, 94–99; and my discussion at the end of this essay. For a second case similar to that of Timarkhos, see Dem. 22 *Androtion* 21–32. For the ancient sources for the tax on prostitutes, see T. Lenschau, *RE* 22.1 (1953) col. 265, s.v. *pornikon telos.*

4. The sources for these cases will be cited in detail later in this essay.

5. See esp. Plato *Menexenus* 235e and 249d; Aiskhines Sokratikos F9 Krauss; Clement *Stromateis* 4.19, 122–23; Plutarch *Pericles* 24; Philostratus *Lives of the Sophists* 2.257 (= DK 82A 35); and Athenaeus 219b. The comic poets routinely call Aspasia a whore: Ar. *Acharnians* 526–29; Eupolis F 98K.; and Kratinos F 241K. (whence the standard modern misconception that she was a *hetaira* or of lax sexual morals).

6. Dodds 1951, 189.

7. Momigliano 1971c, 516: Momigliano writes specifically of the decree of Diopeithes, and of Anaxagoras, Protagoras, and Sokrates.

8. For the family, see most notably Soph. *Antigone,* and, for the hetaireia, see, e.g., And. 1 *Mysteries* 51 and 2 *Return* 7.

9. ἐγὼ γὰρ ἡγοῦμαι πόλιν πλείω ξύμπασαν ὀρθουμένην ὠφελεῖν τοὺς ἰδιώτας ἢ καθ' ἕκαστον τῶν πολιτῶν εὐπραγοῦσαν, ἀθρόαν δὲ σφαλλομένην.

10. εἰ δὲ μὴ ταὐτὰ ἡγοῦνται σφίσι τε αὐτοῖς συμφέρειν καὶ τῶι ὑμετέρωι κοινῶι, δυσμενεῖς ἂν τῆι πόλει εἶεν.

11. See Dem. 20 *Leptines* 118; 23 *Aristocrates* 96; 39 *Boeotus* 1.40; 57 *Eubulides* 63; and MacDowell 1978, 44. Cf. the alleged dictum of Perikles ([Lys.] 6 *Andocides* 10) that in cases of *asebeia* courts should follow unwritten as well as written law (and on this passage, see Ostwald 1986, 530–32).

12. Although praised by Lefkowitz 1981, 110–11, and Stone 1988b, 37 n. 1, most scholars have remained largely unconvinced by Dover's arguments. For negative judgments, see, e.g., Ostwald 1986, 194–98, 528–36; Brickhouse and Smith 1989, 19, 32–33; Stadter 1989, 297–99; see also Kerferd 1981, 21 n. 7, calling Dover "excessively sceptical." Dover has returned to some of these themes in "Anecdotes, Gossip and Scandal" = 1988, 45–52. (One bibliographic oddity: although published in 1976, Dover's *Talanta* article is often cited with the date 1975, for example, by Ostwald 1986; Stadter 1989; and Farrar 1988, in her text [e.g., p. 45 n. 3], but not bibliography.)

13. See *Souda* Π 2365 = 1.4.201 Adler, cf. Σ Plato *Republic* 600c; Welcker 1833, 637–38. Contrast Ostwald 1986, 533 n. 26, who leaves open the evaluation of this tradition, on the grounds of inadequate evidence (although on p. 277 he rejects it).

14. For the sources on these traditions, see Chroust 1973, 177. See also the biographical sketch of Aristotle in Hesychius of Miletos (p. 27 Flach), mentioning his death by hemlock. Cf. the tradition that Aristotle turned to philosophy at the age of thirty (comparing Protagoras *ap.* Plato *Meno* 91e and, *i.a.,* Jesus Christ).

15. See Ps.-Ammonius *Vita Aristotelis;* Seneca *Dialogi* 8.8.1; Aelian *Varia*

Historia 3.36, with Dover 1976, 41–42 = 1988, 147–48, citing Düring 1957, 341–42, and suggesting that the ultimate source for this statement might be the Peripatetic Hermippos. P. Stadter points out to me that this argument depends on the assumption that Aristotle regarded Prodikos as a philosopher.

16. See Rosenberg 1915, 217–19, arguing that the story was an invention of Aiskhines Sokratikos (on whom see below) based on a comedy; Adcock, *CAH* 5.478; Gomme 1956, 187; Jacoby, *FGrHist* 3b Suppl. 2.396–97; Donnay 1968, 29–30; Dover 1976, 28 = 1988, 138; Prandi 1977, 19 n. 38; Montuori 1988, 207 n. 33; Lefkowitz 1981, 110; Stone 1988a, 233–36; cf. Frost 1964, 395–96.

17. *POxy* 1176 frag. 39 X 15 ff. On these biographical practices, see Momigliano 1971a, 70, 80; Lefkowitz 1981, esp. ix, 75–76, 84–85, 88–91, and 110–13, and (esp. for Euripides) *ead.* 1987, 149–66, esp. 150–53. (One may contemplate what might have been thought about Euripides from Satyros, if Aristophanes' play had been lost.)

18. On this report, see Dover 1976, 29 = 1988, 139.

19. On Ephoros *FGrHist* 70 F196, which accepts Aristophanes' explanation of the cause of the Peloponnesian War, see Dover 1976, 29–30 = 1988, 138–39.

20. See, e.g., F 46K. = Plutarch *Pericles* 33.8, from Hermippos' *Moirai* of 430, addressing Perikles as "king of the satyrs" (on this date of this play, see Geissler 1925, 25). Note that Pheidias also was accused of procuring women for Perikles (Plutarch *Pericles* 13) and that, also according to Plutarch *Pericles* 13, the fifth-century writer Stesimbrotos of Thasos spread the "completely unfounded and shocking" accusation that Perikles seduced his own son's wife.

21. See Ostwald 1986, 195 and Stadter 1989, 297. Stadter contends that Aiskhines cited Perikles' behavior at the trial as an example of Aspasia's influence, "and the argument would be without force if there were not a basis in fact." This does not, however, show why the tradition could not be based on the contents of a play.

22. On the dependent value of the testimony of Antisthenes, see Stadter 1989, 297. The other sources for this incident (Athenaeus 589e, the scholiast to Ar. *Knights* 969, [Lucian] *Amores* 30) are also apparently derived from Aiskhines (see Stadter 1989).

23. See Hesychius and the *Souda*, s.vv. The *Menexenus* suggests that Aspasia may have become a standard figure for fantastic speculation.

24. We perhaps cannot rule out the possibility that the epithet is Plutarch's addendum to Aiskhines' account, taken from a comedy or a volume of *Komoidoumenoi* independently of Aiskhines and included simply to identify Lysikles.

25. See, e.g., Diogenes Laertius 2.60 (Aiskhines "never quitted Sokrates") and Themistius 34.5.

26. Melanthios *FGrHist* 326 F3 (= Scholiast RV Aristophanes *Birds* 1073); Krateros *FGrHist* 342 F16; cf. [Lys.] 6 *Andocides* 17, dated 400/399 (or soon after); and Diodorus 13.6.7. See also Jacoby *FGrHist* 3b Suppl. i: 199–200; ii: 166 n. 16; and 1959, 20. As Jacoby points out, the reference to Diagoras in Ar. *Birds*, a datable play, probably underlies the 415/4 dating, but this

may nonetheless be tenable (with Ostwald 1986, p. 275). See also Dover 1976, 26–27 = 1988, 137–38.

27. Cf. Thuc. 6.27.2: after the mutilation of the Herms, "a decree was proposed guaranteeing immunity to anyone, citizen, alien, or slave, who knew of any other sacrilegious act that had taken place and would come forward with information about it" (trans. Warner).

28. For Diogenes, see Demetrios *FGrHist* 228 F42 (= F91 Wehrli), and, for Demokritos, see *id.* F41 (= F92 Wehrli), both from Demetrios' *Defense of Sokrates.* See Dover 1976, 38 = 1988, 145–46, also citing Demokritos' remark, "I came to Athens and no one knew me" (DK 68B 116).

29. Lefkowitz 1987 wrote about this in connection with the *vitae* of Euripides; cf. her general conclusion about extant poets' biographies, that "virtually all the material in all the lives is fictional" (Lefkowitz 1981, viii).

30. See also Minucius Felix *Octavian* 8 (which apparently derives from Cicero) and the *Souda,* s.v. Πρωτάγορας.

31. F5 Diels, *ap.* Sextus Empiricus *Adversus Mathematicos* 9.56.

32. See Momigliano in Long 1978, 81 n. 14. This is accepted by Dover in an "additional note" appended to the reprint of his *Talanta* article: 1988, 158.

33. For different parts of the argument as thus far presented, see Burnet 1928, 111–12; Dover 1976, 34–37 = 1988, 142–45; Stone 1988a, 237–39; and cf. Finley 1977, 613. Note also that Timon of Phleious was fond of reporting scandalous material: e.g., that Plato plagiarized an early Pythagorean source in his *Timaeus* (Aulus Gellius 3.17.4). Kerferd 1981, 43, accepts the traditional account of book-burning because he claims it is consistent with Timon F5 and also Philochoros F217 (mentioned below). Both claims are false.

34. Athenaeus 218b = Eupolis F146a, bK.; cf. Diogenes Laertius 9.50.

35. On Plato's chronology for Protagoras, see K. von Fritz, *RE* 45 (1957), coll. 908–11 (s.v. "Protagoras"); Kerferd 1981, 42; Davison 1953, 33–37.

36. See Walsh 1984, 101–6, with references. The chronological inconsistencies of Plato's dialogues are discussed by Athenaeus (505f–506a) specifically in connection with the *Protagoras* (although his detailed criticisms of this text are not cogent).

37. Derenne 1930, 55.

38. Hippasos: Iamblicus *De Vita Pythagorica* 88, cf. 247, and *De Communi Mathematica Scientia* 77.18 ff.; Empedokles: Telauges *ap.* Diogenes Laertius 8.74; Diagoras: Athenaeus 611a.

39. In reports of philosophers' trials, the ambiguous meaning of the verb φεύγειν (to flee; to be tried) may have proved a source of confusion.

40. For 411: Diogenes Laertius 9.54, *AP* 29.1; for 404; *AP* 35.1, Xen. *Hell.* 2.3.1.

41. Perikles: Plutarch *Pericles* 36; democratic theory: Plato *Protagoras* 322c–d; Thourioi: Herakleides Pontikos *ap.* Diogenes Laertius 9.50.

42. On the date of the *Suppliants,* see Boegehold 1982, 151–52, with references.

43. See Dover 1968, lxxx–lxxxii.

44. All of these reports occur in Diogenes Laertius 2.12–14. On Sotion, Satyros, and Hermippos, see Momigliano 1971a, 79–81.

45. On Satyros, see Lefkowitz 1984, 339–43.

46. See, e.g., Montuori 1988b, 147–200, with earlier versions in *id.* 1984, 153–204; and 1967, 103–48.

47. Gershenson and Greenberg 1962, 346–48, cited by Stone 1988b, 241. Cf. Connor 1971, 96 n. 13, inclining to the view "that both authors [Sotion and Satyros] are . . . freely embroidering the only sure fact: that the Athenians did at some point take legal action against Anaxagoras." See also Rosenberg 1915, 217: "Irgendeine reale Überlieferung über den Anaxagorasprozess existiert also nicht."

48. The tendency is very clearly demonstrated in biographical traditions about Plato: see the excellent treatment of this topic by Riginos 1976.

49. See Brickhouse and Smith 1989, 32, and also Mansfeld 1980, 82, arguing that Sokrates' "sally would make little sense . . . if Anaxagoras had not, like Sokrates, been accused before a dikasterion."

50. Jacoby 1959, 41 n. 159, also denied that *Apology* 26 implies any trial of Anaxagoras. Stone 1988b, 242–43, collects passages in Plato where one would expect "some reference to his prosecution if it had really happened," including the *Phaedo*.

51. Anaxagoras' chronology is a separate question that cannot be considered here. However, the standard recent treatment by Mansfeld 1979, 39–69, and 1980, 17–95, is unacceptable.

52. See Habicht 1961, 1–35.

53. See Rosenberg 1915, 215, and Dover 1976, 40 = 1988, 147.

54. See Lefkowitz 1991. For a recent argument that an important aspect of the Athenians' complaint against Sokrates was his devaluation of sacrifice (an attitude that also had Spartan overtones), see Connor 1991.

55. In the same year that Sokrates was tried, Andokides was acquitted of improperly participating in the Mysteries, even though he was clearly guilty of sacrilege in 415 (see And. 2 *Return* 7, 10, and Thuc. 6.60) and in 399 was arguably in violation of the terms of ἀτιμία imposed upon him.

56. For a full discussion of this and other issues pertaining to Damon, I may refer to my monograph tentatively entitled "Music, Philosophy, and Politics in Fifth-Century Athens: A Study of Damon of Oa."

57. See, in particular, Carcopino 1905.

58. See Brückner 1915, 21, and Hoepfner 1976, 210.

59. For Kharmides, the son of Glaukon, as Damon's student, see [Plato] *Axiochus* 364a. For Drakon as Damon's student and Plato's teacher, see Olympiodorus *In Platonis Alcibiadem Commentaria* 2.43–44 (*Vita Platonis*); cf. *Anonymous Prolegomena to Platonic Philosophy* 2.28–30 (= p. 7 Westerink). However, given the practice of ancient biographers, the description of Plato's teacher Drakon as Damon's student could be an improper inference from Damon's importance in the *Republic*. On the sources for Damon, see Wallace 1991.

60. See, e.g., Macran 1902, 2: "Some years ago . . . Sir Robert Stewart

delivered a lecture in Trinity College, Dublin, on the Music of Distant Times and Places; and illustrated it by specimens from various nationalities and periods, an ancient Greek hymn being included in the number. It was the unanimous verdict of all the musicians present that, while the music of less civilized nations was often crude, barbarous, and monotonous in the highest degree, the Greek hymn stood quite alone in its absolute lack of meaning and its unredeemed ugliness; and much surprise was expressed that a nation which had delighted all succeeding generations by its achievements in the other arts should have failed so completely in the art which it prized and practised most."

61. See Boegehold 1991; cf., for example, Xen. *Anab.* 6.1.5–13, for various martial dances by soldiers in arms, performed to the rhythm of the aulos.

62. See, e.g., *Iliad* 9.185–91; *Homeric Hymn to Hermes* 416–96; and Euripides *Heracles* 867–79, 892–99.

63. See *Odyssey* 19.457; Aesch. *Eumenides* 306–11, 328–33; Theophrastus *ap.* Athenaeus 624; and Pliny *Natural History* 38.2.21.

64. Terpander F12 Gostoli (= Demetrios of Phaleron *ap.* Scholia E Q to *Odyssey* 3.267 = p. 144.8 ff. Dindorf), F14a (= Philodemos *De Musica* 1 F30.31–35, p. 18 Kemke = F 35.31–35, p. 221 Rispoli), F14b (= Philodemos *De Musica* 4. col. 19.4–19 = p. 63 Neubecker), and F15 (= Diodorus 8.28 *ap.* Tzetzes *Chiliades* 1.385–92).

65. Plutarch *Instituta Laconica* 238c, reporting also that the ephors fined Terpander for including "just one extra string" on his lyre.

66. Finley 1966, 1–4.

67. Maintaining the state's precedence over individual rights has, of course, been a characteristic of recent Eastern European regimes. For various historical and other reasons, however, these regimes have also sought to control individual thought.

68. *AP* 40.2; Ar. *Birds* 186; and Thuc. 6.60.

69. Cf. Rhodes 1972, 191: "The American *Declaration of Independence* regards life, liberty and the pursuit of happiness as inalienable human rights, and the twentieth-century scholar may be pardoned (if not positively lauded) for treating the death sentence as a major issue, but the society which allowed the immediate killing of an adulterer caught in the act might well not share our views."

70. See Halperin 1990, 97–99; and Winkler 1990, 56–57.

71. A second explanation has been proposed by Dover 1978, 103–9, and Halperin 1990, 94–97, for Athenian restrictions on the rights of male prostitutes. In their view, such individuals had voluntarily forfeited the democratic citizen's right of bodily inviolability and therefore placed themselves in a subordinate position, together with women, foreigners, and slaves. One difficulty with this thesis is that male prostitutes did not lose, for example, the right to vote in the Assembly or to serve in the Boule (Dem. 22 *Androtion* 30), and therefore they cannot be said to have entirely "resigned [their] . . . standing as citizen[s]" (Dover [p. 104] quoted with approval by Halperin [p. 97]). I do not deny that complex attitudes helped shape Athens' legal restrictions concerning male prostitutes. After all, those who hired out their bodies for work on an-

other man's *estate* were not in any way excluded from participating in government. However, according to the sources I have presented, the critical issue for the restriction in question—that is, the potential danger that magistrates, Assembly speakers, and others, if morally reprehensible in certain ways, might sell away the state's best interests—also applied to state debtors and others for whom sexual conduct was not relevant. (By contrast, bribery was always a central concern in Athenian politics.) Merely voting in the Assembly would not in itself pose any great danger.

I also question Winkler's contention (1990, 60–61) that prosecutions in connection with male prostitution "had very little to do with sex and everything to do with political ambitions and alliances." The point at issue is not that this charge just happened to be a useful tool against political opponents. Rather, the charge had everything to do with the conjunction of a particular sexual attitude by the Athenian demos (on the complexities of which, see Cohen 1987) and participation in government. That is, the Athenians publicly and officially refused to allow those who sold their bodies for sex to participate in city administration.

72. Momigliano 1971b, 779. For a preliminary discussion of the association, esp. in the area of morality, of toleration with democratic ideology, and control with conservative thought, see Cohen 1984, 123–26.

Works Cited

Boegehold, Alan L. 1982. "A Dissent at Athens *ca* 424–421 B.C." *GRBS* 23:147–56.

———. 1991. "Archaic Greece: An Era of Discovery." In *New Perspectives in Early Greek Art*. Studies in the History of Art 32. Center for Advanced Study in the Visual Arts. Symposium Papers xvi. Washington, D.C.: National Gallery of Art. Distributed by the University Press of New England. Hanover, N.H. Edited by D. Buitron-Oliver, 15–21. Washington, D.C.

Brickhouse, Thomas C., and Nicholas D. Smith. 1989. *Socrates on Trial*. Princeton: Princeton University Press.

Brückner, A. 1915. "Mitteilungen aus dem Kerameikos." *Athenische Mitteilungen* 40:1–26.

Burnet, John. 1928. *Greek Philosophy: Thales to Plato*. London: MacMillan.

Burnyeat, Myles. 1988. "Cracking the Socrates Case." Review of Irving F. Stone, *The Trial of Socrates. New York Review of Books* 35.5 (31 March 1988): 12–18.

Carcopino, Jerome. 1905. "Damon a-t-il été ostracisé?" *REG* 18:415–29.

Chroust, Anton-Hermann. 1973. *Aristotle: New Light on His Life and on Some of His Lost Works*. Notre Dame, Ind.: University of Notre Dame Press.

Cohen, David. 1984. "Work in Progress: The Enforcement of Morals. An Historical Perspective." *Rechtshistorisches Journal* 3:114–29.

———. 1987. "Law, Society and Homosexuality in Classical Athens." *P&P* 117:3–21.

Connor, W. Robert. 1971. *The New Politicians of Fifth-Century Athens.* Princeton: Princeton University Press.

———. 1991. "The Other 399: Religion and the Trial of Socrates." *Georgica: Greek Studies in Honour of George Cawkwell, Institute of Classical Studies.* London: Bull. Supp. 58: 49–56.

Davison, J. A. 1953. "Protagoras, Democritus and Anaxagoras." *CQ* 3:33–45.

Derenne, Eudore. 1930. *Les Procès d'Impiété: Intentés aux Philosophes à Athènes au Vme et au IVme Siècles avant J.-C.* Liège: H. Vaillant-Carmanne. Bibliothèque de la Faculté de philosophie et lettres de l'Université de Liège, fasc. 45.

Dodds, E. R. 1951. *The Greeks and the Irrational.* Berkeley: University of California Press.

Donnay, Guy. 1968. "La Date du Procès de Phidias." *AC* 37:19–36.

Dover, K. J. 1968. *Aristophanes' "Clouds."* Oxford: Oxford University Press.

———. 1976. "The Freedom of the Intellectual in Greek Society." *Talanta* 7:24–54 = Dover 1988, 135–58.

———. 1978. *Greek Homosexuality.* New York: Random House.

———. 1988. *The Greeks and Their Legacy.* London: Basil Blackwell.

Düring, Ingemar. 1957. *Aristotle in the Ancient Biographical Tradition.* Gothenburg: Almquist and Wiksell.

Farrar, Cynthia. 1988. *The Origins of Democratic Thinking.* Cambridge: Cambridge University Press.

Finley, John H., Jr. 1966. "Politics and Early Greek Tragedy." *HSCP* 71:1–13.

Finley, Moses I. 1977. "Censura nell'Antichità Classica." *Belfagor* 32:605–22.

Frost, Frank J. 1964. "Pericles, Thucydides Son of Melesias, and Athenian Politics before the War." *Historia* 13:385–99.

Geissler, P. 1925. *Chronologie der altattischen Komödie: Philologische Untersuchungen* 30. Berlin: Weidmann.

Gershenson, Daniel E., and D. A. Greenberg. 1962. *Anaxagoras and the Birth of Modern Physics.* New York: Blaisdell.

Gomme, Arnold W. 1956. *A Historical Commentary on Thucydides* Vol. 2. Oxford: Oxford University Press.

Habicht, Christian. 1961. "Falsche Urkunden zur Geschichte Athens im Zeitalter der Perserkriege." *Hermes* 89:1–35.

Halperin, David M. 1990. "The Democratic Body: Prostitution and Citizenship in Classical Athens." In *One Hundred Years of Homosexuality,* 88–112. London: Routledge.

Hoepfner, W., ed. 1976. *Kerameikos 10, Das Pompeion und seine Nachfolgerbauten.* Berlin: de Gruyter.

Jacoby, Felix. 1959. *Diagoras ὁ ἄθεος.* Abh. deut. Akad. Wiss. Berl. 3. Berlin: Akademie Verlag.

Kerferd, G. B. 1981. *The Sophistic Movement.* Cambridge: Cambridge University Press.

Lefkowitz, Mary R. 1981. *The Lives of the Greek Poets.* Baltimore: Johns Hopkins University Press.

———. 1984. "Satyrus as Historian." *Atti del XVII Congr. Intern. di Papirol.,*

339–43. Naples: Napoli Centro Internazionale per lo studio dei papiri ercolanesi.

———. 1987. "Was Euripides an Atheist?" *SIFC* (ser. 3) 5:149–66.

———. 1991. "Commentary on Vlastos." *Proceedings of the Boston Area Colloquium in Ancient Philosophy* 5:239–46.

Long, Anthony A. 1978. "Timon of Phlius: Pyrrhonist and Satirist." *PCPhS:* 68–91.

MacDowell, Douglas M. 1978. *The Law in Classical Athens.* Ithaca: Cornell University Press.

Macran, Henry S. 1902. *The Harmonics of Aristoxenus.* Oxford: Oxford University Press.

Mansfeld, Jaap. 1979. "The Chronology of Anaxagoras' Athenian Period and the Date of His Trial, I: The Length and Dating of the Athenian Period." *Mnemosyne* 32:39–69.

———. 1980. "The Chronology of Anaxagoras' Athenian Period and the Date of His Trial, II: The Plot against Pericles and His Associates." *Mnemosyne* 33:17–95.

Momigliano, Arnaldo. 1971a. *The Development of Greek Biography.* Cambridge, Mass.: Harvard University Press.

———. 1971b. "Empietà ed Eresia nel Mondo Antico." *RSI* 83:771–91.

———. 1971c. "La Libertà di Parola nel Mondo Antico." *RSI* 83:499–524.

Montuori, Mario. 1988a. "Aspasia of Miletus." In *Socrates: An Approach,* 201–26. Amsterdam: Gieben. Trans. of "Di Aspasia Milesia." *Socrate: Un Problema Storico.* Naples 1984 = "Di Aspasia Milesia." *Corolla Londiniensis* 1 (1981):87–109 = "Di Aspasia Milesia." *AFLN* 20 (1977–78):63–85.

———. 1988b. "On the Trial of Anaxagoras." In *Socrates: An Approach,* 147–200. Amsterdam: Gieben (for an earlier version, see id. *Socrate. Un Problema Storico,* Collana de ric. e analisi stor. VIII, 153–204 [Naples: ed. Napolitana 1984]).

Ostwald, Martin. 1986. *From Popular Sovereignty to the Sovereignty of Law: Law, Society, and Politics in Fifth-Century Athens.* Berkeley: University of California Press.

Prandi, Luisa. 1977. "I Processi contro Fidia Aspasia Anassagora e l'Opposizione a Pericle." *Aevum* 51:10–26.

Rhodes, Peter J. 1972. *The Athenian Boule.* Oxford: Oxford University Press.

Riginos, Alice S. 1976. *Platonica: The Anecdotes concerning the Life and Writings of Plato.* Leiden: Brill.

Rosenberg, A. 1915. "Perikles und die Parteien in Athen." *Neu. Jahrb. f. d. Klass. Altert.* 18 vol. 35:217–19.

Stadter, Philip A. 1989. *A Commentary on Plutarch's "Pericles."* Chapel Hill: University of North Carolina Press.

Stone, Irving F. 1988a. *The Trial of Socrates.* Boston: Little, Brown.

———. 1988b. "Was There a Witch Hunt in Classical Athens?" *New York Review of Books* 34 (21 January 1988): 37–41.

Wallace, Robert W. 1991. "Damone di Oa ed i Suoi Successori: un'Analisi delle Fonti." In *Harmonia Mundi*, edited by R. W. Wallace and B. MacLachlan, 30–54. *QUCC*. Supp. 5. Pisa: Ateneo.

Walsh, John. 1984. "The Dramatic Dates of Plato's *Protagoras* and the Lessons of *Arete*." *CQ* 34:101–6.

Welcker, F. 1833. "Prodikos v. Keos." *RhM* 2:637–38.

Winkler, John J. 1990. "Laying down the Law: The Oversight of Men's Sexual Behavior in Classical Athens." In *The Constraints of Desire: The Anthropology of Sex and Gender in Ancient Greece*, 45–70. London: Routledge.

Witnessing and False Witnessing:
Proving Citizenship and Kin
Identity in Fourth-Century Athens

‎📜📜📜📜📜📜📜📜📜📜📜📜📜

ADELE C. SCAFURO

It is a well-known phenomenon of Attic life that no central or local archive preserved a written record of the births of polis inhabitants. The absence of such a record appears from a modern perspective all the more startling in view of the strict requirements for citizenship that were set out in Perikles' famous enactment of 451/0. According to that law as cited by [Aristotle] *AP* 26.4, "whoever has not been born of two *astoi* parents has no share in the polis."[1] Plutarch refers to the same legislation as a *nomos* (law) about *nothoi* (bastards) and reports that in accordance with it "only those born from two Athenians were Athenians."[2] The law was either annulled or simply disregarded toward the end of the Peloponnesian War.[3] But it was reinstated in 403/2 in the same terms by a decree proposed by Nikomenes, with a proviso adding that it should not be enforced against individuals born before 403/2.[4] Another law is recorded as having been proposed in the same year by a person named Aristophon; by that law, "whoever was not born from an *aste* was to be a *nothos*."[5] The effect of these laws appears to be clear: children born of mixed unions would lack both *politeia* (citizenship) and *ankhisteia* (membership in the group of *ankhisteis*, or kinsmen).[6] Further legislation, passed sometime around the middle of the fourth century, made the pretense of a (citizen) marital union between a citizen and foreigner illegal.[7] The law that provides the penalties for such conduct are recorded in [Demosthenes] 59 *Neaera*.[8] "If an alien man is dwelling together in marriage (συν-οικῆι) with an *aste* under any circumstance whatsoever, let any Athenian for whom it is lawful bring an indictment before the *thesmothetai*; if he is convicted, let him and his property be sold and a third part be given to him who secured conviction. And if an alien woman is dwelling together with an *astos,* let it be in the same way, and let him who is dwelling with the alien woman be liable for 1,000 *drakhmai"* (16).[9] As Harrison has observed, before the "new" laws, "mixed marriages had been discouraged indirectly by the disabilities falling on the children; now the parties to any such marriage are to be subject to heavy fines if convicted of a γραφή before the court of the thesmothetai."[10]

An individual's descent and his or her ability to prove it would be of the utmost importance in any situation in which his or her political status or relationship to kin could be called into question by the law. A candidate for deme enrollment might be rejected in the first instance and then make an appeal to a *dikasterion;*[11] a demesman might be struck off the register by his fellow demesmen in an extraordinary general scrutiny as happened in 346/5;[12] or the *demarkhos* might claim to have lost the register.[13] A *graphe xenias* could be brought against a person alleged to be masquerading as a citizen. The issue in these cases would depend on the dubious person's ability to prove his birth from two Athenian parents— perhaps decades after their deaths. The more specific *graphe xenes engues* could be brought against a man who had allegedly given away an alien woman in marriage as if she were his kinswoman. The issue in such a case would depend on the precise identification of the woman's parents.[14] Prosecutions for these last two offenses (graphai xenias and xenes engues) would probably arise out of personal or political animosities, or from a desire for self-enrichment; the polis employed no public prosecutors.[15] But disputes over polis status could arise in other ways as well. A citizen or freedman who had been wrongfully enslaved might be haled into freedom (*aphairesis eis eleutherian*) by the extrajuridical action of a sympathetic assertor. But if the alleged owner denied the validity of that removal, he could ensure a court hearing by demanding sureties and lodging a *dike exaireseos* against the assertor.[16] The issue in the case would depend on the ability of the wrongfully enslaved citizen to prove the identity of his parents or of the freedman to prove his nonslave status. Or a question of status might arise in an inheritance dispute: a more distant relation might claim that the putative heir was a nothos and so ineligible to inherit.[17] Once again, the ability to prove the identity of parents is essential.

This essay examines the ways in which Athenian society and institutions during the fourth century compensated for the absence of archival birth records. In the citizenship and inheritance disputes that we find in the orators, the most important evidence for proving identity is that supplied by live witnesses who were present at communal events of personal significance to the individual whose status is questioned. The personal significance of these communal events is that they all demand acknowledgment of the celebrated person's descent and of his or her participation in the witnessed event. In the first part of this essay, I provide a survey of such events; these are fairly well-known and so may be quickly reviewed.[18] John K. Davies has drawn attention to many of them in order to show how Athenian institutions and administrative or legal decisions buttressed and reinforced the descent group.[19] Jean Rudhardt has called attention to the fact that a father's acknowledgment of his son combines a number of civic and religious acts, none of which, in isolation, can be pointed to as the definitive act that confirms a child's identity as his father's son.[20] Sally C. Humphreys has shown how important it was for Athenians to have witnesses to all sorts of events (including those discussed here) and transactions that might be of legal import in the future.[21] Using, heuristically, the valuable work of these and other scholars, I draw out the implications especially for the scenario of citizen identification in the courts of Athens. Because citizen identity does not depend on a simple proof of the legal qualification of being born from two parents, but rather on the production of a broad array of witnesses who testify to an individual's descent and participation in a variety of kin and communal events, then having such witnesses and participation in such events must be seen as important qualifications for being Athenian.

In the second part of this essay, I briefly examine proofs of citizenship and kin relationships in the orators. The use of witnesses for identification as exemplified there is not a foolproof system. Often the best witnesses—relatives and friends who had been present at communal events that took place long ago—are dead; or these same witnesses, if alive, are open to the sometimes well-grounded suspicion of lying in the interest of kin and friendship, or even payment. In the third part of this essay, I examine the *dike pseudomarturion* (suit for false witnessing) and argue that it was used as a remedy for the deficiencies and abuses of the system of status identification in fourth-century Athens. The remedy, alas, appears no better than the illness. Such a flat-out assessment, however, while true from a modern perspective familiar with impersonal bureaucratic procedures of documentation, overlooks an essential feature of the system of identification in Athens: that witnessed participation in communal events as a function of being born Athenian was perceived by Athenians as tantamount to "being Athenian."

Communal Events

Numerous events in the biological and political life cycles of Athenian males were celebrated or formally acknowledged by kin, community, or civic groups. Long before a boy became a citizen, indeed, on the fifth day after his birth, the *amphidromia,* a purification ritual, would be celebrated.[22] On the seventh (*hebdome*) or tenth day (*dekate*) after birth, there would be another celebration, when the infant was given a name.[23] These celebrations marked the father's acceptance of the infant into his oikos. The father's acknowledgment of paternity, witnessed by friends and relatives who attended the ceremonies, could later be used as evidence that in disputes concerning inheritance or citizenship the son is not a nothos.[24] Other kin and community groups would likewise have the opportunity to witness a father's acknowledgment of an infant or child's paternity and birth from a lawful marriage.[25] A father might, for example, introduce his son to his *gennetai.* He would take hold of the altar and swear that the child was his own son born from a wedded wife; the gennetai would thereby become witnesses to the son's parentage.[26]

Local phratries performed three ceremonies on the third day (called *Koureotis*) of the Apatouria.[27] The first was the offering of the *meion,* a sacrifice that was apparently made by fathers to whom sons had been born during the previous year.[28] The second offering, the *koureion,* was another sacrifice presented by the father that may have coincided with the adolescent's formal (second?) entry and enrollment into the phratry.[29] The third offering was the *gamelia,* a sacrifice presented to his fellow *phrateres* by a young man at the time of his marriage.[30] Sons appear to have been introduced to their fathers' phratries on two occasions, once as infants or young children, and later, perhaps before they became ephebes.[31] Because some of our evidence connects phratry introductions with sacrifices or with the timing of the third day of the Apatouria, modern writers sometimes say imprecisely, or at least without warrant, that sons were introduced into the phratry at the meion and koureion.[32] Isaeus 8 *Ciron* 19 provides the form of words presumably used at the first introduction: "Our father, after we were born, introduced us to the phrateres, having sworn in accordance with established laws, that he was introducing [children born] of an aste and pledged woman."[33] The formula appears elsewhere, with slight alteration.[34] Occasionally, gennetai and phrateres are mentioned together as the groups to whom a son is introduced—whether in one ceremony or two is not always clear.[35] Most frequently, however, we hear that a son is introduced to phrateres alone.[36] Phratry members, if called upon at some later time, could testify to the parentage of the infant, boy, or man whose ceremony—the meion, koureion, gamelia, and introductions (if different from the meion and koureion)—they had attended.[37] While phratry membership was not legally required of citizens, the converse was true: birth from Athenian parents was a prerequisite for membership in a phratry.[38]

Athenian males were formally enrolled by their deme as citizens at the age of eighteen. [Aristotle] *AP* 42.1–2 describes procedure and requirements:

> It is men born of citizens on both sides who share in citizen rights and they are enrolled among the demesmen when they have reached the age of eighteen. Whenever they are being enrolled, the demesmen decide by vote under oath, first, whether they appear to have reached the age which the law prescribes—and if they do not so appear, they return to being "boys" once again—and secondly, whether [each one] is free and was born in accordance with the laws. Then, should they vote against him as being *not* free, he appeals to the jury-court, and the demesmen choose five of their number as accusers; if it is decided [by the court] that he has no right to be enrolled, the polis sells him [into slavery], but if he wins the demesmen are obliged to enroll him. After this the *boule* scrutinizes those who have been enrolled, or if it is decided that someone is younger than eighteen, the demesmen who enrolled him are fined.[39]

While the account here may be incomplete and not accurate in every respect,[40] I shall only single out for brief comments three features—none of them unambiguous—of the requirements for citizenship: (1) that boys are required to be a certain age at the time of enrollment,[41] (2) that they need to be free, and (3) that they must be born in accordance with the laws. As for (1) age, it should be noted that because Athenians kept no birth records, evidence of age might be difficult to establish.[42] That the boys be (2) free, I have understood as referring to their status (i.e., free as opposed to slave);[43] that they be born in accordance with (3) the laws, I have with hesitation accepted as referring to the laws that require both mother and father to be Athenians.[44] Presumably, witnesses to the boy's parentage would have to be present at his enrollment to testify to the three criteria.[45] Attestation of age, status, and Athenian birth are interrelated in an important way: the assertion that a boy was born free eighteen years ago to a particular Athenian couple (XY) could, for example, be countered by a statement that X was living with *xene* Z at that time, not aste Y. A candidate rejected by his demesmen in the fourth century could appeal their decision before a dikasterion. In such an appeal, the rejected candidate would be the defendant against the deme's claim as presented by five prosecutors. Presumably, the defendant would call in witnesses to his parentage and to his parents' participation in communal events. We have no certain reports of such cases.[46] On the other hand, we do have reports of appeals arising from the extraordinary general scrutiny that was set in motion by the decree of Demophilos in 346/5.[47] The next section of this essay briefly examines some of the proofs put forward by Euxitheos (Demosthenes 57 *Eubulides*) in his appeal at

the time of that scrutiny. The procedure offered the defendant the opportunity to present his case before a panel of dikasts that was representative
of the entire body of citizens; local prejudice would be far less pervasive.
But the method of identification would be the same: dependence on witnesses to kin and communal events.

It is a justifiable inference from available evidence that each deme
kept a register of its members (*lexiarkhikon grammateion* or *koinon
grammateion*) and that such lists were therefore constitutive of deme
members and, collectively, of the citizen body.[48] The lists are mentioned
numerous times in the orators, sometimes as a lexiarkhikon grammateion, less frequently as a koinon grammateion; usually, a man's name is
said to be written up in them when he is enrolled in a deme.[49] We shall
consider below what use might have been made of such documents for
the purpose of identifying citizens.

Descent is again a matter of importance at the scrutinies of officials
before their entry into public office. [Aristotle] *AP* 55.3 describes the
questions asked of each man chosen to one of the nine archonships:

> "Who is your father and to what deme does he belong? And who is your
> father's father, and your mother, and your mother's father, and to what
> deme does he belong?" Then they ask whether he has an ancestral
> Apollo and a household Zeus, where their sanctuaries are, whether he
> has family tombs and where they are, whether he treats his parents well
> and pays his taxes, and whether he has served on the military expedi-
> tions. Having asked these questions, [the examiner] says: "Call the wit-
> nesses to this statement." Then, when he has presented his witnesses, [the
> examiner asks]: "Does anyone wish to bring a charge against this man?"

One interesting feature of scrutiny for public office is the use of live
witnesses. Although the candidate would certainly have passed the age of
deme enrollment and his name would be included in his deme list, that list
is not mentioned and does not appear to serve any documentary function.
Live witnesses are preferred. The successful candidate not only passes
scrutiny, he also acquires another "credential." The witnesses at his scrutiny may be used as witnesses of descent, if ever his citizen status comes
into dispute at a later time. In that case, they will be witnesses both of
descent and of the successful acceptance of their testimony at the scrutiny.

All these communal events—the amphidromia, dekate, introduction
to gennetai, the phratry ceremonies (meion, koureion, enrollment, gamelia), as well as deme enrollment and scrutiny for public office—required
an acknowledgment of a male's descent from two Athenian parents. Such
communal events therefore provided the opportunity for numerous men
(and women, at least at the amphidromia and dekate) to witness that

acknowledgment. Witnesses to an earlier communal event would be useful at the next such event: e.g., a witness to the name-giving ceremony would be useful at the meion, and a witness at the meion would be useful at the koureion. Once the youth is registered in a phratry, and then in his deme, he has safely secured his civic identity: his membership in phratry and deme would be written down; his descent from two Athenian parents would appear to be duly authenticated—yet live witnesses are required once again at scrutinies for public office.

Women were not citizens as men were. They were not registered in demes, and probably were not registered in phratries, either.[50] Yet by Perikles' citizenship law of 451/0 B.C. and its re-enactment in 403/2, a son was required to be born of two Athenian parents in order to be a citizen. And according to a law attested for the mid-fourth century, pretense of marriage between a citizen and a xene was liable to severe penalties. How, then, did a woman acquire her Athenian identity?[51] In a way similar to that used by men—by witnesses to her descent at kin and communal events and by participation in some of those events. Purification rituals (amphidromia) would be offered after the birth of a female infant. Her name-giving day would be celebrated on the seventh or tenth day. Her own descent would be directly acknowledged and affirmed when her son was introduced into a *genos,* phratry, and deme, or if he underwent scrutiny for public office. If a phratry required that a son be born of a woman who had been "pledged" to her husband by engue, then presumably witnesses of that transaction would have to be present.[52] One phratry appears to have required that the name of a son with his patronymic and demotic, together with his mother's name with patronym and father's demotic, be inscribed and posted at a common meeting place. Another copy, written on a white-washed board, was to be displayed by the priest in a sanctuary; this was to take place in the son's first year or the year in which he celebrates the koureion, in order that the phrateres may know those who are going to be introduced.[53] If this is a proper interpretation of *IG* 2² 1237, 117–25, then we have an instance of the actual publication of a woman's name and descent group that would be open to public scrutiny, at least temporarily.[54]

There would be other occasions when a woman's descent would be implicitly acknowledged. Her marriage would be celebrated at the gamelia when her husband offered a sacrifice to his phrateres. Although she probably would neither become a member of the phratry nor be present at the phratry celebration, her husband would want his phrateres to know her name (or more importantly, her descent) and to be aware that she was Athenian—that is, he would lay the groundwork for their sons' acceptance into the phratry at a later time. The marriage of a son or daughter to another Athenian would be another implicit acknowledgment of a woman's own descent. When her husband pledged their daughter in marriage to a son-in-law, he may have used some variation of the formula that we find repeated in plays of New Comedy: "I give [so-and-so] to you for the ploughing of *legitimate* children."[55] If she took some prominent role in the celebration of public sacrifices or other religious ceremonies reserved for astai, her participation as an aste might be observed. If she took part in the funeral rites for the dead in her natal oikos, her participation might be noted and her relationship observed. There was ample occasion, then, for a woman's descent to be acknowledged and witnessed, and for her aste status and relationship to a particular oikos to be confirmed. At many of these communal events (her son's enrollment in phratry and deme and his scrutiny for public office), she herself would probably not be present. But her name would be mentioned, and her descent would be open to public examination. Acceptance of the son into one of these groups was, after all, an acceptance of both his mother's and father's Athenian descent.

The importance of marriage for providing opportunities for the confirmation of a woman's status and descent is exemplified by a reverse scenario: the case of a divorced woman. In the fourth century, divorce was required if a man discovered that his wife had been unfaithful and if the *moikhos* was successfully prosecuted; and divorce would naturally happen if a woman were convicted of *xenia* (because the marriage would not have been legal, "divorce" can only be used in a nontechnical sense).[56] The latter woman would be sold into slavery, and her 'cohabitor' would be fined a thousand drakhmai. A "seduced woman" would have no easy time finding a second husband, unless, perhaps, she were provided with a very large dowry.[57] Divorced and remaining unmarried, such a woman would lose the qualification of being Athenian—not by any law, but by the practical circumstance that she would lose the opportunities for the acknowledgment of her descent and the recognition of her oikos. If she already had children, their descent from an identifiable husband could be questioned at any enrollment or scrutiny; she would be excluded from participation in public religious sacrifices (her attendance was proscribed by law: [Dem.] 59.87); she would lose, in effect, the opportunity for the communal confirmation of her descent and status.

Women who were divorced for innocent reasons might easily come under suspicion of infidelity (her husband had divorced her to avoid prosecuting the moikhos and suffering infamous publicity) or alien birth (her husband had divorced her to avoid the thousand drakhmai penalty if the true status of his alien "wife" were discovered); the reiteration of reasons for divorce in the orators supports this thesis. It would be best for the divorced woman both to have witnesses to account for the divorce (e.g., that her husband was required to marry an *epikleros*) and to remarry as soon as she could.[58] Marriage, participation in an oikos, and participation in all permissible kin and communal events that stemmed from membership and that conferred recognition and acknowledgment were desirable—and necessary for identity as an Athenian woman.

Living witnesses to kin and communal events were invaluable for constructing proofs of descent. Athenians in the fourth century still viewed witnesses as superior to "archival documents." If a deme register is said to be lost (a circumstance reported in Dem. 57 *Eubulides* 26, 60–61), or if a man's name has been struck from the register (Dem. 57 and Is. 12 *Euphiletus*), then that document can be of no value in those cases. But other circumstances under which we might think that "archival documents" would be of assistance demonstrate that Athenians routinely preferred witnesses:

1. A man who has been struck from a deme list might use the inclusion of his name in a phratry list as evidence of his citizenship.

2. A man undergoing scrutiny for public office might advert to a phratry or deme list as evidence of his citizenship.

3. A woman whose identity is being established in an inheritance dispute might use a deme list or phratry list that included her son's name, to demonstrate that her son had passed these earlier scrutinies that had "certified" her own aste status. The list would only have been useful evidence, of course, if we knew for certain—and we do not—whether any deme or phratry ever recorded the son's name as X son of Y (father) and Z (mother) and not simply X son of Y.[59]

Litigants in cases that require status identification never bring such documents into court—at least as far as we can tell without having the witness testimonies available. Instead, a man struck from a deme list brings live witnesses, among whom are included his phrateres and demesmen.[60] Live witnesses testify to a candidate's identity at a scrutiny for public office. Women's identifications are likewise made without adverting to any documents.[61] It is easy to postulate reasons why this should be so: the deme list would probably be in the hands of the demarkhos; any copy of a deme list would have to be authenticated by the demarkhos as a genuine document or copy; and so the appearance of the demarkhos or other demesmen as witnesses would supersede the importance of the list itself. The preference for live witnesses noted here is in accordance with fourth-century practice in regard to other kinds of documents such as contracts and wills.[62]

Witnesses to the kin and communal events discussed above therefore served important functions—not only to confirm a person's descent at a tenth-day celebration or phratry enrollment but also to provide testimony of that event if it were ever required in the future. That second function is surely not merely a *post facto* one.[63] That the types of event witnessed in citizenship cases and inheritance disputes are so similar, that is, that they appear to follow a pattern, suggests that the polis recognized and expected that a *polites* and *politis* would provide just such testimonies as credentials. The selected events seem natural and pertinent enough for such use: this is what a polites does, this is what a politis or aste does—he or she becomes known to the community and acknowledged by it. Being observed and collecting witnesses are part of that process. This is not to say that Athenians were by practice cynical, paranoid, deceitful, or quintessentially busybodies—although the orators and writers of New Comedy provide us with examples enough of these characteristics. Rather, a life that is celebrated, that is oriented toward membership in kin and communal groups, and that is scrutinized on so many different occasions creates witnesses. Everyone knew that, and everyone gathered witnesses.

Proving Citizenship and Kin Identity in the Orators

A brief consideration of arguments of citizen and status identity in the orators will show the prominent position given to witnesses of kin and communal events. Demosthenes 57 *Eubulides* is an appeal before a dikasterion against the decision of the demesmen of Halimous to reject the speaker (Euxitheos); the case occurred during the general scrutiny of deme lists that was decreed by Demophilos in 346/5.[64] We do not know the precise grounds for the Halimousians' rejection of Euxitheos, but the latter's arguments indicate that the demesmen had probably claimed that his parents were not citizens: his father spoke with a foreign accent, and his mother sold ribbons in the marketplace and had hired herself out as a wet-nurse. In the final sections of the speech, Euxitheos summarizes his defense by putting it all neatly into the question and answer form, as it were, of a scrutiny for public office. The artifice of the form deserves comment: it creates an aura of authority as a scrutiny is staged in a trial, which is, in essence, the ultimate scrutiny—a scrutiny, then, within a scrutiny, a scenario well-known to the audience, who will recognize their dual role as dikasts sitting in judgment and as witnesses of Euxitheos' descent. I quote it here at length because it is the fullest account of a citizen's proof of status and identity that I know of:

> Recall the following points and see with how many just arguments I have come before you. For just as you examine the thesmothetai, I in the same way shall examine myself before you. "Sir, who was your father?" "My

father? Thoukritos." "Do any relatives testify that you are his son?" "Yes, indeed. First of all, four cousins, then, a son of a cousin, then the husbands of his female cousins, then the phrateres, then the gennetai of Apollo Patroios and Zeus Herkeios, then those who share the same tombs, then the demesmen who testify that he frequently passed scrutiny and entered office and those who manifestly voted for him." As for the facts, then, that pertain to my father, how could I prove them to you more justly or more clearly? I shall call my relatives before you, if you like. And now hear the facts that pertain to my mother. My mother is Nikarete, the daughter of Damostratos of Melite. What relatives of hers give testimony? First of all, a nephew; then two sons of another nephew; then a son of a cousin, then the sons of Protomakhos, who was my mother's former husband; then Eunikos of Kholargos, who is the husband of my sister, the daughter of Protomakhos; then my sister's son. Above all, the phrateres and the demesmen of her kin have given testimony. What more, accordingly, could you require? For, as to the fact that my father married my mother according to the laws and that he offered a gamelia for the phrateres—this has been testified to. And in addition to this evidence, I have demonstrated that I myself have shared in all those privileges that befit free men (ἐλευθέρους). Therefore, if you altogether justly and fitly give your verdict in my behalf, you will keep your oaths.[65]

Because the status of Euxitheos' parents has been called into question, he must prove that both his father and mother were citizens. To prove his father's civic identity, he calls upon living individuals of various relation to his father, Thoukritos, to testify that he was in fact his father. The order of relationship is important: he begins with those associated with him in the private and smaller realm of the oikos, then gradually branches out to include his father's fellow phrateres, gennetai, and those who share the same places of burial, and finally he comes to the civic realm of fellow demesmen who testify to his father's passing scrutiny and holding public office. The witnesses in behalf of Thoukritos had testified earlier in the speech, almost exactly in the order as reported in the summary—except that there he had reserved the final testimony for the gennetai who share common burial ground.[66] We do not have the depositions of these witnesses, but it appears from Euxitheos' description that they testified to the scrutinies passed (ἐξητασμένος 24) by Thoukritos and Euxitheos before gennetai, phrateres, and deme, and to the fact that Thoukritos had passed scrutiny for public office (ἦρξεν δοκιμασθείς 25). Thoukritos' foreign accent had been explained by an account—duly testified to by prepared depositions—that he had been taken prisoner during the Decelean War, sold into slavery, taken to Leukas, and brought back to

Athens and ransomed after a long lapse of time. Upon arrival in Athens, he received his share of property from his uncles (18–19).[67] All traces of this account have been omitted from the summation, undoubtedly because the speaker considers that he has already refuted the arguments of his opponents and because it was more effective not to remind the dikasts at the end of his speech of the specific charge that had been made against his father.

Euxitheos follows the same order in reporting witnesses of his mother's status, beginning with witnesses to her natal oikos and then gradually branching out to include witnesses to her marital oikoi and finally mentioning the phrateres and demotai of his mother's male kin. Thus, first the surviving relatives on the male side, and then the surviving male relatives on the female side, represent the natal oikos.[68] Next the male offspring of Protomakhos, Nikarete's former husband, testify to the earlier marital oikos.[69] Then comes Eunikos of Kholargos, the man who married the daughter of Protomakhos and Nikarete, and then his son. Finally, the speaker cites the testimony of the phrateres and demotai of his mother's male relatives. The phrasing is of interest: the phrateres and demotai cannot give testimony directly about her; she is neither a member of the phratry or deme—but they give testimony that her kinsmen are members. The speaker then tags on the information that his father had married her mother according to the laws and had offered a gamelia for the phrateres in behalf of his wife. That important information had been set out in more detail earlier in the speech (40–43): that Nikarete's brother, Timokrates, had given her in marriage to Protomakhos; that Protomakhos, when he had divorced her in order to marry an epikleros, had persuaded his friend Thoukritos to take her; and that Thoukritos had received her through engue from Timokrates in the presence of his own uncles and other witnesses who will give testimony. Moreover, Protomakhos had by Nikarete a son and daughter, the latter of whom he had given away in marriage (to Eunikos); though Timokrates is now dead, his deeds bear witness that she was an aste and politis.

The information in the earlier sections (40–43) focusing upon the mother's marriage corresponds with the information that had been given about Thoukritos' participation in phratry and deme life. Marriage—legally sanctioned marriage effected through engue—is the proof that can be offered that a woman is an aste and a politis. The speaker is careful to show on what grounds Protomakhos had divorced Nikarete—the divorce had nothing to do with either the woman's status or moral character. That argument is further supported by Protomakhos' treatment of his daughter, that is, the fact that he gave her away in marriage. Witnesses to betrothal and to the gamelia thus become witnesses to a woman's aste status. Everything depends on the credibility of the witnesses—and the discrediting of the motives of the opponent.

All the witnesses to the mother's status had testified earlier in the speech—in slightly different order from that in the summation.[70] The order in the summation is again for rhetorical effect. Notable here is the absence of all mention of the earlier testimony about the legality of selling ribbons in the market or employment as a wet-nurse. Like the omission of the account of his father's foreign accent, it is more effective not to recall the specific charges at the end of the speech.

The major portion of Euxitheos' defense—and his summary of it— had to do with proving the citizen status of his father and mother. If they were both citizens (or citizen and aste), then he has the right to citizenship. Only a small segment of defense and summary deals directly with himself—in the summary (69), the statement that he has had a share in everything that befits free men (*eleutheroi*), and in the narrative (46), that he has the witnesses to prove this, that is, that he was introduced into phratry, enrolled among demesmen, chosen by the latter to draw lots for the priesthood of Herakles, and scrutinized successfully for public office. The weak point in this case, as Sally C. Humphreys has suggested, may have been the lack of attestation to Euxitheos' birth: no relatives come forward to testify to the *amphidromia* or *dekate*. The omission might have been noticeable; the chronology of Thoukritos' absence during the war and its relation to the date of Euxitheos' birth remain vague.[71]

The same type of proof appears in speeches concerning disputed estates. Indeed, the resemblances are so close that it appears almost as if there were a set formula. There are many circumstances under which an inheritance might be disputed and that would require the precise identification of kin. We shall single out one here: claimant X objects to claimant Y's claim on the grounds that claimant Y is illegitimate. Both Isaeus 3 *Pyrrhus* and Isaeus 6 *Philoctemon* are cases of this sort. In the former, claimant Y (son of Phile, grandson of Pyrrhos) had maintained that the estate of his mother's father should be his, because his mother was an epikleros; claimant X (the alleged sister of Pyrrhos, who is represented by her son, the speaker) argues in the oration that Phile's mother had not been legitimately married to Pyrrhos, and therefore both Phile and her son are illegitimate. Against Phile's status, he argues:

And do not forget about the marriage feast for the phratry. This proof is the most important for his evidence. For it is self-evident that, if he [Pyrrhos] had been persuaded to marry this woman by engue, he also would have been persuaded to give a marriage feast for her to the members of the phratry and to introduce to them the child, who has been declared to be this woman's daughter, as his legitimate offspring. And in his deme, since he was in possession of a household worth three talents, if he had been married, he would have been compelled in behalf of his wedded wife to entertain the wives at the Thesmophoria, and to perform for her all the other fitting public duties in the deme from the rather considerable substance of his property. (3.79–80)[72]

In Isaeus 6, we hear another claimant X objecting that claimants Y are illegitimate, again attacking the status of the mother:

That these children are in fact legitimate (γνήσιοι), let him [Androkles] prove, just as each of you would do. For they are not legitimate if he mentions the mother's name, but if he proves that he is telling the truth— by providing kin who know that she was married to Euktemon, and demesmen and phrateres, if they have ever heard or have any knowledge that Euktemon carried out public services on her behalf, and where she has been buried, in what sort of tomb, and who has ever seen Euktemon performing the customary rites over her, and whether her sons still go to offer sacrifices and libations, and who of the citizens or of the slaves of Euktemon has ever seen these rites being performed. All these details constitute a proof—and not mere invective. (6.64–65)

The format of the proof of a woman's identity and status (here, as legitimate wife) is well-established in Isaeus 6 and 3: witnesses to betrothal or to the marriage feast for the phrateres, the deme's and phratry's knowledge of her husband's public service on her behalf, her participation in public cults, her place of burial.[73]

Although the polis gives no formal civic identity to a woman, nevertheless it is in her interest to establish one. She does this through her father and husband, through their phrateres and fellow demesmen, by their testimony to her betrothal and marriage and to her participation in public cults and by their acceptance of her husband's oaths on various occasions that his children are born from an aste and *enguete*. Of interest is the claim made by the speaker of Isaeus 6 *Philoctemon* that the name of the mother is not enough to make her children legitimate (64). He refers to his opponent's earlier identification of the woman as a Lemnian named Kallipe, the daughter of Pistoxenos, and scoffs, "as though it were enough for them merely to produce the name of Pistoxenos" (13). The speaker here argues that the names must be backed up by evidence and the testimony of relatives. We may assume that a name on a list would not be sufficient for this litigant: witnesses to kin and communal events constitute the best proof of a woman's status.

It is difficult to prove that witnessing in inheritance and citizenship disputes was of greater significance than witnessing in other sorts of case. Witness testimony *was* important in all cases that came before a dikasterion. Stephen Todd has calculated the frequency with which witnesses are called for testimony in Attic orations and has observed "a striking difference between the use of witnesses in public and private disputes."[74] The greatest frequency occurs in the twenty-five speeches concerned with private property where it reaches 13.8 per 100 sections; in the one preserved speech in a prosecution for xenia, there are 13 depositions in 124 sections.[75] The frequency with which witnesses appear in these particular cases does suggest that witness testimony may have been of greater service in them than in other sorts of cases.

Moreover, there is something qualitatively different about witnesses to status identity and witnesses to other sorts of "facts," events, or business transactions. Witnesses to status identity are providing an individual with the credentials that will constitute his or her civic identity. It is conceivable that Attic law recognized the weightiness of this responsibility by allowing convictions for false witnessing that arose out of inheritance and xenia cases to provide grounds for retrial. There is some evidence, moreover, that suggests that retrial was permitted after successful false witnessing trials *only* in cases that arose out of inheritance disputes, trials for xenia, and false witnessing. That evidence is discussed in the next section of this essay. Whether that evidence is conclusive and so could support a claim that Athenians felt that witnesses to status and identification were a distinctive set of witnesses or were witnesses to particularly distinctive facts and events, we can still say the following: Athenians of the fourth century had established a procedure for identifying citizenship and status in which the inscribing of a name on a deme list played a part, but the whole picture—and the ability to re-create it—was more important than the part in isolation. Being "Athenian" was of the utmost importance for the inhabitant of Athens. Therefore witnesses to one's Athenian status were the most important witnesses an individual could have.

The Dike Pseudomarturion

The system was obviously fallible. It put at a disadvantage those who were unable to amass witnesses after the lapse of years and favored those who could produce a plethora of kin, phrateres, and fellow demesmen to produce a "documentary picture" of longstanding communal acceptance. In the fourth century, legal measures tried to ensure the integrity of witnesses. A *dike kakotekhnion* could be brought against a litigant who had suborned a witness.[76] A *dike pseudomarturion* could be brought against witnesses who were alleged to have given false testimony, or to have provided testimony contrary to the laws (e.g., the use of hearsay evidence was contrary to the laws except in clearly articulated, permissible circumstances such as reporting the views of a dead man).[77] The dike pseudomarturion was an *agon timetos;* the penalty was a fine; a person convicted three times would be disfranchised (And. 1.74; Hyp. 2.12). Because the dike pseudomarturion would be directed against the opponent's witnesses and not against the opponent himself, the penalty can hardly be thought of as a compensation. Some scholars have therefore hypothesized that the dike kakotekhnion may have served this purpose.[78] In certain cases, a plaintiff who had successfully convicted someone of false witnessing would be allowed a retrial (*anadikia*). Theophrastus tells us that retrial was permitted after successful convictions of false witnessing in cases arising from xenia, false witnessing, and disputed estates.[79] Theophrastus' evidence will be presented briefly below. Although I have taken a position on how that evidence should be treated, the issues are too complex for detailed argumentation in this essay.[80]

In discussing the procedure for initiating a dike pseudomarturion and the effect of a conviction on the original case, we must distinguish generally between (A) false witnessing suits arising from a procedure called *diamarturia,* a "formal assertion of a fact by a witness who was in a position to know it,"[81] and (B) false witnessing suits arising from trials. In the fourth century, most of the cases of diamarturia about which we have specific information arise out of inheritance disputes. In these cases, a person (X) who claimed he was the heir to an estate (a descendant of the deceased or son adopted *inter vivos* or by testament) could protest the claim of any other person (Y) who had applied to the arkhon for *epidikasia* (an adjudication hearing in an inheritance dispute); he (X) would make his protest by a diamarturia, a declaration that the estate was not adjudicable, and would himself provide testimony to support his claim or provide witnesses to do this for him. A dike pseudomarturion could arise out of this situation if the second claimant (Y) challenged X's deposition by an episkepsis (an objection), claiming that the testimony was false (e.g., Y could assert that X or X's witness had lied that Y is illegitimate, or that X or X's witness has fabricated an adoption into the family of the deceased); claimant X or his witness(es) would then be charged with false witnessing and brought to trial.[82] False witnessing suits belonging to this category (A) disrupted the adjudication hearing and were decided first. The verdict in such cases might affect the original hearing: for example, if the defendant were acquitted and his statements about claimant X's relationship to the deceased were proven true, then the plaintiff (if he were a competing claimant) would probably lose his claim to the estate.[83]

Litigants involved in false witnessing cases belonging to category B (cases arising from trials) followed a different procedure. Before the verdict was given in the original trial (e.g., for assault or impiety), either litigant could make an episkepsis to the testimony of his opponent's witnesses.[84] By making such an objection, the litigant appears to have reserved the right to proceed against his opponent's witnesses with a dike pseudomarturion. The original trial would not be disrupted, and the verdict would be delivered.[85] If the penalty were monetary, it would probably have to be paid before the trial for false witnessing took place.[86] Where the penalty was death, we are less certain. No evidence conclusively indicates that a death penalty would be postponed.[87] However, because it appears that an individual convicted of xenia would be imprisoned rather than enslaved before the false witnessing trial, some scholars have extrapolated that a death penalty would likewise be postponed.[88]

False witnessing suits could be brought against alleged false witnesses in any trial (with the possible exception of homicide cases) and in adjudication hearings in inheritance disputes. Given that fact, we might expect witnesses to be charged with lying about all sorts of things in all sorts of cases. While that expectation is to some degree borne out by imputations of false witnessing in the orators, we also find that one type of alleged lie appears rather frequently: that about the status of an individual. Moreover, the evidence suggests that such allegations emerged most frequently in two kinds of dispute: about inheritance and xenia. In this final section of my essay, I shall argue that trials for false witnessing became a specific remedy or even normal procedure for dealing with the deficiencies of the identification system. The preponderance of false witnessing suits arising out of inheritance and xenia disputes is symptomatic of the special importance attached to witnessing in cases of identifying a person's status and relationship to kin. My argument will take the following route: (1) an examination of false witnessing suits that demonstrates the statistical prevalence of such suits that arise out of inheritance disputes, (2) the evidence that connects xenia disputes with false witnessing, and (3) conclusions.

False Witnessing and Inheritance Disputes

There are eight extant speeches (belonging to seven trials) in which alleged false witnesses are prosecuted or defended (see table 1). Four trials (Is. 2 *Menecles*, 3 *Pyrrhus*, 6 *Philoctemon*, and [Dem.] 44 *Leochares*) arise from diamarturiai concerning an inheritance dispute.[89] One trial (Dem. 29 *Aphobus*) arises from a guardianship case and is ultimately connected with an inheritance dispute; one ([Dem.] 46 and 47 *Stephanus*, both speeches belonging to the prosecution in the same trial) arises (probably) from a *dike blabes* but is ultimately concerned with the speaker's attempt to recover money that he believed his former guardian had embezzled from his father's estate;[90] and one ([Dem.] 47 *Evergus*) arises from a suit for assault. Of six other dikai pseudomarturion that are specifically mentioned in Attic orations (as having taken place, or as having been dropped, or as being still undecided), five arise from inheritance disputes (three from the same disputed estate: Is. 5 *Dicaeogenes*) and one from an action for slander (Lys. 10 *Theomnestus* 22–25).

On the basis of this catalogue of fourth-century dikai pseudomarturion, it is easy to see that far the greatest number arise out of diamarturiai that are a part of inheritance disputes: there are nine such cases (Is. 2; 3; 6; [Dem.] 44; the allusions to earlier or pending suits in Is. 5.9, 12, 17; Is. 3.2–4; Is. 11.45–46). Two arise from cases in which the treatment of a will or an estate is a central issue (Dem. 29, [Dem.] 45/46),[91] and two arise from other suits (assault and slander). Why do so many false witnessing cases arise out of inheritance disputes? The most obvious answer is this: within the legal structure that developed to settle such disputes, the only *procedural* way for claimant X to demonstrate either that claimant Y has made a false claim of relationship to the deceased or that Y has based a claim on an inauthentic will was to issue a diamarturia and then defend that assertion if Y objected and initiated a dike pseudomarturion against him. What is a *remedy* for false witnessing in other kinds of dispute is *standard procedure* in inheritance disputes.

The answer that has just been given to the question, "Why do so many false witnessing cases arise out of inheritance disputes?" begs that very question—or at least conceals a deeper one: Why should this procedure (diamarturia followed by episkepsis and a dike pseudomarturion) have been established in the first place? The answer is again obvious: while witness testimony was important in all trials, it had a privileged position in trials that demanded the identification of kin and status. As the speaker in Isaeus 4 *Nicostratus* 17 says—tendentiously, but no doubt in harmony with the gut feelings of the dikasts: "And apart from these matters, you must put your trust in wills through the agency of witnesses—by whom one can also be deceived (for otherwise there would be no denunciations of false witnesses (*pseudomarturion episkepseis*), whereas you put your trust in kinship relationships (*ankhisteiai*) through your own witnessing. For kin make their claims in accordance with the laws which you have set down."

Disputes that depend on the precise identification of a person's status (legitimate or illegitimate) and of his or her relationship to kin require a documentation that the Attic bureaucracy (and I use that term loosely), particularly in regard to the female members of the community, had not established; without an archival mechanism to record births, adoptions, and marriages, the testimony of living witnesses would be heavily relied upon and distorted easily—either by the ravages of time or by more corrupt motivation. The institution of birth, adoption, and marriage records would have put an end to many of these disputes before they reached court. However, such a solution did not materialize—the use of live witnesses was too firmly entrenched a part of the system to allow for substitution or innovation. The remedy—which became normal procedure in inheritance disputes—appears to be a protraction of the illness.

Were status or kin identifications crucial issues in these trials? A presentation of false witnessing suits in tabular form, identifying both the original case out of which the false witnessing trial developed, as well as the subject of the disputed testimony in the later trial, will help clarify the issues. An (S) in the third column indicates that status identification plays a significant role in the side of the case represented in the extant speech; in the case of "references to specific false witnessing trials," (S) indicates that status identification is likely to have played a significant role.

In half the trials that originate out of disputes over estates (and I include here Dem. 29 and [Dem.] 45/46), the plaintiff, defendant, or *sunegoros* (advocate) must prove or disprove his own or someone else's status or relationship to the deceased (Is. 2; Is. 3; Is. 6; [Dem.] 44; Is. 3.2–4; Is. 11.45–46 [cf. Ps.-Dem. 43.29], Dem. 29). "Status identification" is obviously an important issue in the trial against Philonides (Is. 2); his sunegoros (the alleged adopted son of Menekles) must prove the truth of the defendant's statement that he (the sunegoros) had been adopted legitimately by Menekles twenty-three years ago (see the summary of proofs in cc. 44–45).[92] Status identification is again an important issue in the trials against Nikodemos (Is. 3) and Xenokles (Is. 3.2–4), where Phile's legitimacy (and hence the legality of her mother's marriage to Pyrrhos) are crucial to the two cases. The plaintiff in Isaeus 6 must disprove the legitimacy of the heirs brought forward by Androkles. The plaintiff against Theopompos' witnesses (Is. 11.45–46 and [Dem.] 43.29) probably must prove that Phylomakhe I was the full sister of Polemon.[93] The plaintiff in [Dem.] 44 must disprove the legality of Leokhares' postmortem adoption into the family of Arkhiades and demonstrate his father's relationship to that family. In each of these cases, testimony of status or relationship to the deceased must be established.

Demosthenes 29 *Aphobus* III is somewhat different. In that trial, Demosthenes speaks in behalf of Phanos, who had testified in his behalf in an earlier successful trial against Aphobos for misconduct of the guardianship of the estate left to Demosthenes. Apparently, before that earlier suit had been decided, Aphobos had asked Demosthenes to hand over Milyas, foreman of his deceased father's sword factory, for examination under torture, and Demosthenes apparently had refused, on the grounds that Milyas was not a slave (Dem. 27.19–22 and 29.20). Phanos is then alleged to have given false testimony when he said that Aphobos had admitted before the public arbitrator that Milyas was a free man. This last case involves a question of status in a much different way from the other dikai pseudomarturion arising from inheritance disputes. Disputes over the status of a person offered or demanded for purposes of examination under torture appear occasionally in the orators.[94] One instance in which a speaker envisions a scenario from which a false witnessing suit could have arisen involves such a dispute. In [Demosthenes] 49 *Timotheus* 55–56, the speaker, who is seeking repayment of a debt, claims that Timotheos refused to provide a deposition that Aiskhrion was free and not a slave (and so could not be subjected to examination under torture); the speaker conjectures that Timotheos feared that if he did so depose, then he (i.e., the speaker) would bring a suit for false witnessing and afterward proceed against Timotheos for subornation (kakotekhnia).[95] Suits for false witnessing in such cases as Demosthenes 29 *Aphobus* may have been used as a tactic to win back compensation for a penalty that had been assessed at the original trial or else as a pretext (not sanctioned by law) to postpone that payment. It is conceivable that the speaker of [Demosthenes] 49 *Timotheus* may have had some such strategy in mind for the future but had been obstructed from its deployment by his clever adversary. The availability of the dike pseudomarturion as the means by which to implement these ulterior motives, *through an examination of status,* is established.

That half the number of false witnessing trials involve issues of status is a significant statistic. It supports the thesis articulated above that the dike pseudomarturion was especially relevant to trials in which the identification of kin and status is important. An answer to an objection to this thesis will clarify my argument. The objection is this: the predominance of false witnessing suits that emerge out of inheritance disputes is due to the accidental preservation of so many inheritance speeches by Isaeus; there were probably many other false witnessing trials that arose out of all sorts of court actions. The false witnessing/inheritance trials may only have been preserved because they were of greater interest to contemporary readers (as displaying the lives of the rich and quarrelsome) than, for example, false witnessing trials that arose out of suits for assault. It is therefore incorrect to infer that false witnessing trials became a special remedy for trials that involved issues of status and identity. The rebuttal is a reiteration of a point made earlier: it is true that what is a remedy for

TABLE 1. False Witnessing Trials in the Orators

Orations Belonging to False Witnessing Trials

Oration and Speaker	Original Dispute or Trial	Disputed Statement of Defendant in False Witnessing Trial
Is. 2 *Menecles* defense of Philonides speaker: son of Eponymos (= son-in-law of defendant) plaintiff: Menekles' brother	Diamarturia/inheritance	Son of Eponymos was adopted legally by Menekles I (who had been legally married to the daughter of Eponymos) (S)
Is. 3 *Pyrrhus* plaintiff's speech vs. Nikodemos speaker: nephew of Pyrrhos in behalf of Pyrrhos' sister (= speaker's mother)	Diamarturia/inheritance	Nikodemos had given his sister (Phile's mother) to Pyrrhos in marriage (S)
Is. 6 *Philoctemon* plaintiff's speech vs. Androkles speaker: advocate for Khairestratos	Diamarturia/inheritance	Euktemon had legitimate sons, and Philoktemon made no will (S)
[Dem.] 44 *Leochares* plaintiff's speech vs. Leokhares speaker: advocate for Aristodemos (= son of plaintiff)	Diamarturia/inheritance	Arkhiades had children whose legitimacy was rightfully established according to statute (chap. 46) (S)
Dem. 29 *Aphobus* III defense of Phanos speaker: Demosthenes plaintiff: Aphobos	Guardianship/will	Aphobos admitted before arbitrators that Milyas was free (Aphobos had demanded Milyas for torture, chap. 14) (S)
[Dem.] 45/46 *Stephanus* plaintiff's sp. vs. Stephanos speaker: Apollodoros	A *paragraphe* instituted by Phormion to block the *dike blabes* that Apollodoros had initiated vs. Phormion; Ap. had claimed that Phormion embezzled money owed to his father's estate	Apollodoros refused Phormion's challenge before the arbitrator to identify an alleged copy of his father's will (chap. 8)

Continued on next page

TABLE I—*Continued*

Orations Belonging to False Witnessing Trials

Oration and Speaker	Original Dispute or Trial	Disputed Statement of Defendant in False Witnessing Trial
[Dem.] 47 *Evergus* plaintiff's sp. vs. Euergos and Mnesiboulos speaker: Anon. plaintiff	*Dike aikeias* (won by Theophemos who used testimony of Euergos and Mnesiboulos)	Anon. plaintiff had refused to admit as a witness a female slave whom Theophemos had offered to deliver up before the arbitrator

References to Specific False Witnessing Trials

Oration and Litigants in False Witnessing Trial	Original Dispute or Trial	Disputed Statement of Defendant in False Witnessing Trial
Is. 3 *Pyrrhus* 2–4 nephew of Pyrrhos vs. Xenokles	Inheritance	Phile was the legitimate daughter of Pyrrhos (S)
Is. 5 *Dicaeogenes* 9 Polyaratos vs. witnesses for Dikaiogenes III	Inheritance	Probable statement: Dikaiogenes III was adopted as sole heir to Dikaiogenes II
Is. 5 *Dicaeogenes* 12 Menexenos II vs. Lykon	Inheritance	Dikaiogenes III was adopted as sole heir to Dikaiogenes II
Is. 5 *Dicaeogenes* 17 Menexenos II and III vs. Leokhares	Inheritance	Probable statement: Dikaiogenes III was adopted as sole heir in authentic will
Is. 11 *Hagnias* 45–46 Sositheos (?) vs. witnesses of Theopompos (cf. [Dem.] 43.29)	Inheritance	Probable statement: Polemon, the father of Hagias II, had no full sister Phylomakhe I (S)
Lys. 10 *Theomn.* 22 and 25 Theomnestos vs. witness of Lysitheos, Dionysios	Slander (*kakegoria*)	Testimony about shield
Total: 13	Inheritance: 9 "ultimately inheritance": 2 (Dem. 29; and [Dem.] 45/46)	

false witnessing in other trials is standard procedure in inheritance disputes and that therefore the standard procedure will inevitably appear as a special category in our record over and over again. But that such a procedure became standard attests to the deficiency in the system; birth, adoption, and marriage records would have put an end to many of these disputes; but witnessing was so firmly established as the method of identification that only claims of false witnessing could undo the identifications of witnesses.

In sum, the link that I have posited between false witnessing trials and inheritance disputes is not a phenomenon that can be explained only by the accidental preservation of certain orations rather than others. Rather, the link is symptomatic of the dependence upon witnesses in disputes of identity and status. I am not claiming that the dike pseudomarturion was instituted in the first place to handle such disputes; but I am claiming that the suit, as it was used, came to be recognized as the method to establish disputed identity before the law. This claim is further supported by its links with prosecutions for xenia.

False Witnessing and Xenia

Our one fully preserved speech that belongs to a prosecution for xenia ([Demosthenes] 59 *Neaera*) yields no evidence for a connection with a dike pseudomarturion. But we should not expect the prosecution in such a case to be making claims of false witness against the defendant's witnesses whose depositions have not yet been delivered. Nor do we find evidence for false witnessing suits arising out of status disputes in allusions elsewhere to *specific* trials for xenia; however, much of this evidence is very fragmentary.[96] But in Demosthenes 57 *Eubulides* and Isaeus 12 *Euphiletus,* both appeals from the decision of demesmen to strike a man from the deme register, the speakers make allusions to the possibility of false witnessing suits arising from these trials (Dem. 57.53 and Is. 12. 4, 6, and 8). Furthermore, that indictments and trials for false witnessing actually arose from citizenship disputes rather frequently is suggested by two sources:

First, an off-hand statement by the speaker of Demosthenes 24 *Timocrates* 131, who is arguing that the horrors of imprisonment for being a state debtor should not be exaggerated to such a degree that punishment should then be withheld when it is fully warranted: "And do not allow them to be overly upset about going to prison while they have your money, but make them subject to the laws. For men convicted of xenia are not overly upset about staying in that place until the trials for pseudomarturia are over, but they remain there and do not think it necessary to go about at large by appointing sureties [as bailsmen]."

Second, a scholiast to Plato *Laws* (937 c–d) adduces a citation from book 7 of Theophrastus' *Nomoi* in the course of discussing Plato's (problematic) measure that a dike pseudomarturion justified the reopening of the original suit when over half the evidence given by the witnesses had been successfully overturned.[97] The scholiast, who appears to treat Plato's measure as if it were a real one, cites Theophrastus, who provides a more restrictive list of cases that allowed retrial: "A judgment that is retried (*anadikos krisis*). If either all the witnesses or more than half were convicted of giving false testimony, the case was tried over again. Not in the case of all actions are retrials allowed, but, as Theophrastus says in book 7 of *Nomoi*, only in cases of xenia, pseudomarturia, and *kleroi* (estates)."

The second passage is much debated;[98] the issue that concerns us here is whether Theophrastus' restricted list of types of case that are allowed retrial in the event of a successful dike pseudomarturion is correct. Those who claim that it is not argue that Theophrastus has given us, as a selective list, examples of types of case that could be penalized by enslavement or loss of family or of full citizen rights.[99] Those who argue that it is correct have the direct text of Theophrastus to support them, as well as evidence of *anadikia* from the orators in cases of citizenship and inheritance.[100] Moreover, the statistical evidence of false witnessing cases corroborates the justifiable expectation that cases in which successful prosecution allows retrial would be more frequent than those that do not. The second view of Theophrastus' evidence is to be preferred, although it cannot be conclusively demonstrated.[101]

At the very least, Demosthenes 24.131, by itself, allows us to conclude that successful prosecutions for xenia were not infrequent, that unsuccessful defendants in such cases initiated dikai pseudomarturion against the prosecution's witnesses and that the successful conclusions of such suits allowed retrials for the original charge of xenia. In such cases, the dike pseudomarturion was a remedy—even if it appears to be a protraction of the illness. Decisions on xenia were democratic in the sense that they were made by dikasts representative of the citizen population. But those decisions were at the same time accompanied by all of the disadvantages of that democracy, most relevantly, its bureaucratic incapacity to record the births, adoptions, and marriages of its citizens. If the "preferred view" of Theophrastus' text is accepted, we could go further and claim that Athenians thought that disputes concerning the identification of citizen and familial status were so significant—*and so liable to error*—that they warranted the privilege of retrial.[102]

A man convicted of xenia would thus be likely to resort to a dike pseudomarturion. A conviction of his opponent in that trial would give him the chance to stand trial again for xenia. Presumably, he would be in a better position this time around. But if he lost in the second try, he could keep his case alive and go after his opponent's witnesses once again. If he lost the false witnessing trial and if he were tenacious, he could sue his opponent's witnesses from the false witnessing trial—for false witnessing. It is logically conceivable that such a case could go on for years in the courts—provided enough witnesses remained alive to give their true or false accounts. The dike pseudomarturion was not a weapon that could guarantee the testimony of truthful witnesses, but it could guarantee a stage for witness testimony. Successful acquittal on a charge of xenia at a retrial (or first trial) may not have been the end of the matter, however: a charge for *doroxenia*, for winning acquittal for xenia through bribery, could be brought against such a defendant.[103] Such a charge most likely entailed impugning the testimony of the defendant's witnesses, on the ground that it was suborned. If so, then we have another instance of the overlapping of procedures that are a regular feature of the Athenian legal system: doroxenia would cover the same ground as a dike kakotekhnion, but it would be specifically tailored for cases of xenia—and it was a graphe, not a dike—anybody could bring the indictment.[104] Its very existence attests to the special concern of Athenians to establish citizen status through witnessing techniques.

As an addendum to the evidence from the orators that links false witnessing with status and kin identifications, it can be pointed out that the most frequent scenario of false witnessing in New Comedy has to do with the same sorts of identifications. In two plays, *Sikyonios* and *Poenulus* (5.2), characters approach potential witnesses in an attempt to suborn them to give false testimony about a woman's birth.[105] In the *Andria*, a character suspects that a witness has been suborned to give this same kind of information. In both *Sikyonios* and *Andria*, the "false testimony" would enable women of dubious status to be identified as Athenian women, and, in the *Andria*, would enable the woman's son to have Athenian citizen status, too.[106] In the *Phormio*, the background for the dramatic action of the play is a trial at which one character presented false testimony (which will turn out, fortuitously, to have been true) about a young man's proximity of relationship to an alleged epikleros.[107] In *Poenulus* (3.1), a scene is rehearsed and dramatized: a pimp is trapped into harboring a slave (rather than a foreigner, as he had thought) and accepting a great sum of money from him; he is then charged with theft. In this last situation, the pimp's false impression of his client's status is the basis of his alleged crime. Moreover, witnesses had been rehearsed onstage to observe his treatment of the client.

In all these plays, the status or identity of the person who is testified about is of crucial significance for determining (1) whether the witness' testimony is false (*Sikyonios, Poenulus* 5.2, *Andria, Phormio*), or (2) whether the act they have witnessed is criminal (*Poenulus* 3.2). That witnesses are called upon to give testimony so frequently about status or identity is not so surprising in the context of New Comedy in which so many plots depend upon the identification of citizen status for the happy citizen marriages that so frequently conclude them. Indeed, witnesses to citizenship and status appear in far more plays than those listed here. What is surprising is that the scenarios of false witnessing (in *Sikyonios, Poenulus, Andria, Phormio*) should conform so well with the significant constellation of false witnessing in fourth-century orations that was identified earlier.

Conclusions

The foregoing examination of the types of trial from which dikai pseudomarturion emerged in the fourth century led us first to focus on the preponderance of such dikai that arose out of inheritance disputes. Further examination of the type of alleged falsifications revealed that, in half the cases, testimony about the identification of a person's status or relationship to the deceased was impugned. An interesting exception to this evidence was the case of Demosthenes 29 *Aphobus* III, in which testimony about the status of an alleged free man whom one party had asserted was a slave and demanded for examination under torture was impugned. The appearance of this case suggested that cases of pseudo-marturia might be categorized under some other principle; for example, rather than clustering together cases that emerged from inheritance disputes, it might be useful to constellate those cases that arose from impugning statements about the status of individuals. Suits that dealt with citizenship were an obvious quarry. Although our sources did not yield references to specific false witnessing suits arising from prosecutions for xenia, enough evidence appeared to support a view that such suits were numerous in the fourth century. This evidence came from the scenarios of false witnessing suits envisioned by the speakers in Isaeus 12 *Euphiletus* and Demosthenes 57 *Eubulides;* from the speaker's remark in Demosthenes 24 *Timocrates* 131 about the men convicted for xenia awaiting the outcome of false witnessing trials while in prison; from Theophrastus' instancing of the rule by which successful false witnessing suits allowed retrial in cases about citizenship, false witnessing, and estates; and from the supplementary evidence of New Comedy. If, then, we are right in thinking that there were numerous trials for false witnessing arising from citizenship disputes in the fourth century, then we can note their connection with those false witnessing cases arising from inheritance disputes over status or kin identification: that litigants are able to impugn testimony on these related issues so frequently points clearly to the functional incapacity of the Attic bureaucracy to identify its polis inhabitants. On the basis of the evidence collected here, we may hypothesize that the dike pseudomarturion developed in such a way as to remedy that incapacity and that the courts themselves became a stage for identifying the status and kin identities of polis inhabitants. The courts became, in a sense, a live archival recording session that could create such identities through trials and that could have such identities erased through retrials. Witnesses to status and kin identity, then, played an extraordinary role on that Attic stage.

Notes

I thank Alan L. Boegehold, C. Patterson, W. F. Wyatt, and, esp., E. Stehle, for reading and offering suggestions on earlier versions of this essay.

1. [Aristotle] *AP* 26.4: καὶ τρίτωι μετὰ τοῦτον ἐπὶ Ἀντιδότου διὰ τὸ πλῆθος τῶν πολιτῶν Περικλέους εἰπόντος ἔγνωσαν μὴ μετέχειν τῆς πόλεως ὃς ἂν μὴ ἐξ ἀμφοῖν ἀστοῖν ἦι γεγονώς.

2. Plutarch *Pericles* 37.2–5: νόμον ἔγραψε [Περικλῆς] μόνους Ἀθηναίους εἶναι τοὺς ἐκ δυεῖν Ἀθηναίων γεγονότας. The two reports (Plutarch's and [Aristotle's]) may represent two independent traditions, with [Aristotle] representing an annalistic source. See Patterson 1981, 2.

3. The law of 451/0 was still in force in 414 (Ar. *Av.* 1646–70). The basis for the argument in favor of annulment comes from D. L. 2.26 (which depends on [Aristotle]), where it is reported that "the Athenians because of the shortage of men passed a vote (ψηφίσασθαι), with a view to increasing the population, that a man might marry one *aste* and have children from another (γαμεῖν μὲν ἀστὴν μίαν, παιδοποιεῖσθαι δὲ καὶ ἐξ ἑτέρας). Although the decree is not dated, Müller 1899, 786–811 suggested that it belongs soon after the Sicilian disaster. He is followed by Wolff 1944, 85–86 and by Jacoby (*FGrHist* 3b, Suppl. 2, 381 n. 35), who thinks it "more likely" than an annulment in 429. For a different view, that there was neither annulment nor lapse, and that the legislation of 403/2 was part of the codification of Athenian law that began in 411, see Walters 1983, 325–27.

4. Nikomenes' proposal is reported by Eumelos *FGrHist* 77 F 2 (= scholiast to Aeschin. 1 *Timarchus* 39): Εὔμηλος ὁ Περιπατητικὸς ἐν τῶι τρίτωι Περὶ τῆς ἀρχαίας κωμωιδίας φησὶ Νικομένη τινὰ ψήφισμα θέσθαι μηδένα τῶν μετ᾽ Εὐκλείδην ἄρχοντα μετέχειν τῆς πόλεως, ἂν μὴ ἄμφω τοὺς γονέας ἀστοὺς ἐπιδείξηται, τοὺς δὲ πρὸ Εὐκλείδου ἀνεξετάστως ἀφεῖσθαι.

5. Athenaeus 13.577C mentions the law (νόμος) of Aristophon, citing it from book 3 of Karystios' *Hypomnemata* (= Karystios fr. 11 Mueller *FHG* 4.358): ὃς ἂν μὴ ἐξ ἀστῆς γένηται νόθον εἶναι. Some scholars appear to assume that Nikomenes' *psephisma* and Aristophon's *nomos* are the same (e.g., MacDowell 1978, 66); others distinguish the two (e.g., Sealey 1987, 23 and n.

52; Walters 1983, 322; Jacoby *FGrHist* 3b, Suppl. 1, 161 and Suppl. 2, 144 nn. 27–28). Harrison 1968, 26 n. 1 suggests that "possibly Aristophon's law made the rule retrospective and Nikomenes' decree simply reversed this particular clause."

6. I am deliberately sidestepping the controversial issue whether Perikles' law envisioned that only children born of legitimate marriages (as opposed to less formal unions) were to be citizens. A recent discussion of that question, with a full survey of earlier scholarly views, is Patterson 1990, 40–73.

7. Sealey 1984, 126 suggests that the laws cited in [Dem.] 59. 16 and 52 would have been passed after Isaeus 6, which was delivered in 364 (6, 14). In the latter speech, "no penalties were invoked against Euktemon, although he treated his union with Alke as marital cohabitation when he introduced her son to his phratry." Sealey further suggests that "the revision of the list of citizens in 346/45 may provide the context in which the law was passed." But Sealey rightly remains tentative: "Alternatively, perhaps the law was already in existence but no one came forward to prosecute Euktemon."

8. For the date of the oration (ca. 340 B.C.), see Schaefer 1858, 179–84. On the authenticity of the laws cited at [Dem.] 59. 16 and 52, see Lipsius 1905–15, 419 n. 163.

9. The Greek text of the law appears in Patterson's essay in this volume, n. 16. Any translation of the law calls for an interpretation of its meaning; particularly troublesome are the meanings of the verb συνοικῆι and the phrase τέχνηι ἢ μηχανῆι ἡτινιοῦν. For a discussion of different scholarly opinions of this Skylla and Kharybdis, see Harrison 1968, 26–28. I have translated the law according to my interpretation, which is similar to Walters 1983, 321 and n. 21, that "what the law penalizes is the fraudulent pretense of Athenian marriage." All translations in this essay are my own, unless otherwise indicated.

10. Harrison 1968, 26.

11. [Aristotle] *AP* 42.1–2. We do not know when the appeal was instituted; *AP* 42 reports contemporary conditions, ca. 333–25. It is possible that several lost speeches for which we have only the titles arose out of appeals to a dikasterion from a deme decision (Is. [Thalheim frag. 6] Πρὸς Βοιωτὸν ἐκ δημοτῶν ἔφεσις and Din. Κατὰ Κηρύκων [λόγος περὶ τινος ἀποψηφισθέντος] and Κατὰ Μοσχίονος ἀπογραψαμένου αὐτὸν Νικοδίκου).

12. Harpocration s.v. διαψήφισις cites Androtion (*FGrHist* 324 F 52) and Philochoros (*FGrHist* 328 F 52) for the fact that the scrutinies took place in the archonship of Arkhias (346/5); also schol. Aeschin. 1 *Timarchus* 77 and *argum.* Dem. 57 *Eubulides;* contemporary allusions in Aeschines 1. 77, 86, 114–15; 2 *Embassy* 182; allusions to universal scrutinies as a recent event: Dem. 57. 2, 15, 49, 58, (in chap. 7, the scrutinies are said to have arisen from a *psephisma*). For discussion, see Jacoby *FGrHist* 3b, Suppl. 1, 157–58, 161–62, and the debate between Diller 1932 and 1935 and Gomme 1934 concerning whether there was a standing law that enabled the Assembly to decree a general scrutiny. We do not know whether other general scrutinies occurred in the fourth century. Jacoby's open-minded observation (158) is worth remembering: "Tradition in regard to an examination of the whole citizens' list (i.e., of the registers of all

demes) is poor, or rather (with the exception of the year 346/5 B.C.) it is non-existent."

Concerning Isaeus 12 *Euphiletus:* while some scholars (e.g., Diller 1932) think that Dionysius of Halikarnassos (*Isaeus* 17) has mistakenly attributed the speech to a trial that resulted from a general scrutiny, there is no certain way to determine the circumstances that led to the court action (whatever it was) for which the speech was written; however, the issue is clearly citizenship. For detailed discussion, see Diller 1932 and Wyse 1904, 714–17.

13. Dem. 57 *Eubulides* 26. 60–61. We do not know whether such abuses of the system happened frequently.

14. The law is cited at [Dem.] 59 *Neaera* 52: "If any man give away an alien woman to an Athenian man as if she were his kinswoman, let him be disfranchised and his property be given to the state, and a third part be given to him who secured conviction." The Greek text of the law is given in Patterson's essay in this volume, n. 20.

15. Charges of alien citizenship or illegitimacy were frequently made against politicians in comedy and public speeches; see Connor 1971, 168–70, who views such charges as challenges to political leadership. For personal animosity as a motive in bringing a charge of alien citizenship, see the opening of [Dem.] 59 *Neaera* and Patterson's essay in this volume. The graphe xenias is considered in more detail later in my essay.

16. On aphairesis and subsequent court action, see: Harrison 1968, 178–80; Lipsius 1905–15, 636–43; Thalheim 1958, 1548. There appears to be no difference in meaning whether the term δίκη ἀφαιρέσεως or δίκη ἐξαιρέσεως is used. Harpocration discusses the suit under ἐξαιρέσεως δίκη and refers to a lost speech by Isaeus (᾿Ισαῖος ἐν τῆι ὑπὲρ Εὐμάθους εἰς ἐλευθερίαν ἀφαιρέσει). There are five references to aphairesis in the orators (including one intended case): Lys. 23 *Pancleon* 9–11; Aeschin. 1 *Timarchus* 62–63; [Dem.] 58 *Theocrines* 19; Isaeus frs. 15–17 (Thalheim) *Eumathes;* and [Dem.] 59 *Neaera* 40. Two further references in Isocrates (17 *Trapeziticus* 13 and 49 and 12 *Panathenaikos* 97) are problematic and may represent abuses of the procedure; see Thalheim 1958, 1548.

17. Isaeus 6 *Philoctemon* 47: ἐκεῖ μὲν γὰρ ἔστι νόθωι μηδὲ νόθηι ⟨μὴ⟩ εἶναι ἀγχιστείαν μήθ᾿ ἱερῶν μήθ᾿ ὁσίων ἀπ᾿ Εὐκλείδου ἄρχοντος.

18. Although these events are much discussed and frequently cited, many of them are problematic because of vague or scanty ancient testimony and the suspiciousness of some of the later testimony. Among the authors I cite below, I single out Ledl, Deubner, Wyse, Rudhardt, Labarbe, Gould, Cole, and Hedrick as scholars who treat the evidence judiciously. Much of it is too exiguous to allow for safe conclusions, and readers should be wary of descriptions of these events (esp. of phratry celebrations) in secondary literature.

19. Davies 1977–78, 105–21.

20. Rudhardt 1962, 39–61, esp. 58–60.

21. Humphreys 1985, 313–69.

22. For the ancient and late lexicographical sources that allude to the *amphidromia,* see Stengel 1958, 1901–2. For the confusion of ancient and lex-

icographical sources over the celebrations on the fifth, seventh, and tenth day after birth, see Deubner 1952, 374–77. For recent interpretations, see Garland 1990, 93–94 and Golden 1990, 23–24.

23. For the ancient and lexicographical sources, see Deubner 1952, 374–77.

24. Evidence from the tenth-day ceremony had been given for a claimant in an inheritance dispute (Isaeus 3 *Pyrrhus* 6, 30, 33–34) and for one party in two arbitrations (Dem. 39 *Boeotus* 22 and [Dem.] 40 *Boeotus* 28). The first arbitration probably involved a dispute about the rightful use of a name and so involved the issue of paternity, and the second arbitration concerned the recovery of a mother's dowry.

25. The Χοαί appears to be another celebration for children, which Deubner 1932, 115 calls "eine Art *confirmatio*." Participation in this festival is not attested in reports of witness depositions.

26. And. 1 *Mysteries* 127 reports that Kallias, "when the boy was already a grown child, introduced him to the Kerykes, saying he was his own son." When one member objected, the Kerykes voted according to their law, "that a father who has sworn that he is introducing his own son can introduce him. Kallias took hold of the altar and swore that the boy was his legitimate (γνήσιον) son born from Khrysilla." That Andocides reports that "the boy was already a grown child" (τὸν παῖδα ἤδη μέγαν ὄντα) is probably meant to cast suspicion on the introduction (so MacDowell 1962); probably it was more usual (and therefore freer from suspicion) to introduce an infant (cf. Lys. 30.2, which, however, concerns an introduction to a phratry). It is possible that in the introduction to the gennetai at And. 1.127, we are to see the gennetai acting for the phratry, whose ceremony at the Apatouria is mentioned in the preceding chapter; Andrewes 1961, 6 offers this as a tentative suggestion.

27. For a collection of the evidence and interpretation of these three sacrifices, see Deubner 1932, 232–34; for the specific celebrations, see nn. 28–32 below.

28. Attested only at *IG* 2² 1237.5, 60 and in later lexicographical sources: e.g., Harpocration s.v. *meion; Etymologicum Magnum* s.v. κούρεον. Hedrick 1984, 169–73 collects citations of scholiasts and lexicographers. Hedrick 1990, 26 n. 24 points out that "it is nowhere explicitly stated that the meion was offered for children in their first year." For interpretation and survey of scholarly views, see Labarbe 1953, 361–62.

29. Hedrick 1984, 169–74 collects citations of scholiasts and lexicographers on the koureion.

30. On the gamelia, see esp. Hruza 1892, 133–45; Wyse 1904, 363–64; Ledl 1907, 217–18; both Wyse and Ledl offer salutary criticisms of Hruza. On the related question concerning whether women were introduced into the phratry, see n. 50 below.

31. On the problematic nature of the two introductions, see Rudhardt 1962, 57 n. 81. On the age of a son at the sacrifice of the koureion, see Deubner 1932, 234; on age and for interpretation in general, see Labarbe 1953, 358–94.

32. The phratry enrollment described at Isaeus 6 *Philoctemon* 21–22 takes

ADELE C. SCAFURO

place when the koureion is offered; in *IG* 2² 1237, 26–29, the candidate under-
goes scrutiny (*diadikasia*) a year after the koureion is celebrated—but during
the same celebration (i.e., the third day of the Apatouria, Koureotis). Elsewhere the orators mention sacrifices at the time of phratry introduction without specifying the name of the sacrifice: And. 1 *Mysteries* 126; [Dem.] 40
Boeotus II 11–15, 81–83; [Dem.] 43 *Macartatus* 11–14; Isaeus 7 *Apollodorus*
13–17; and Isaeus 8 *Ciron* 18–20.

33. ὅ τε πατὴρ ἡμῶν, ἐπειδὴ ἐγενόμεθα, εἰς τοὺς φράτορας ἡμᾶς εἰσήγα-
γεν, ὀμόσας κατὰ τοὺς νόμους τοὺς κειμένους ἦ μὴν ἐξ ἀστῆς καὶ ἐγγυητῆς
γυναικὸς εἰσάγειν. For other instances of infant introduction, but to both
phrateres and gennetai, see n. 36 below.

34. Dem. 57 *Eubulides* 54. Apparently, not all phratries had the same strict
requirement concerning the limitation of admission to male children born of a
woman who had been pledged by *engue* to her husband. The strongest pieces
of evidence that phratries did not always contain the "strict requirement" are
Isaeus 7 *Apollodorus* 16, and *IG* 2² 109–11. See Sealey 1984, 121–22.

35. [Dem.] 59 *Neaera* 59–61; and Isaeus 7 *Apollodorus* 15–17. In the latter
passage, Thrasyllos claims he was adopted by Apollodoros after the death of
the latter's son. "At the time of the Thargelia," he says, "he brought me to the
altars and to the gennetai and the phrateres. They have a law, whenever anyone
introduces someone—whether his own natural son or an adopted one—that
[the introducer] must swear an oath upon a victim that he is introducing [an
entrant] born from an aste and born in the right way; . . . even after he has
done this, the others still must vote, and if the vote is favorable, then—and not
before—they inscribe his name on the official register." For an elucidation of the
relations between phrateres and gennetai in this passage, see Andrewes 1961, 5.

36. It is often difficult to determine whether the "introduction" refers to
that of an infant or of an older boy. Here I add an indication of the son's age, if
the text has provided one; the abbreviation "ad." is appended if the child is
being adopted: Isaeus 2 *Menecles* 14 (young man, see chap. 18; ad.); Isaeus 3
Pyrrhus 73–76 (witnesses depose that an epikleros was not introduced, see n.
50 below); Isaeus 6 *Philoctemon* 22 (a boy: ὁ πρεσβύτερος τοῖν παίδοιν, 21);
Isaeus 10 *Aristarchus* 8 (ad.); Isaeus 12 *Euphiletus* 3; Dem. 39 *Boeotus* 4, 20;
[Dem.] 43 *Macartatus* 12–14 (παῖς; ad.); and *POxy.* 2538 col. 2, 24–27 (at the
age of three or four: restored text). Our fullest report of procedure for entry
into a phratry is *IG* 2² 1237; at the preliminary inquiry (anakrisis), each candidate must be supported by three witnesses who are among his (father's) thia-
sotai. These witnesses must give evidence, undergo questioning, and swear an
oath by Zeus Phratrios (71 ff.). On the meaning of *anakrisis* in l. 72, see
Hedrick 1990, 56–57, 70–71.

37. Testimony about "phratry events" by phrateres appears frequently.
About the meion: see n. 28 above. Concerning introduction into phratry: Dem.
39 *Boeotus* 4–5, 20; [Dem.] 44 *Leochares* 44; Isaeus 2 *Menecles* 14–16; Isaeus
3 *Pyrrhus* 73–76 (phrateres testify that the alleged epikleros was never introduced to phratry); Isaeus 6 *Philoctemon* 22; Isaeus 7 *Apollodorus* 16–17;
Isaeus 10 *Aristarchus* 8; Isaeus 12 *Euphiletus* 3; and *POxy.* 2538 col. 2, 24–27.

Concerning election of member as phratriarkhos: Dem. 57 *Eubulides* 23–24. Concerning gamelia: Isaeus 3 *Pyrrhus* 76 (witnesses depose that there was no gamelia); and Isaeus 8 *Ciron* 18–20.

38. According to Hedrick's 1990 interpretation of the decrees of the Demotionidai, if the Demontid phratry rejects a member during the extraordinary scrutiny, that individual may appeal to the deme Dekeleia. If so, then the deme is shown to be very interested in the qualifications of phrateres. The relationship between phratry and deme in regard to citizen identification deserves further study.

39. The translation is that of Whitehead 1986, 101–2.

40. E.g., it has been viewed as unlikely that the criteria of age tested by the *boule* and of status tested by the courts would have been tested separately— "both bodies would examine all relevant criteria" (Whitehead 1986, 102; so also Rhodes 1981, 500–502).

41. There has been some dispute whether men were registered after reaching their seventeenth or eighteenth birthday. Golden 1979, 35–38 persuasively argues the latter view, as does Rhodes 1986, 497–98.

42. Dem. 39 *Boeotus* 27 is pertinent here: Mantitheos is arguing that he, rather than his stepbrother ("Boiotos"), has the right to the name Mantitheos; the former's case is stronger if he is the elder (or rather, if he was introduced to the phratry before "Boiotos"). Mantitheos attempts to argue that "Boiotos" was younger in this way: "I remember seeing him, before he became a relative of mine, casually, as one might see someone else, and thought him younger than I, to judge by appearance (ὅσ' ἐξ ὄψεως), much younger; but I will not insist upon this, for it would be silly to do so." Humphreys 1989, 182–85 has made a strong case that both "Boiotos" and Mantitheos were born ca. 378 (*contra* Rudhardt 1962, 41–43, who had argued that "Boiotos" was the elder).

43. ἐλεύθερος in the first of the two clauses εἰ ἐλεύθερός ἐστι καὶ γέγονε κατὰ τ[ο]ὺς νόμους is used in its "normal" meaning here, "free" as opposed to "slave." While ἐλεύθερος sometimes does denote a man with citizenship, the requirement of citizenship is conveyed by the second clause ("[whether each one] was born in accordance with the laws"); so Rhodes 1981.

44. Following Rhodes 1981. The omission of a phrase "in marriage" (i.e., "born of parents in wedlock according to the laws") has been taken by some to mean that children born out of wedlock to two Athenian parents would still be citizens. Others, however, understand the phrase κατὰ τ[ο]ὺς νόμους as referring to marriage. See Patterson 1990 for relevant bibliography.

45. Compare the requirement for three witnesses to attest a boy's parentage for enrollment in a phratry at *IG* 2² 1237, 71 ff.

46. See n. 11 above, and, on Isaeus 12 *Euphiletus*, see n. 12 apud fin. There are indications that there were abuses in the system of deme enrollment (e.g., Dem. 57 *Eubulides* 26, 60–61, and [Dem.] 44 *Leochares* 44). See Whitehead 1986, 291–301.

47. On the decree of Demophilos, see n. 12 above and Whitehead 1986, 106–9.

48. We do not possess any of these grammateia and so must infer their

ADELE C. SCAFURO

contents from other sources: (1) inscriptions: *IG* I³ 138.6 dated by D. Lewis
ante 434, which records that demarkhoi are to exact payment from hippeis and
[hoplitai] "from [those written up] ἐς τὸ λεχσιαρχικὸν γρ⟨α⟩μματ[εῖον . . .";
SEG 2.7, 20, a deme decree of the Halimousioi granting honors to a Khari-
sandros orders that the decree be written up in the koina grammateia; (2)
references in the orators, usually in the context of the enrollment of a demesman (Dem. 57.26; 44.35 and 37; Isaeus 7.1 and 27; and Lycurgus 76); and (3)
more particular references in the orators: (a) Dem. 57.60: Euxitheos maintains
that his opponent's father, when he was demarkhos of the Halimousioi,
claimed to have lost the koinon grammateion; a voting (διαψηφίσασθαι) on
deme members followed; and (b) the deme scrutinies that attended the whole-
sale revision of deme lists in accordance with the decree of Demophilos in
346/5. For the evidence for the revision reported in the orators and later writers, see n. 12 above.

For a summary presentation of the knotty problems concerning when such
grammateia were first created, the meaning of lexiarkhikon, and whether the
thetes were included, see Whitehead 1986, 35 n. 130, and, more generally,
Rhodes 1981, 497. Osborne 1985, 72–73, pointing to *SEG* 2.7, argues that the
grammateion was the demarkhos' "minute book"; he claims it was not a public
document, and so "there was no public list of demesmen and no public list of
citizens." Such inferences are not justifiable.

49. Dem. 57.26; 44.35 and 37; Isaeus 7.1 and 27; and Lycurgus 76.

50. During the scrutiny of a man for public office, the name of his father's
deme is asked for, but his mother's is not. As Sealey 1987, 19 points out, "she
did not belong to a deme . . . a woman's relation to the deme was the indirect
connection through her husband." If we define citizen status in Athens as
"deme membership," then women were not citizens. But the process of identification for both men and women shows that the criteria of "being Athenian"
were broadly conceived and differed according to gender. To call the one a
citizen, and the other not, is correct from a limited constitutional perspective,
but otherwise misleading. On citizen terminology, see n. 51 below.

Concerning the question whether women were introduced into the phratry,
see the judicious presentation of ancient evidence by Wyse 1904, 363–64 with
reference to earlier scholarship, and the detailed argument by Ledl 1907, 173–
227, that women were not introduced except in a nontechnical way (223). Cole
1984, 235–38 reviews the evidence once again and offers sound criticism
against more recent attempts to connect women with phratries. With one exception, only late lexicographers or commentators mention the introduction of
women; the exception appears in a tricky passage of Isaeus (3 *Pyrrhus* 73),
where the speaker argues that because a particular epikleros was not introduced by her father into phratry, she was therefore not legitimate. The best
explanation is found in Sealey 1987, 18.

51. I am not here offering a definition of aste, but an examination of the
means that could be used to prove an Athenian woman's descent and identity;
nevertheless, the various criteria of identification—once recognized as such—
do become part of the definition. Important studies of citizenship terminology

have been made by Patterson 1981, 151–74, and 1987, 49–67. On the important role that participation in ritual would play in an Athenian woman's life, see Cole 1984, 238–44, who focuses on the rite of *arkteia* at Brauron. Cole rightly sees such rituals as parallels to phratry rituals performed for boys and young men: "At Athens a girl may not have been publicly recognized by her father's phratry, but there were rituals associated with the maturation process of girls and young women" (238). However, a woman's participation in rituals is not without political significance for her identity as an Athenian woman and lawfully married wife; e.g., the speaker of Isaeus 8 *Ciron* 20 adduces as evidence of his mother's status the fact that she presided at the Thesmophoria. It is possible that participation even in the rituals for girls may also have had a similar political significance, i.e., marking the girls as "growing up Athenian."

52. Engue of mother required: Dem. 57 *Eubulides* 54; Isaeus 8 *Ciron* 19. Importance of witnesses at this transaction: Dem. 30 *Onetor I* 21 (Demosthenes is attempting to refute Aphobos' statement that Onetor had given Aphobos a talent as dowry for his sister): "For no one who concludes such a transaction—not only with such a man as this, but with anyone—would do so without witnesses. But this is why we celebrate marriages and summon our closest kin and friends, because it is not a trivial event, but because we are entrusting [to others] the lives of our sisters and daughters, in whose behalf we especially look for security."

53. *IG* 2² 1237, 114–26: Μενέξενος εἶπεν· δεδόχθαι τοῖς φράτερσι περὶ/ τῆς εἰσαγωγῆς τῶμ παιδῶν τὰ μὲν ἄλλα κα/τὰ τὰ πρότερα ψηφίσματα, ὅπως δ' ἂν εἰδῶσι οἱ/φράτερες τοὺς μέλλοντας εἰσάγεσθαι, ἀπο/γράφεσθαι τῶι πρώτωι ἔτει ἢ ὧι ἂν τὸ κούρεο/ν ἄγει τὸ ὄνομα πατρόθεγ καὶ τὸ δήμου καὶ τῆ/ς μητρὸς πατρόθεν καὶ τοῦ [δ]ήμου πρὸς τὸν/φρατρίαρχον, τὸν δὲ φρατρία[ρ]χον ἀπογραψ]/αμένων ἀναγράψαντα ἐκ[τιθέναι ὅπου ἂν Δεκ]/ελέες προσφοιτῶσι, ἐκτιθ[έναι δὲ καὶ τὸν ἱερέα]/ἀναγράψαντα ἐν σανιδ[ίωι λευκῶι ἐν τῶι ἱερ]/ῶι τῆς Λητοῦς. τὸ δὲ φρ[ατερικὸν ψήφισμα ἀναγρ]/[άψαι εἰς τὴν σ]τήλην [τὴν λιθίνην τὸν ἱερεα ——].

54. See n. 59 below.

55. For the occurrence of the formula in New Comedy, see Gomme and Sandbach 1973, 531.

56. Divorce required for infidelity after a successful prosecution of a moikhos: [Dem.] 59 *Neaera* 87; marriage with a xene: [Dem.] 59 *Neaera* 16.

57. That Stephanos was able to marry off his alleged daughter Phano, first to Phrastor and then to Theogenes, is probably not unrelated to the amount of dowry he was able to offer ([Dem.] 59 *Neaera* 50, 71–72). Davies 1977–78, 113: "But for the political dimension Stephanos would very probably have got away with it, for he chose his sons-in-law with care. The position of each made it foolish for him to enquire too closely into the status and legitimacy of the woman being offered to him as a wife—Phrastor because he was a poor peasant being offered via the dowry a bribe to keep quiet, Theogenes because, though a poor man inexperienced with public affairs, he had suddenly become Basileus by the luck of the draw and needed a wife to perform the Basilinna's rituals on behalf of the State."

ADELE C. SCAFURO

58. Examples of reasons for divorce in the orators: Isaeus 2 *Menecles* 8; and Dem. 57 *Eubulides* 40–41. Men in New Comedy who are considering divorce or withdrawal from an engagement usually express concern for the reputation of the woman involved: Menander *Epitrepontes* and *Fabula Incerta;* and Terence *Phormio* and *Hecyra* (based on originals by Apollodoros of Karystos).

59. It of course seems natural and logical that both parents' names should appear on a list of deme or phratry members if that list is to serve the function of identifying members, esp. because it is a requirement for admission that the boy be a son of two Athenians. (This is the same natural and logical rationale that leads Jacoby *FGrHist* 325 F 17 Suppl. 2, 162 n. 4 to accept Didymus' report that women were introduced to the phratry at the gamelia.) But we simply have no authoritative evidence on this point. One unweighty report might support our natural and logical assumption: at Dem. 57.51, the speaker argues, as an absurdity, οὐ γὰρ ἂν ξένην καὶ ξένον τοὺς ἐμαυτοῦ γονέας ἐπιγραψάμενος μετέχειν ἠξίουν τῆς πόλεως. But the inclusion of both parents here may simply be for rhetorical effect. Lists of names in deme documents cite the individual demesmen as X son of Y; but these lists are always designated for specific purposes; e.g., to acknowledge a payment (*SEG* 24, 197), or a number of honorands (*IG* 2² 1197). Ought we to assume that the deme register followed a different procedure? It is questionable whether we possess any full phratry lists; Flower 1985, 232–35, arguing against Premerstein 1910, 103–17, maintains that *IG* 2² 2344 is a full phratry list rather than a list of members of a *thiasos* within the phratry. In that list, members are cited as X son of Y; but perhaps not all phratries would follow the same procedure. The most interesting evidence appears in the "motion of Menexenos" that is affixed to the decrees of the Demotionidai (*IG* 2² 1237; see n. 53 above); here we definitely have evidence of lists that include the name of the mother, as well as the name of her father and his deme. But it is unclear whether these lists were preserved *after* the introduction; the nature of their explicit purpose "in order that the *phrateres* may know those who are going to be introduced" suggests they served a temporary function—like the publication of names required by the Catholic church before marriage. See Ledl 1907, 215–23 for a sound discussion of lists. He rightly sees in the motion of Menexenos strong circumstantial proof that there were no local marriage registries, and he cites (215) the daydreams of earlier scholars who have thought that women were registered on phratry lists.

60. See the discussion of Dem. 57 *Eubulides* later in this essay.

61. See esp. [Dem.] 43 *Macartatus* 35–37, where witness depositions are presented, attesting to the existence of Phylomakhe I as the sister of Polemon. The witnesses present hearsay evidence (to the effect that "so-and-so says that he heard from X [usually an older relation] that Polemon had a sister, Philomakhe, born of the same father and mother"). Documents would have been useful in such cases as these, where the individual whose status is questioned has been dead for some time. That documents were not so used does not mean that such documents did not exist; it means that they were not used for purposes of identification.

62. See Pringsheim 1961, 401–20; Harvey 1966; and Thomas 1989.

63. This important function of witnessing has been demonstrated by Humphreys 1985, 313–65, and esp. 325.

64. See n. 12 above. This speech has been the subject of many discussions; I single out the following (in addition to references cited in n. 12 above): Haussoullier 1884, 38–52; Ledl 1907, 175–90; Osborne 1985, 146–51; Humphreys 1986, 59–62; and Whitehead 1986, 296–301.

65. Dem. 57.66–70.

66. The order of testimony in the body of the speech is: male relatives (21) and husbands of female relatives (22) testify that Thoukritos was συγγενής to themselves (22), and ἀμφοτέρωθεν Ἀθηναῖος (23); then the phrateres and gennetai, and, after them, the demesmen along with kinsmen in regard to the phrateres to prove that Euxitheos had been elected phratriarch (23); later others testified that Thoukritos was allotted office and passed scrutiny (25); lastly, the members of the γένος sharing common burial ground (28). Osborne 1985, 148 speculates that Euxitheos "may have produced no demesmen who were not also kin."

67. The relevance of the detail (18)—that at Leukas he fell in with Kleandros, the actor—is not transparent; possibly Kleandros was so famous that all in Athens knew of his stay and hence mention of his name confers verisimilitude to the story.

68. This slightly alters the order in 38–39: first, mother's nephew; then, grandson of the sister of the speaker's grandmother, whom the speaker designates a "cousin" in 68 (ἀνεψιαδοῦς = son of a first cousin); then, the mother's nephew.

69. Because earlier the speaker said that his mother had one son by Protomakhos (43), the plural number in 68 might mean that Protomakhos' son(s) by his second marriage are also bearing witness.

70. The depositions of phrateres and demotai (40) appeared before the depositions of Protomakhos' family (43); following the latter were the depositions of those present at his mother's betrothal to the speaker's father and phrateres testifying to the marriage feast (43); then Eunikos of Kholargos and his son (43).

71. Humphreys 1986, 62.

72. See n. 50 above.

73. A similar pattern of proof is offered in Isaeus 8 *Ciron,* in which the speaker must refute his opponent's claims that Kiron had no daughter (whom the speaker claims was his mother, cc. 1–2) and that the speaker's mother did not even have citizen status (43). The speaker presents testimony concerning those who betrothed her and those present at the betrothal (17), and testimony that his father gave a marriage feast to three friends and relatives, that the father gave a marriage banquet (gamelia) to his phrateres, that the wives of the demesmen chose his mother to preside at the Thesmophoria, that his father had introduced his children to his phrateres, having declared on oath in accordance with the established laws that he was introducing children ἐξ ἀστῆς καὶ ἐγγυητῆς γυναικός (18–19, with summary at 29). These are all the right cre-

dentials for his "proof"; unfortunately, it looks as if he has no relatives as first-hand witnesses and must rely on hearsay (14, 29).

74. Todd 1990, 31–32, with a chart on 39; the quote appears on 31.

75. Todd 1990, 32 and 39 for the figure from speeches concerned with family property; the figure from [Dem.] 59 is mine. I have not broken down Todd's category of "family property" disputes into cases that required kin and status identification and cases that did not.

76. *Dike kakotekhnion:* mentioned at [Dem.] 46.10; 47.1; 49.56. See Leisi 1908, 139–41; Lipsius 1905–15, 783; MacDowell 1978, 245.

77. I have used the somewhat cumbrous phrase "false witnessing" in trans-lating *dike pseudomarturion* rather than the misleading translation "perjury"; see Todd 1990, 36. For the two situations in which the dike could be applied: [Dem.] 47.1: "In my opinion the laws are good, oh dikasts, which permit to suits [i.e., to those already undertaken] another trial for pseudomarturia, in order that, if a person deceived the dikasts by having provided witnesses who testify falsely or by having invoked challenges that never took place or deposi-tions contrary to the law, there may be no gain for him, but the wronged litigant, if he had put in a protest to the testimony and come to you and proven that the witnesses have testified falsely in the case, may exact a penalty from them and hold as liable to an action for kakotekhnia (subornation of testi-mony) the one who brought them forward." For the circumstances allowing the admission of hearsay: [Dem.] 46.6–9; 57.4; Isaeus 3.18–27; and Aeschin. 2.19. See further, on the dike, Leisi 1908, 121. For the possibility that there had formerly been a graphe in use for such charges, see MacDowell 1978, 244.

78. E.g., Leisi 1908, 141; Behrend 1975, 148–50.

79. Szegedy-Maszak 1987, F5 (= schol. Plato *Laws* 937d).

80. Behrend 1975, 131–56 is the best guide on these issues. As to the ques-tions, what kind or how much evidence had to be overturned or how many witnesses had to be convicted of giving false testimony before a retrial of the original case became permissible, see n. 97 below.

81. MacDowell 1978, 212. For diamarturia, see Harrison 1971, 124–31; MacDowell 1978, 212–13, 217–18. In the fourth century, a diamarturia usually proceeds out of a *diadikasia* for an inheritance. It would be interesting to know more about the cases referred to by Harpocration (s.v. *diamarturia*) in lost speeches of Isaeus and Hyperides, a *dike apostasiou* and a *graphe aprostasiou.* For notice of a diamarturia from an *anakrisis,* see Boegehold 1982, 1–6.

82. For dikai pseudomarturion arising out of diamarturiai in inheritance cases, see Berneker 1972, 1372–73; Harrison 1971, 124–31.

83. This point is generally agreed upon (Harrison 1971, 129). However, there is much disagreement about the effect of a plaintiff's success; see Har-rison 1971, 129–30, with summary of earlier views.

84. For discussion of the procedure and the function of episkepsis in it, see: Leisi 1908, 124–30; Lipsius 1905–15, 778–83; and Calhoun 1916, 365–87, with criticisms of earlier views.

85. According to *AP* 68.4, the herald first asks, as the dikasts are preparing to cast their votes, whether either adversary objects to the witness testimonies;

no objections can be made once the voting has begun. [Aristotle] immediately continues with the next stage in the trial's procedure, viz., the herald's directions for the casting of votes. Lipsius 1905–15, 781 understands this to mean that the original trial is not disrupted.

86. We do not have much evidence on this point, but [Dem.] 47 *Evergus* 49 clearly indicates that the speaker, who had lost the original trial for assault, was liable to pay the penalty before the false witnessing trial took place. Instead of paying the penalty, however, the speaker claims (49–51) to have made a private agreement with his successful adversary about its postponement; he also says he was "trusting in his claim of false witnessing." His opponent could presumably have pursued him with a *dike exoules;* instead, he is alleged to have retracted the private agreement by taking the law in his own hands and carrying off the speaker's household possessions.

87. Harrison 1971, 196 discusses the absence of anadikia for homicide cases without considering whether false witnessing charges could be brought. Possibly he thought that because no retrial was permitted, a false witnessing suit would be of no consequence.

88. E.g., Lipsius 1905–15, 781; MacDowell 1978, 244 assumes the death penalty would be postponed, but offers no grounds for the assumption. Dem. 24 *Timocrates* 131, which is discussed briefly later in this essay, provides the evidence for postponement of enslavement following conviction in a xenia trial.

89. It is not absolutely certain that [Dem.] 44 *Leochares* is a false witnessing suit (e.g., the speaker says in chap. 7: ἔστιν γὰρ ὁ μὲν ἀγὼν οὑτοσὶ κλήρου διαδικασία); but the argument presented in chaps. 34–44 (and especially in chap. 42) makes it seem very likely that it was. See Harrison 1971, 129 n. 2.

90. That the original case was a *dike blabes* is argued by Harrison 1971, 116 n. 2 against Lipsius 1905–15, 725–26, who argues for a *dike aphormes.*

91. For the centrality of the will in the original dispute from which the false witnessing suit stems in Dem. 29, see esp. chaps. 6 and 44; the centrality of an inheritance dispute is evident throughout [Dem.] 45 and 46.

92. The plaintiff in this trial had not denied the existence of the will by which his adversary's sunegoros had been adopted *inter vivos* twenty-three years ago, but rather its validity (he claimed that it was made under the undue influence of a woman). In order to argue against this, the sunegoros tries to establish his status as the legitimate (adopted) son and adduces the testimony of phrateres, demotai, and orgeonai (16). The issue in the various false witnessing trials alluded to in Is. 5 is quite different; it is not a question of the existence or validity of one will, but of deciding the authenticity of competing wills.

93. See Humphreys 1986, 63–67.

94. Lys. 4 *Trauma* 14; Isocr. 17 *Trapez.* 14–17; and [Dem.] 49 *Timotheus* 55–56, discussed above.

95. It is not uncommon for a speaker (A) to claim that his adversary (B) is giving false testimony or for a speaker (A) to offer arguments in anticipation of his opponent's (B's) claim that his (A's) witnesses are testifying falsely (see, e.g., Dem. 41 *Spudias* 16). Two such anticipatory arguments are made in cases

involving disputed disfranchisements. In Dem. 57 *Eubulides* 53, the speaker argues that his relatives who are giving testimony about his identity would not have chosen to undergo the risk of perjuring themselves. Similarly, in Isaeus 12 *Euphiletus* 4–8, the speaker provides an extended argument from probability that neither he nor other kin are giving false testimony about Euphiletos' identity.

96. (1) *POxy.* 2538: This fragment may have been (a) part of the defense in a trial for xenia, or (b) part of an inheritance dispute, or (c) part of an appeal to the thesmothetai for re-enrollment on a deme list. (The first two suggestions were made by the editors [p. 38] of the fragment; the third suggestion appears to be Thompson's [1968, 149–50].) (2) *POxy.* 2537, which seems to be a list of hypotheses of Lysias' speeches, records (verso, 33–41) that there were three speeches for xenia. (3) Harpocration s.v. notheia, mentions a speech against Kalliphanes for xenia; he questions Lysias' authorship (= Lys. frag. 71 Thalheim). The editors of *POxy.* 2538 suggest that "from the title and the citation—νοθεῖα. τὰ τοῖς νόθοις ἐκ τῶν πατρώιων διδόμενα οὕτω καλεῖται. ἦν δὲ μεχρὶ χιλίων δραχμῶν.—[the speech against Kalliphanes] may be supposed to have concerned a man accused of ξενίας because his mother was not a citizen" [39]. The editors also suggest that this speech may be the one summarized in *POxy.* 2537, 39–41. (4) Hyp. (Jensen) frag. Or. 15 (title only): *kata Demeou xenias.* (5) References to other trials for xenia preserved in the orators: (a) Lys. 13 *Agoratus* 60: Certain individuals plead with Aristophanes not to run the risk of a trial for xenia; the circumstances are unclear as to why he would run this risk. (b) Isaeus 3 *Pyrrhus* 37: Speaker asks if his uncle (Pyrrhos) would have married the sister of a man (Nikodemos) "who, when he was charged with xenia by a member of the phratry to which he said he belonged, by four votes obtained his citizenship rights?" (c) Dem. *Ep.* 3.29: A politician named Pythias is said to have been prosecuted for xenia and barely escaped being sold into slavery.

97. As Szegedy-Maszak 1981, 28–29 points out, the scholiast does not reduplicate the wording of Plato's measure when he discusses retrial. Plato had said: "In the case of all those whose evidence has been convicted at trial, i.e., when it has been proven that they have given false testimony and provided the victory for the prosecutor, if some of such testimony, to the extent of more than half of it, be condemned, the trial that was lost on the basis of this testimony is to be retried" (937 c5–d2). On the other hand, the scholiast has quantified the number of witnesses rather than, as Plato does, the evidence as a whole. Harrison 1971, 192–95 discusses "whether there was any rule governing the number or character of the witnesses who had to be convicted in order to allow a reopening of the original case" (193–94) and is surely right to conclude (195) that we do not have enough evidence to decide.

98. For a full treatment of the passage and earlier scholarship, see Behrend 1975, 131–56.

99. So, e.g., Leisi 1908, 133; Lipsius 1905–15, 955–57; Bonner and Smith 1938, 265; and Berneker 1972, 1271. The general argument of these scholars is that anadikia protected the citizen who, because of false witnesses, was threat-

ened with enslavement or loss of citizen rights or of oikos, for none of which could there be financial compensation.

100. Behrend 1975, 139–48 has collected the evidence for retrials from the orators; retrials appear in cases of inheritance and xenia, but none originates from false witnessing trials.

101. Perhaps the riskiest business in using the scholiast or his citation of Theophrastus to support either view is the problem raised but not treated by Harrison 1971, 194 with n. 3, that neither the scholiast nor Theophrastus indicates that the rule applied to Athens. Szegedy-Maszak 1981, in his collection of Theophrastus' *Nomoi*, includes twenty-three fragments positively attributed to that work and three more whose attribution is almost certain. In only one fragment are the laws of other cities explicitly discussed (F 21, on laws of sale); in two others (FF 15 and 22), the customs of other cities are explicitly mentioned. For a work that originally consisted of twenty-four books, we are rather badly off to make a judgment on whether the fragment quoted in the text above is about Athenian law or belonged to a discussion of, let us say, Mytilenean law. My only contribution to the alleviation of this risky business is to suggest that the scholiast may not have been interested in non-Attic law.

102. This explanation of the limited extent of anadikia differs from earlier ones (see Behrend 1975) that view the causative factor as the suitability and availability of restitution: while a subsequent and successful dike katatekhnion might win compensation for an innocent man who had been convicted of a charge that entailed the payment of a monetary fine, that same dike could not compensate an innocent man who had been convicted of a charge that brought the loss of his estate or freedom—hence the allowance of anadikia. But that explanation does not tell us why other charges punishable by atimia were not included; nor does it offer an explanation of retrial for false witnessing. According to my suggestion (which is adumbrated by Lämmli 1938, 137), it was a recognition of the failure of the mechanism of identification that allowed for the exceptional cases of retrial. Regardless of the specific type of procedure or case from which a false witnessing charge arose, a great many would concern the identification of individuals. While this is obviously the concern (as demonstrated above) in false witnessing trials arising from inheritance disputes and trials for xenia, it would also be the concern in subsequent false witnessing trials that might arise out of false witnessing trials where the original case was an inheritance dispute or charge of xenia.

103. [Aristotle] *AP* 59.3 and Harpocration s.v. *parastasis* and *doroxenia*.

104. On the overlap of this graphe with the dike pseudomarturion and other procedures, see Rhodes 1981, 662.

105. Gratwick 1982, 101–3 has made the plausible suggestion that Plautus may have contaminated his play with the scene from *Sikyonios* or with some other similar scene.

106. For a convincing account of the citizenship scenario in Terence's *Andria* and in the Menandrian original, see Steidle 1973.

107. The best explanation of the procedure envisioned in *Phormio* can be found in Brown 1980, 195 and involves no discrepancy between the Greek

original and Terence's account of the events that led to the marriage: "In this play [Terence's *Phormio*] we have (according to Phormio's fiction) an 'heiress' who is poor and whose nearest male relative has to be forced by legal action to assume responsibility for her. We know about such cases from Dem. 43.54 ἀπογραφέτω δὲ τὸν μὴ ποιοῦντα ταῦτα ὁ βουλόμενος πρὸς τὸν ἄρχοντα. Phormio has acted as ὁ βουλόμενος, and we may assume that the arkhon referred the matter to a court after the usual preliminary hearing (*anakrisis*)." At *Phormio* 399–401, the young man who was prosecuted by Phormio is said to have made no protest to the testimony at the trial; this is probably a reference to an episkepsis; no suit for false witnessing can arise.

Works Cited

Andrewes, A. 1961. "Philochoros on Phratries." *JHS* 81:1–15.
Behrend, Diederich. 1975. "Die ἀνάδικος δίκη und das Scholion zu Plato Nomoi 937 d." In *Symposion 1971*, edited by Hans Julius Wolff, 131–56. Cologne: Böhlau Verlag.
Berneker, Erich. 1972. "ψευδομαρτυρίων δίκη." In *RE* 23.2:1372–73.
Boegehold, Alan L. 1982. "A Lid with Dipinto." In *Studies in Attic Epigraphy History and Topography Presented to Eugene Vanderpool. Hesperia:* Supplement 19:1–6.
Bonner, Robert J., and Gertrude Smith. 1938. *The Administration of Justice from Homer to Aristotle.* Vol. 2. Chicago: Chicago University Press.
Brown, Peter G. McC. 1980. "Terentian *Imitatio*." Review of Eckard Lefèvre, *Der Phormio des Terenz und der Epidikazomenos des Apollodor von Karystos. CR* 30:194–96.
Cole, Susan G. 1984. "The Social Function of Rituals of Maturation: The Koureion and Arkteia." *ZPE* 55:233–44.
Connor, W. Robert. 1971. *The New Politicians of Fifth-Century Athens.* Princeton: Princeton University Press.
Davies, John K. 1977–78. "Athenian Citizenship: The Descent Group and the Alternatives." *CJ* 73:105–21.
Deubner, Ludwig. 1932. *Attische Feste.* Berlin: Akademie Verlag.
———. 1952. "Die Gebräuche der Griechen nach der Geburt." *RhM* 95:374–77.
Diller, Aubrey. 1932. "The Decree of Demophilus, 346–345 B.C." *TAPA* 63:193–205.
———. 1935. "Scrutiny and Appeal in Athenian Citizenship." *CP* 30:302–11.
Flower, Michael. 1985. "*IG* II². 2344 and the Size of Phratries in Classical Athens." *CQ* 35:232–35.
Garland, Robert. 1990. *The Greek Way of Life.* Ithaca: Cornell University Press.
Golden, Mark. 1979. "Demosthenes and the Age of Majority at Athens." *Phoenix* 33:35–38.
———. 1990. *Children and Childhood in Classical Athens.* Baltimore: Johns Hopkins University Press.

Gomme, Arnold W. 1934. "Two Problems of Athenian Citizenship Law." *CP* 29:123–40.

Gomme, Arnold W., and F. H. Sandbach. 1973. *Menander: A Commentary.* Oxford: Oxford University Press.

Gould, John. 1980. "Law, Custom and Myth: Aspects of the Social Position of Women in Classical Athens." *JHS* 100:38–59.

Gratwick, A. S. 1982. "Drama." In *The Cambridge History of Classical Literature.* Vol. 2, *Latin Literature,* 77–137. Cambridge: Cambridge University Press.

Harrison, A. R. W. 1968. *The Law of Athens.* Vol. 1, *The Family and Property.* Oxford: Oxford University Press.

———. 1971. *The Law of Athens.* Vol. 2, *Procedure.* Oxford: Oxford University Press.

Harvey, F. D. 1966. "Literacy in the Athenian Democracy." *REG* 79:585–635.

Haussoullier, Bernard. 1884. *La Vie Municipale en Attique: Essai sur l'organisation des dèmes au quatrième siècle.* Paris.

Hedrick, Charles W., Jr. 1984. "The Attic Phratry." Ph.D. thesis, University of Pennsylvania. Ann Arbor.

———. 1990. *The Decrees of the Demotionidai.* Decatur, Ga.: Scholars Press.

Hruza, Ernst. 1892. *Die Ehebegründung nach attischem Rechte.* Erlangen: Deichert. Reprint. New York: Arno Press, 1979.

Humphreys, Sally C. 1985. "Social Relations on Stage: Witnesses in Classical Athens." *History and Anthropology* 1:313–69.

———. 1986. "Kinship Patterns in the Athenian Courts." *GRBS* 27:59–62.

———. 1989. "Family Quarrels." *JHS* 109:182–85.

Jacoby, Felix. 1923–58. *Die Fragmente der griechischen Historiker.* Leiden: E. J. Brill.

Labarbe, Jules. 1953. "L'âge correspondant au sacrifice du κούρειον et les données historiques du sixième discours d'Isée." *BAB* 39:358–94.

Lämmli, Franz. 1938. *Das attische Prozessverfahren in seiner Wirkung auf die Gerichtsrede.* Paderborn: Ferdinand Schöningh.

Ledl, Artur. 1907. "Das attische Bürgerrecht und die Frauen I." *WS* 29:173–227.

———. 1908. "Das attische Bürgerrecht und die Frauen II." *WS* 30:1–46.

Leisi, Ernst. 1908. *Der Zeuge im attischen Recht.* Frauenfeld: Verlag Huber. Reprint. New York: Arno Press, 1979.

Lipsius, Justus H. 1905–15. *Das Attische Recht und Rechtsverfahren.* Leipzig: O. R. Reisland. Reprint. Hildesheim: Georg Olms Verlagsbuchhandlung, 1966.

MacDowell, Douglas M. 1962. *Andokides on the Mysteries.* Oxford: Clarendon Press.

———. 1978. *The Law in Classical Athens.* London: Thames and Hudson.

Müller, Otto. 1899. "Untersuchungen zur Geschichte des attischen Bürger- und Eherechts." *Jahrbücher für classische Philologie* Suppl. 25:661–866.

Osborne, Robin. 1985. *Demos: The Discovery of Classical Attika.* Cambridge: Cambridge University Press.

Patterson, Cynthia. 1981. *Pericles' Citizenship Law of 451/0 B.C.* New York: Arno Press. Reprint. Salem, N.H.: Ayer, 1987.

———. 1987. *"Hai Attikai:* The Other Athenians." *Helios* 13:49–67.

———. 1990. "Those Athenian Bastards." *CA* 9:40–73.

Premerstein, Anton von. 1910. "Phratern-Verbände auf einem attischen Hypothekenstein." *Ath. Mit.* 35:103–17.

Pringsheim, Fritz. 1961. "The Transition from Witnesses to Written Transactions in Athens." In *Gesammelte Abhandlungen,* edited by Fritz Pringsheim. Vol. 2, 401–20. Heidelberg: Carl Winter. Universitätsverlag. First published in *Festschrift Simonius* 1955:287–97.

Rhodes, Peter J. 1981. *A Commentary on the Aristotelian* Athenaion Politeia. Oxford: Clarendon Press.

Rudhardt, Jean. 1962. "La reconnaissance de la paternité sa nature et sa portée dans la société athénienne." *MH* 19:39–61.

Schaefer, Arnold. 1858. *Demosthenes und seine Zeit.* Vol. 3.2. Leipzig: B. G. Teubner. Reprint. New York: Arno Press, 1979.

Sealey, Raphael. 1984. "On Lawful Concubinage in Athens." *CA* 3:111–33.

———. 1987. *The Athenian Republic.* University Park: Pennsylvania State Press.

Steidle, Wolf. 1973. "Menander bei Terenz." *RhM* 116:303–47.

Stengel. *"Amphidromia."* In *RE* 1.2:1901–2.

Szegedy-Maszak, Andrew. 1981. *The Nomoi of Theophrastus.* New York: Arno Press. Reprint. Salem, N.H.: Ayer, 1987.

Thalheim, T. 1958. "ἐξαιρέσεως δίκη." In *RE* 6.2:1548–49.

Thomas, Rosalind. 1989. *Oral Tradition and Written Record in Classical Athens.* Cambridge: Cambridge University Press.

Thompson, Wesley E. 1968. "An Interpretation of the 'Demotionid' Decrees." *SO* 62:51–68.

Todd, Stephen. 1990. "The Purpose of Evidence in Athenian Courts." In *Nomos: Essays in Athenian Law, Politics, and Society,* edited by Paul Cartledge, Paul Millett, and Stephen Todd, 19–40. Cambridge: Cambridge University Press.

Walters, Kenneth R. 1983. "Perikles' Citizenship Law." *CA* 2:314–36.

Whitehead, David. 1986. *The Demes of Attica 508/7–ca. 250 B.C.* Princeton: Princeton University Press.

Wolff, Hans Julius. 1944. "Marriage Law and Family Organization in Ancient Athens: A Study on the Interrelation of Public and Private Law in the Greek City." *Traditio* 2:43–95.

Wyse, William. 1904. *The Speeches of Isaeus.* Cambridge: Cambridge University Press. Reprint. New York: Arno Press, 1979.

The Case against Neaira
and the Public Ideology of
the Athenian Family

𝍫𝍫𝍫𝍫𝍫𝍫𝍫𝍫𝍫𝍫𝍫𝍫𝍫𝍫𝍫

CYNTHIA PATTERSON

A reader familiar with the conventional view of Athenian civic ideology, that of exclusive male political egalitarianism, must find remarkable ironies in the speech and case against Neaira. To mention only the most obvious, this speech, the sole surviving prosecution on the charge of *xenia* (false claim to Athenian status), is delivered by the son of a former slave against a woman—and a former slave woman at that. Invoking the holiest of Athenian laws, Apollodoros, the son of the former slave Pasion, calls upon the Athenians to guard the sacred purity of their Athenian body— and throw Neaira back into slavery! We are certainly familiar with the zealous patriotism of new citizens and the xenophobia of those who were only recently *xenoi* themselves. But in prosecuting a woman, Apollodoros is drawn beyond the celebrated privileges of voting and judging to a consideration of the broader essential nature of membership or participation in the polis and in particular to its connection with Athenian family membership. That the familial relationships of husband-wife and parent-child have significance beyond the courtyard gate need hardly be emphasized, but what is particularly striking in this speech is the way in which Apollodoros draws upon the public ideology of family and household— that is, the nexus of values and beliefs which gave public meaning and status to both the marriage relationship and the household (*oikos*) that relationship created. In short, this is the ideology of citizenship as "family membership" in the extended "family of families" that was classical Athens.

By making the responsibilities of Athenian family members to one another and to the public world of the polis the ideological basis of his attack, Apollodoros presents Neaira, and her infiltration into one Athenian oikos, as a threat to (or violation of) the collective identity of all Athenian oikoi. Apollodoros counts on moving his audience not so much with crafted argument (the speech most likely comes from his own amateur pen)[1] as with an appeal, backed up with frequent citation of law, to the essential connection between family and city privilege. Although he was himself an "adopted" (*poietes*) member of the Athenian community, I think we can assume that Apollodoros did not misread his audience and can also read the case for ourselves as an instructive counterweight to the prevailing and deeply ingrained individualistic bias in modern perceptions of Athenian society. In emphasizing the importance of "family ideology" in classical Athens, I am in no way advocating a return to the long influential patriarchal and patrilineal paradigm of ancient society put forth by Fustel de Coulanges in 1864—a paradigm of, as Momigliano put it, an "earthly paradise of gentes worshipping their ancestors."[2] Rather, I would like to focus attention on the ways in which the operational unit of the oikos, with its related kin and associated members uniquely constituted by every marriage, both allowed and constructed an Athenian's public identity and participation.

A focus, however, on the rights and interests of individuals rather than responsibilities of households is a deeply ingrained modern habit,[3] and, as a protreptic introduction to my "group dynamics" reading of Apollodoros' attack on Neaira, I offer first a tale from Herodotus. The tale is a shocking one to modern sensibilities and not often emphasized or fully told.[4] Perhaps it may today "shock" or at least "nudge" those with comfortable Aristotelian ideas about "citizenship"—as consisting of a neat and rational set of political rights—into a willingness to think about the nature of Greek community membership along unaccustomed lines.

Book 9 of Herodotus' *Histories* opens with Mardonios' march back into central Greece and Attika in the spring of 479. Unable to dislodge the Athenians from the Greek alliance, he sacked the city once again—as once again the Athenians watched the fires from their "polis-in-exile" on the island of Salamis. Still, Mardonios could not believe the Athenians' stubborn tenacity would last and so sent one last messenger, a certain Hellespontine Greek named Mourykhides, to offer once again special terms to the Athenian Boule on Salamis. At this point, says Herodotus:

> One of the bouleutai, a man named Lykides, expressed the opinion that the best course would be to admit the proposals which Mourykhides brought, and to submit them for approval to the general assembly of the people. This was his expressed opinion—whether he had been bribed by Mardonios to express it or really thought so. In any case the Athenians, both those in that Boule and those outside, were so enraged when they

heard it that they surrounded Lykides and stoned him to death. Mourykhides they allowed to depart unharmed. With all the uproar in Salamis
over Lykides, the Athenian women [*hai gunaikes ton Athenaion*] soon
found out what had happened; whereupon, without a word from the
men, they got together, and each one egging on her neighbor and taking
her along with the crowd, flocked to Lykides' house and stoned his wife
and children. (5, trans. de Selincourt, modified)

Herodotus offers no comment on this act of communal, male and
female, violence—an act of pure "democratic" consensus at the expense
of individual life and liberty—but quietly and quickly moves on to the
stalled negotiations between Athens and the Peloponnesians. However,
the identification of the Athenian citizen with his or her oikos and of the
Athenian woman with her polis and its perceived interest is unmistak-
able. This is not a heartwarming picture of women at work about their
civic duties—nor of women as an excluded "other" with interests separate
from those of the male citizenry. Rather, what we are given is a brutal
story of one man's oikos being destroyed in response to his taking a
political position perceived as threatening to the polis: the other males
stone Lykides while the complementary female members of other Athenian oikoi then obliterate the remainder of Lykides' oikos—again to blot
out their threat to the polis itself. The story, for all its brutality, reveals the
seriousness of family identity, and in this case even a symmetry between
male and female participation in both oikos and polis, with a force beyond that of the choral lines in the *Lysistrata* often quoted to this point:
"I too have a share in the common service (*eranos*): I contribute sons"
(651).[5]
    Nonetheless, the dominant view today takes citizenship as a bundle
of political rights and denies that women were part of the "citizens' club"
that was classical Athens. Feminine forms of the term "citizen" (*aste* or
politis) are taken as empty names; or, if the notion of "female citizenship"
is implied (at times unavoidably, as in reference to the citizenship law
requiring birth from "two citizen parents"), this is explicitly understood
to be mere place-holding or reflection of male relatives' authentic citizen
status.[6] Such an attitude seems erroneous—and ultimately based on the
assumption that the public/private distinction in classical Athens neatly
corresponds to male/female spheres of responsibility. Herodotus' tale,
however—and no less the case against Neaira, whom Apollodoros wants
the jurors to "stone" with their votes—shows women's involvement in,
and commitment to, the public life of the polis (whether we choose to call
it "citizenship") to be both significant and substantial.[7]
    Similarly, Ste. Croix's argument that women are a distinct class in

Greek society, marked by the exploitation of their reproductive labor, is qualified by his admission that there may be more significant class criteria for women—and by his admission that the issue deserves "further thought."[8] Child-bearing did decisively and essentially (in Athens if not in Plato's Republic) distinguish men from women, but the context in which child-bearing took place—for example, an Athenian *oikia* as opposed to a public brothel—would decisively distinguish one woman from another. If we say that as members of Athenian households, Athenian women were "exploited," we need to recognize also that they were themselves "exploiters" of the non-Athenian and the nonfree.

For better or worse, Athenian women should be seen as standing within the citizen class as participants in the polis in ways marking them off in law and in public consciousness from the non-Athenian and the nonfree—as we could say, share-holders rather than place-holders. Their share was not congruent with that of the male Athenian, and to a great extent it was identified and exercised—as the fate of Lykides' family reveals—in connection with the oikos or household. But while mediated through the oikos, the woman's share in the public good as seen, for example, in the care and lament for the dead or the ritual celebration of fertility and marriage—was not only publicly recognized but also legally enforced. Moreover, both male and female Athenians were active share-holders in the property and fortunes of their oikoi and polis.[9] However difficult it may be to define the woman's share (Aristotle does not even try), it is not a mere token and not limited to the payment of a child-bearing "tax." Indeed, a closer appreciation of the participation of the Athenian woman through her oikos in public life and public ideology may very well contribute to a better understanding of the distinctiveness of classical Athenian society and history. And in considering the case against Neaira, we need to remember that it is after all *Neaira* who (at age fifty-five or thereabouts) is on trial for *xenia* (usurpation of citizenship) in [Demosthenes] 59, and to ask just what this trial means not only for Neaira herself but also for the oikos of which she is a part.

At this point I can imagine (and have heard) an objection to the effect that the attack on Neaira or on any woman (e.g., the wife of Lykides) is simply a way of getting at a man. In order to ruin Stephanos, with whom Neaira is apparently living, Apollodoros attacks the character and status of his "wife." Is the woman simply a pawn in the power game of individual male politicians? Is she drawn in as the quarrel escalates, just as Briseis is drawn into the quarrel of Akhilleus and Agamemnon—or, to take a more recent example from American popular culture, as the wife of an aluminum-siding salesman is drawn into a quarrel with a rival salesman in the film *Tin Men*?[10] While it is clear that Apollodoros would not have been interested in Neaira if she were not living with Stephanos, the case against Neaira is nonetheless not so much aimed at one individual, Stephanos or Neaira, as at the oikos they have allegedly created by the act of *sunoikein,* literally, "to set up an oikos together."[11] As an individual, Stephanos stands to be fined one thousand drakhmai if Neaira is convicted, but as head of an oikos he potentially loses much more. If Neaira is convicted of acting as his wife, then the legitimacy of the entire oikos is called into question. It is not clear what immediate legal effect a guilty verdict would have on the children of the oikos (apparently three sons and a daughter, 121, cf. 38), but it certainly put them, and through them Stephanos, in a highly vulnerable position.[12] Stephanos could come out of the case with his individual citizen rights intact, but his oikos in shambles. Similarly, Neaira is not liable on her own to the *graphe xenias*—but only as the alleged wife of Stephanos. In order for her to be guilty, the whole household of Stephanos must be implicated. Individual family members in this case must "sink or swim" with the whole—the oikos or household group. In sum, even if the personal motive for this charge is to "get" Stephanos, our interest here lies in the societal motive— the protection of family and civic legitimacy—to which Theomnestos and Apollodoros so fervently appeal.

Prologue by Theomnestos

So much by way of introduction to a nonindividualistic "group dynamics" reading of the case against Neaira. The introduction to the speech itself, to the litigants and their quarrel, is provided by Apollodoros' brother-in-law and son-in-law, Theomnestos, son of Deinias, who is the official prosecutor of the case (he has *"grapsasthai Neairan ten graphen,"* 1). Theomnestos declares (in Herodotean fashion) that Stephanos, Neaira's "husband," was the "first to do wrong" and openly asserts that he and his kinsman Apollodoros are simply out for revenge. Although Theomnestos speaks only for the first few minutes (fifteen chapters) of the speech, his brief sketch of past family history establishes the themes of family loyalty and civic legitimacy that form the basis of this prosecution.

When the Athenian demos saw fit to make the freed slave Pasion an Athenian citizen (in the 380s), Deinias, the father of Theomnestos, favored the granting of that gift. Indeed, he was so impressed by the good will—and no doubt the good fortune—of Pasion's household that some years later he gave his daughter as wife to Pasion's son Apollodoros (at the latest by 365). And when Apollodoros reciprocated by treating Theomnestos as truly "one of the family" (considering him *"oikeios,"* 2),

Theomnestos in turn married his own niece, the daughter of Apollodoros and his sister (at the latest in 349). So this happy family—and its property—was even more tightly bound together. What is more, the marriages establish that Apollodoros is properly incorporated into the civic community of Athens. His daughter, legitimately married to Theomnestos, is a public symbol of that incorporation. Thus, two women, a mother and daughter—and, from another perspective, a sister and a wife—connect the lives and interest of Apollodoros and Theomnestos. The evocation of these properly anonymous women in the opening moments of the speech may have been intended to call to mind (for the informed juror) an invidious comparison with that other mother-daughter pair, Neaira and her alleged daughter Phano, with their illegitimate and fraudulent oikos.

The "wrong" for which Theomnestos and Apollodoros seek revenge is at first sight a simple political matter: Stephanos successfully prosecuted Apollodoros with a *graphe paranomon,* asking for an exorbitant fine of fifteen talents.[13] As represented by Theomnestos, however, the charge and proposed fine put into jeopardy the well-being of his entire oikos. Besides suffering *atimia* for default on a fine, Apollodoros would not have been able to provide a dowry or find a husband for his younger daughter. Stephanos had threatened the very ability of Apollodoros to function as proper head of household. The oikos itself, as well as its head, risked suffering a kind of atimia—suggesting perhaps what was in store for the oikos of Stephanos. The fine was reduced, but when Stephanos persisted in putting Apollodoros' family at risk with further suits, Apollodoros and Theomnestos "return the *eranos*" and charge that Stephanos' oikos is a fraud, his "wife" is a foreigner, and his "children" are bastards. Theomnestos states: "I have come before you to prove that Stephanos is living with an alien woman contrary to the law; that he has introduced children not his own to his phratry and deme; that he has given in marriage the daughters of *hetairai* (courtesans) as if his own; that he is guilty of impiety toward the gods and that he makes the demos *akuros* (without authority), if it chooses to make anyone a citizen" (13).[14]

After thus introducing his family and the nontrivial nature of the complaint and after expanding on the danger to the public good and public privilege represented by a household such as Stephanos', Theomnestos turns over the case to the "older and more experienced" (in matters of law) Apollodoros.[15] However, Theomnestos has set up the basic terms on which the case will proceed: Stephanos and Neaira's fraudulent "family" relations threaten both the sovereignty of the people and the good will of the gods. The well-being of the Athenian polis depends upon the preservation of elite privilege—at the heart of which lies, as Apollodoros sees it, the privilege of citizen marriage.

Apollodoros on the Career of Neaira

After paraphrasing once again the charge "that Neaira is an alien and lives [as wife] with Stephanos contrary to the laws," Apollodoros launches immediately into a quotation of the relevant law:

"If an alien shall live as husband with an Athenian woman in any way or manner whatsoever, he may be indicted before the thesmothetai by any-one who chooses to do so from among the Athenians having the right to bring charges. And if he be convicted, he shall be sold, himself and his property, and the third part shall belong to the one securing his convic-tion. The same principle shall hold also if an alien woman shall live as wife with an Athenian, and the Athenian who lives as husband with the alien woman so convicted shall be fined one thousand drakhmai." (16)[16]

The quotation of law in this manner is Apollodoros' trademark.[17] (It is remarkable—and somewhat disconcerting—how much Athenian "law" we apparently owe to Apollodoros' "quotations.") Just as Euphiletos, the wronged husband in Lysias 1, recalls dramatically the words he spoke as he struck down the adulterer Eratosthenes, "It is not I who am killing you, but the law itself" (26), so Apollodoros asks his audience in the closing moments of the speech to forget that he, Apollodoros, is speaking and rather "consider that the laws and Neaira here are contending in a suit" (115). For Apollodoros in particular, knowledge of the laws estab-lishes the legitimacy of his citizenship: he has no citizen-born parents, but the laws themselves are his instructors.[18]

In order for the law to convict Neaira (with Apollodoros' help), the jury must be shown two things: first, that Neaira is an alien; second, that she has "set up an oikos with Stephanos." An alien can only be guilty of xenia if he or she is posing as an Athenian—and in the case of a woman this means particularly posing as a member of an Athenian household and exercising the various responsibilities that membership entailed. Apollodoros takes up the initial part of the charge first, and here he seems on solid ground. The topic also gives him an opportunity to describe vividly and at length Neaira's disreputable character. Just as Theom-nestos went back some three decades to detail the "family" background of his prosecution, so Apollodoros also goes back to those same decades to make clear Neaira's disreputable (and improper) familial origins. Apollodoros has entered the Athenian "citizen family" properly, Neaira improperly. The case against Neaira can then be said to be a "story of two families," for the outline of which see table 1.

In the next thirty-three chapters, Apollodoros relates, in as full detail as he can muster, the life and career of the woman Neaira. The story

TABLE 1. Two Lives/Two "Families"

394 B.C.	Apollodoros, son of ex-slave Pasion, a banker, born in Athens	Neaira born, abandoned, found, and reared as prostitute by Nikarete in Corinth	390s B.C.
380s	Pasion given Athenian citizenship (extends to Apollodoros and other children)	Neaira visits Athens when still a "child" in company of Nikarete	Late 380s?
		Neaira returns to Athens with Nikarete and a client	378 (?)
376	Apollodoros comes of age		
		Neaira bought by two Corinthians from Nikarete	370s
		Neaira buys, with help of owners and clients, her own freedom	370s
		Neaira comes to Athens with Phrynion	373
		Neaira flees to Megara	372
		Neaira returns again with Stephanos to Athens (with children?)	371
370	Pasion dies; Apollodoros unhappy with settlement		
			350s ?
By 365	Apollodoros marries sister of Theomnestos	Marriages of Phano?	
By 350	Theomnestos marries his niece		
349	Apollodoros prosecuted by Stephanos	Apollodoros prosecuted by Stephanos	349
Ca. 340	Apollodoros and Theomnestos prosecute Neaira	Apollodoros and Theomnestos prosecute Neaira	Ca. 340
		??verdict??	

begins like the plot of New Comedy and continues with numerous dramatic twists and turns as well. Insofar as we know, however, the requisite "happy ending" is missing. Apparently abandoned as an infant, Neaira was reared as a slave and prostitute. But due to her own unusual combination of beauty, nerve, and determination, she managed to win for herself both freedom and a certain accepted place in Athenian society. (It is important to bear in mind that Neaira is in her fifties when the trial takes place—she is clearly a survivor.) Despite their intrinsic interest, the details of Neaira's legal and social status or of earlier litigation concerning that status are outside of the scope of this essay.[19] What seems clear, however, is that Apollodoros has no trouble establishing the first part of the charge: as he himself says, "I have, then, shown you in my argument, and the testimony of witnesses has proved, that Neaira was originally a slave, that she was twice sold, that she made her living by prostitution of her body" (49). Apollodoros can back up most of his claims with direct testimony of witnesses, many of whom can be found in the pages of Davies' *Athenian Propertied Families*—and perhaps would have appeared in the pages of Neaira's account books as well. That Neaira was a figure well-known to elite Athenian society and a resident alien with a remarkable—if, in Apollodoros' view, disreputable—past can be safely taken as proven. On the other hand, it is also possible to imagine that in the twenty years or so before the trial Neaira had settled into a more "respectable" domestic life, on the surface not so very different from that of the ordinary Athenian woman—until the moment Apollodoros "blew the whistle."

The Plot Thickens: Who Is Phano?

The establishment of alien status is not of itself sufficient to win Apollodoros' case. Neaira must be shown to be acting the part of the wife—to have formed a household with Stephanos (*sunoikein*) and to be (or have been) participating as a wife in the productive and reproductive, as well as the social and religious, activities of an Athenian household. This is clearly a more difficult task, and the argument is accordingly more slippery. Yet it is also most crucial to the success of the whole. In brief, Apollodoros argues that a certain Phano is Neaira's daughter (by an unknown father) and that Neaira and Stephanos have married her twice to Athenian citizens, as though she were Stephanos' own daughter. Apollodoros also cites a law appropriate to this situation: "If anyone shall give an alien woman in marriage to an Athenian man representing her as being related to himself, he shall lose his civic rights and his property shall be confiscated, and a third part of it shall belong to the one who secures his conviction" (52).[20]

This citation presents a puzzle: because the penalty for the action Stephanos supposedly has committed is here said to be atimia, why did not Apollodoros prosecute on this law instead of that on sunoikein—if he were simply aiming at knocking Stephanos out of the political ring? Also, what is the implication for the case as a whole that Apollodoros resorts to attacking Phano here and says nothing of Neaira's supposed sons and their entry into deme and phratry? One implication might be that in attacking the status of these children Apollodoros is not on solid ground and that he finds it more convenient to attack the female child, whose reputation could be slandered simply by association with her supposed "mother" and whose name would in any case not be found on a public register, rather than male children whose public claim to citizenship may never have been questioned and was "provable." The woman was the easier target.[21]

Apollodoros uses his "evidence" that Stephanos has wrongly married the daughter of an hetaira to an Athenian citizen in support of his contention that Neaira as mother of Phano has acted as "wife" to Stephanos. It was apparently true that Phano had been married and divorced twice, but in neither case was the husband able or willing to press a case in the public courts on the basis of the law Apollodoros quotes.[22] Phano's parentage seems to have been a matter of some confusion, but it is important to note that Apollodoros never offers either proof or testimony for his assertion that she is Neaira's daughter.

In this situation—with recalcitrant evidence and apparently some recalcitrant witnesses[23]—Apollodoros shifts upward into a higher rhetorical gear and launches into an outraged account of Phano's marital troubles and civic activities *on the assumption that she is an alien*. A further trick of the argument is the conflation of the identities of the two women—mother and "daughter"—in order to associate Neaira herself as closely as possible with the scandal and outrage (as he paints it) of the younger woman's career. I think it is fair to say that by the end of the speech Apollodoros has created a fictional two-headed monster from the combined personae of Neaira and Phano.

What is it that Phano (and vicariously then Neaira) has done? With laws again ready at hand, Apollodoros charges that Phano has twice usurped the privilege of the Athenian woman. As the wife of a somewhat inexperienced Basileus, she has shamelessly presided over the most sacred and secret (*hagia kai aporrheta*, 73) rites of Dionysos, even though the ancient law inscribed on a stele in the sanctuary of the god in Limnai required that the Basilinna be an aste and a virgin-bride (76).[24] Second, as an "adulteress" and woman of loose morals, she violated the law prohibiting such a woman from public sacrifices (87).[25] Both of these charges beg more questions than they answer: Although Phano was not the Basileus' virgin-bride, it has not been established that she was an alien. Apollodoros has simply encouraged his audience to follow his lead and his conflation of Phano's identity with that of her "mother." Even less is Phano correctly termed a *moikheuomene* (woman caught in "adultery"). According to Apollodoros, the unfortunate Epainetos of Andros was caught by Stephanos as a *moikhos* with Neaira's daughter (65),[26] and he responded by pressing charges against Stephanos for wrongful detention as a moikhos. (He thought he was in a brothel, not an Athenian oikos.) However, the peculiar private settlement of the case by which Epainetos was both ordered to contribute to Phano's dowry *and* offered her services whenever he was "in town" (71)[27] introduces some doubt about Apollodoros' veracity on this point and also some suspicion that Phano may very well have been Stephanos' own daughter. In any case, she was dowered rather than expelled, and that she was caught in "adultery" is again a rhetorical assertion rather than an established fact.

For present purposes, the reality of Phano's sacrilege or the factual basis of Epainetos' case is less important than the emotional content and ideological implications of Apollodoros' narration. The laws Apollodoros cites create a strong positive and negative image of an Athenian woman's civic responsibility, which closely connects legitimate marriage with pious worship. The pure Athenian wife becomes the bride of Dionysos himself, while the polluted adulteress is excluded from *ta hiera ta demotele*. Again, in Apollodoros' construction, the *timai* of Athenian women are epitomized in the responsibilities of the Basilinna—and analogously, for a female citizen to suffer *atimia* is to be *ekbeblemene* (outcast) from the oikia of her husband and from ta hiera of the city (86). It is no accident that Apollodoros builds his attack on these two laws—one on the Basilinna, one on the adulteress; together they present his audience (and us) with a strong demonstration of the way in which women's participation was mediated through the oikos but nonetheless highly significant in the public sphere.

Plataea and the Gift of Athenian Citizenship

Apollodoros is not sure that his audience has understood the real public danger presented by women such as Neaira and Phano or Neaira/ Phano. Therefore, in his last extended rhetorical *and* historical barrage, he demonstrates that the demos of the Athenians itself—the very jury that is listening to him—shares his understanding of the essential nature of

CYNTHIA PATTERSON

Athenian privilege or *timai*. Apollodoros, the child of a freed slave and an "adopted" Athenian citizen, wants his audience to remember the sanctity of the gift of Athenian citizenship. Thus, he recounts the story of the loyal and devoted Plataeans who risked their all for Athens and were rewarded with the gift of citizenship (being made "Athenians").[28] (The contrast with Neaira is so blatant that even Apollodoros does not feel compelled to belabor it.) But in telling at length the dramatic story of the Plataeans (one wonders how the jury stood this extended history lesson!) and in good form quoting the decree by which the Plataeans became Athenians, Apollodoros returns to the theme of marriage and religion. The Athenians thought it right to grant the Plataeans all the privileges of membership in the Athenian polis *except* for the office of archon or any priesthood (106).[29] These privileges were only extended in the next generation to those born from an Athenian woman given in marriage according to the law.[30] Thus the privilege of Athenian citizenship—given for whatever sort of good deeds, whether military, political, or economic—contained at its core the privilege of Athenian marriage and reserved participation in certain critical functions for those who entered the Athenian family by way of Athenian marriage. Thus, even a good Thucydidean military tale ends by upholding the privilege of marriage and family.

In this way, Apollodoros argues that Neaira's behavior strikes at the heart of Athenian privilege. Neaira and Phano, the extension of her mother's alien identity, have taken what even the demos does not allow itself to give, the privilege of native birth. Their fraudulent presence in Athenian households undermines the distinctions upon which the polis is based, making Athene's people indistinguishable from aliens and so corrupting and polluting public cults. In his final appeal Apollodoros calls upon the jury to imagine the rage of their female relatives if "you [have] deemed it right that this woman should share in like manner with themselves in the public ceremonials and religious rites" (*metekhein ton tes poleos kai ton hieron,* 111) and exhorts each juror to consider that he is voting in behalf of the female members of his oikos and for the polis. "I would," he charges them, "have each one of you consider that he is casting his vote, one in behalf of his wife, one of his daughter, one of his mother, and one in the interest of the polis and the laws and of religion, in order that these women may not be shown to be held in like esteem with the harlot" (114). As highly dramatic as this may be, it is more than just another rhetorical flourish on the theme of family feeling. The *teletai* and *hiera* and *timai* that Neaira (and Phano) have usurped belong properly to Athenian women and men: these are deeply felt issues bearing directly on the core of that privilege which is Athenian citizenship—sharing as an Athenian in the polis of Athens.

By the end of his oration Apollodoros has created a vivid image of the proper and improper family and household in Athenian society, as he calls upon the jurors to punish this woman who "treats the city with outrage and the gods with impiety." He has by then to some extent lost sight of the real Neaira and the real Phano. (The verdict is unknown—and even further out of reach is the true identity of Phano.) But whatever the truth of the matter—and it is clear that Stephanos was equipped with his own depositions and witnesses—the ideological force and importance of Apollodoros' argument is, in its main lines, clear and revealing. The values of legitimacy and marriage extend from the private into the public realm and are embedded in a public ideology underpinning the classical Athenian democracy. Marriage is a key element in the public ideology of Athens because it brings, through the oikos it creates, access to privilege and responsibilities in the public realm.

So, if we are attempting to reconstruct the civic ideology of Athens— the web of values, beliefs, principles, and attitudes underpinning the Athenian democracy—we should put at its center the relationship of legitimate marriage and the civic legitimacy that marriage creates. The function and political importance of marriage is a persistent theme of both the legal and the dramatic stage. According to Aeschylus' Apollon, marriage was (ideologically speaking) "stronger than oaths and guarded by the right of nature."[31] To the Athenian audience, whether in the theater or the law court, marriage represented the first political bond of the polis and was a potent symbol of the political order. Therefore, we should not neglect the clear public significance of family identity in classical Athens, nor the ways in which the rules of marriage and legitimacy illuminate the nature of both male and female participation in the Athenian polis.

Notes

1. See Pearson 1966.
2. Momigliano 1983, 136.
3. MacDowell 1989, 10–21, e.g., argues that the essential and formal meaning of oikos is "property" (oikos as referring to persons is then informal or nontechnical) and concludes with the comment: "Athenian law did not recognize rights of families but rights of individuals" (p. 21).

Two recent treatises on Athenian democracy that emphasize the political and social agency of the (male) individual are Ober 1989 and Hansen 1991. While not denying the importance of individual male actors in Athenian history or the political institutions through which they acted, I do think that the different conceptual bases of the Weberian "rational" city (represented in quite different ways by both Ober and Hansen) and the Durkheimian "holistic" city with its emphasis on community and communal experience (see Murray 1990; Scafuro's introduction in this volume) need to be recognized and evaluated.

4. Note, e.g., the neglect or partial neglect in Bury 1902, 172; Sealey 1976, 223. One author who does call attention to this episode of the Persian Wars is Mahaffy 1874—writing at a time of intense interest in the possibility of moral progress and the evolution of human society. He cites the incident as commentary on his own statement that "we have ample evidence in our own day, how nations as civilised as, and far more humane than, the Greeks become cruel not only through revenge, but more inevitably through fear"—but ends by affirming that "such conduct was rare among Athenians at any epoch" (p. 166 and n. 1).

5. τοὐρανοῦ γάρ μοι μέτεστι· καὶ γὰρ ἄνδρας ἐσφέρω. *Lysistrata* 651.

6. See, for example, the authoritative analysis of Davies 1977. Note also references to the "latent" citizenship of women (Sealey 1990, 14).

7. See Patterson 1986 for discussion of the terminology of Athenian citizenship and its implications for female citizenship.

8. Ste. Croix 1981, 99–101. On the question of women's property rights, which Ste. Croix discussed initially in 1970 (Ste. Croix 1970), see Foxhall 1989.

9. Contrary to popular perceptions, Athens was not a strictly patrilinear society in which property rights only descended through—or were restricted to—men. Inheritance of both property and civic status devolved to and through women as well as men; matrilinear as well as patrilinear kin were included in the inheritance network (the *ankhisteia*); and women themselves ought to be recognized as real heirs even if under the legal guardianship of a male relative. See Harrison 1968, 142–49 *with* Foxhall 1989.

10. The quarrel of these modern "heroes" driving Cadillac chariots escalates from a simple "fender bender" accident to the seduction of the rival's wife. Cf. the discussion of this motif in Cohen 1991, 168–69.

11. For the significance of this term in relation to marriage, see Patterson 1991.

12. Presumably a guilty verdict would open the way to further attacks on the citizen status of the sons and on Stephanos' own conduct; e.g., his giving Phano in marriage as though she were his own daughter.

13. For the legal details of this case, see Hansen, 1976. For a political reading of the suit, see Macurdy 1942.

14. . . . καὶ ἐγὼ τοῦτον ἥκω ἐπιδείξων εἰς ὑμᾶς, ξένηι μὲν γυναικὶ συνοικοῦντα παρὰ τὸν νόμον, ἀλλοτρίους δὲ παῖδας εἰσαγαγόντα εἴς τε τοὺς φράτερας καὶ εἰς τοὺς δημότας, ἐγγυῶντα δὲ τὰς τῶν ἑταιρῶν θυγατέρας ὡς αὑτοῦ οὔσας, ἠσεβηκότα δ' εἰς τοὺς θεούς, ἄκυρον δὲ ποιοῦντα τὸν δῆμον τῶν αὑτοῦ, ἄν τινα βούληται πολίτην ποιήσασθαι (13).

Unless otherwise noted, translations of passages from "Against Neaera" are those of the Loeb text with slight modification.

15. On Apollodoros' considerable experience in the courts, see Pearson 1966 and orations 46, 49–50, 52–53 of the Demosthenic corpus.

16. Ἐὰν δὲ ξένος ἀστῆι συνοικῆι τέχνηι ἢ μηχανῆι ἡιτινιοῦν, γραφέσθω πρὸς τοὺς θεσμοθέτας Ἀθηναίων ὁ βουλόμενος οἷς ἔξεστιν. ἐὰν δὲ ἁλῶι πεπράσθω καὶ αὐτὸς καὶ ἡ οὐσία αὐτοῦ, καὶ τὸ τρίτον μέρος ἔστω τοῦ ἑλόντος. ἔστω δὲ καὶ ἐὰν ἡ ξένη τῶι ἀστῶι συνοικῆι κατὰ ταὐτά, καὶ ὁ συνοικῶν τῆι ξένηι τῆι ἁλούσηι ὀφειλέτω χιλίας δραχμάς (16).

I do not consider here the problem of the authenticity of this (and other) laws and documents inserted into the text. Cf. the recent comments of Humphreys 1985b, 316–17, on this question with reference to the classic discussion of Drerup 1898 on this speech.

17. Citation of law in the Athenian courts was itself a rhetorical strategy (see Aristotle's discussion in the *Rhetoric* of how to use laws as "evidence," 1375a–b). Cf. Humphreys 1985a.

18. Cf. Plato *Crito* 50c–d (the Laws to Sokrates): "Did we not, first, bring you to birth, and was it not through us that your father married your mother and begat you?" (trans. Grube).

19. The speech throws interesting light on, in particular, the private arbitration or reconciliation procedures in Athens, which seem to aim at satisfaction of all parties at the expense of strict legality or even consistency. So in one arbitration Neaira is declared to be free and *kuria hautes* but nonetheless will be "shared" by the two men claiming her (46), and in another Epainetos is both required to give Phano a dowry and (if we trust the document inserted into the speech, see n. 16 above) assured that she will be available to him whenever he is "in town" (70–71). For discussion of these procedures, see Scafuro (n.d.).

20. Ἐὰν δέ τις ἐκδῶι ξένην γυναῖκα ἀνδρὶ Ἀθηναίωι ὡς ἑαυτῶι προσήκουσαν, ἄτιμος ἔστω, καὶ ἡ οὐσία αὐτοῦ δημοσία ἔστω, καὶ τοῦ ἑλόντος τὸ τρίτον μέρος (52).

21. For discussion of the strategies and problems inherent in "proving" citizen status, see Scafuro's essay in this volume.

22. Note that Apollodoros asserts that Neaira's sons—Proxenos, Ariston, and Antidorides—were also fraudulently entered upon the citizen registers (38 and 121). Yet he offers no evidence to suggest that the citizen privileges of these men were ever questioned.

23. Note that Theogenes, Phano's second husband, seems to have been "forced" to testify—or so we are told by Apollodoros: καὶ ὅτι ταῦτ' ἀληθῆ λέγω, τούτων ὑμῖν μάρτυρα αὐτὸν τὸν Θεογένην καλῶ, καὶ ἀναγκάσω μαρτυρεῖν (84).

24. According to Apollodoros, the law was inscribed in Attic script and nearly effaced (καὶ αὕτη ἡ στήλη ἔτι καὶ νῦν ἔστηκεν, ἀμυδροῖς γράμμασιν Ἀττικοῖς δηλοῦσα τὰ γεγραμμένα, 76). Was it possibly obsolete? This particular stele seems to have been overlooked by Thomas 1989.

25. I use the term "adulteress" with quotation marks to avoid here the issue of the precise meaning and extent of reference of the noun *moikhos* and the verb *moikheuein*. Although these terms had strong popular associations in classical Athens with the violation of marital relations (see Cohen 1991, 107–8), it is not clear that they could *only* refer to adultery in its modern sense. The fact that Stephanos claimed to have caught Epainetos as a moikhos with Phano

might indeed be taken as evidence *against* reading *moikheia* as adultery, for Phano was not married at the time. However, it can also be argued that part of the "plot" as Apollodoros describes it included the claim that Phano was an Athenian matron within the protective sphere of the laws of adultery (in its modern sense). Note in this connection Apollodoros' reference to the punishment of the adulterous wife in 85–86. Also relevant is the way in which Apollodoros tells this story or attributes this "plot" to Stephanos and Neaira herself earlier in the oration (41–42), thus further conflating the identities of the two women. For opposing views on the meaning of moikheia and for specific discussion of this episode, see Cohen 1991, 108–9, who argues for the narrow meaning, and Cantarella (1991), Foxhall (1991), and Scafuro (n.d.), who all argue in different ways for a more expanded meaning.

26. λαμβάνει μοιχὸν ἐπὶ τῆι θυγατρὶ τῆι Νεαίρας ταυτησί (65).

27. See n. 19 above.

28. In this extended historical digression, usually ignored in discussions of the orators' use of history, Apollodoros shows a remarkable familiarity with Thucydides' account in books 2 and 3.

29. μὴ ἐξεῖναι αὐτῶν μηδενὶ τῶν ἐννέα ἀρχόντων λαχεῖν μηδὲ ἱερωσύνης μηδεμιᾶς, τοῖς δ' ἐκ τούτων, ἂν ὦσιν ἐξ ἀστῆς γυναικὸς καὶ ἐγγυητῆς κατὰ τὸν νόμον (106).

In the law (or "decree about the Plaetaeans") inserted into the text (104), the prohibition against holding religious office is limited to those held ἐκ γένους— on the basis of family membership (e.g., position of priestess of Athene Polias held by women from the *genos* of the Eteoboutadai).

30. An interesting question arises over the status of Apollodoros' own mother, Arkhippe, and that of her two marriages to Pasion and then Phormio. Did Arkhippe become a citizen or remain an alien when her husband Pasion was given Athenian citizenship? And if she did become a citizen, was her second marriage to Phormion (an alien) legal? Whitehead 1986 argues on the basis of this case for an Athenian tolerance of some ambiguity in female citizenship, particularly that of wives of enfranchised aliens. In response, Carey 1991 argues that Arkhippe remained an alien throughout her various marriages—and fell to the status of mistress when Pasion became a citizen.

31. ἐυνὴ γὰρ ἀνδρὶ καὶ γυναικὶ μόρισμος / ὅρκου 'στὶ μείζων τῆι δίκηι φρουρουμένη. *Eumenides* 217–18, trans. Lattimore. These interesting words (about which more could be said) strongly underline the political significance of the "marriage bed," as well as its ideological position at the intersection of the public and private realms. On the interconnections of private and public morality, see Cohen 1991.

Works Cited

Bury, J. B. 1902. *A History of Greece to the Death of Alexander the Great.* London: MacMillan.

Cantarella, Eva. 1991. "Moicheia: Reconsidering a Problem." In *Symposium*

1990: Papers on Greek and Hellenistic Legal History, edited by Michael Gagarin, 289–96. Köln: Böhlau Verlag.

Carey, C. 1991. "Apollodoros' Mother: The Wives of Enfranchised Aliens in Athens." *CQ* 41:84–89.

Cohen, David. 1991. *Law, Sexuality and Society: The Enforcement of Morals in Classical Athens.* Cambridge: Cambridge University Press.

Davies, John K. 1971. *Athenian Propertied Families, 600–300 B.C.* Oxford: Oxford University Press.

———. 1977. "Athenian Citizenship: The Descent Group and Alternatives." *CJ* 73:105–21.

Drerup, E. 1898. "Über die bei den attischen Rednern eingelegten Urkunden." *Jahr. für Cl. Phil.* 24:221–366.

Foxhall, Lin. 1989. "Household, Gender and Property in Classical Athens." *CQ* 39:22–44.

———. 1991. "Response to Eva Cantarella." In *Symposium 1990: Papers on Greek and Hellenistic Legal History,* edited by Michael Gagarin, 297–303. Köln: Böhlau Verlag.

Hansen, Mogens H. 1976. "The Theoric Fund and the *graphe paranomon* against Apollodorus." *GRBS* 17:235–46.

———. 1991. *The Athenian Democracy in the Age of Demosthenes: Structure, Principles, and Ideology.* Oxford: Basil Blackwell.

Harrison, A. H. R. 1968. *The Law of Athens.* Vol. 1, *The Family and Property.* Oxford: Oxford University Press.

Humphreys, Sally C. 1985. "Social Relations on Stage: Witnesses in Classical Athens." *History and Anthropology* 1:316–17.

MacDowell, Douglas M. 1989. "The Oikos in Athenian Law." *CQ* 39:10–21.

Macurdy, G. 1942. "Apollodorus and the Speech against Neaera." *AJP* 63:257–71.

Mahaffy, J. P. 1874. *Social Life in Greece from Homer to Menander.* London: MacMillan.

Momigliano, Arnaldo. 1983. "Fustel de Coulanges, *The Ancient City.*" In *The Family, Women, and Death,* edited by S. C. Humphreys, 131–36. London: Routledge and Kegan Paul.

Murray, Oswyn. 1990. "Cities of Reason." In *The Greek City: From Homer to Alexander,* edited by O. Murray and S. Price, 1–25. Oxford: Clarendon Press.

Ober, Josiah. 1989. *Mass and Elite in Democratic Athens: Rhetoric, Ideology, and the Power of the People.* Princeton: Princeton University Press.

Patterson, Cynthia. 1986. "Hai Attikai: The Other Athenians." *Helios* 13:49–67.

———. 1991. "Marriage and the Married Woman in Athenian Law." In *Ancient History/Ancient Women,* edited by S. B. Pomeroy, 48–72. Chapel Hill: University of North Carolina Press.

Pearson, Lionel. 1966. "Apollodorus, the Eleventh Attic Orator." In *The Classical Tradition,* edited by L. Wallach, 347–59. Ithaca: Cornell University Press.

Ste. Croix, Geoffrey E. M. de. 1970. "Some Observations on the Property Rights of Athenian Women." *CR* 84:273–78.

———. 1981. *The Class Struggle in the Ancient Greek World.* Ithaca: Cornell University Press.

Scafuro, Adele. n.d. *The Forensic Stage: Settling Disputes in Graeco-Roman New Comedy.* Cambridge: Cambridge University Press. Forthcoming.

Sealey, Raphael. 1976. *A History of the Greek City States, ca. 700–338 B.C.* Berkeley: University of California Press.

———. 1990. *Women and Law in Classical Greece.* Chapel Hill: University of North Carolina Press.

Thomas, Rosalind. 1989. *Oral Tradition and Written Record in Classical Athens.* Cambridge: Cambridge University Press.

Whitehead, David. 1986. "Women and Naturalisation in Fourth-Century Athens: The Case of Archippe." *CQ* 36:109–14.

Premarital Sex, Illegitimacy, and Male Anxiety in Menander and Athens

DAVID KONSTAN

Menander's *Epitrepontes* (*Arbitrants*) provides a unique glimpse into the nature of male anxiety in classical Greece over the premarital sexual experience of women. The evidence of this comedy fits with certain other practices and beliefs specific to Greek antiquity, which may in turn shed further light on the attitudes of Athenian males toward women, and more specifically wives, who have had premarital sexual experience. While act 1 of the *Epitrepontes* is severely mutilated, it is evident from scraps and fragments that the opening of the play dramatized the essential facts of Kharisios' estrangement from his wife, Pamphile.[1] Five months after their marriage, while Kharisios was away on a business trip, Pamphile bore a child, which she exposed with the assistance of her nurse. Onesimos, a slave of Kharisios, has informed his master of Pamphile's actions, with the result that Kharisios has abandoned his own home and taken residence at the house of his friend and neighbor Khairestratos, where he has, in addition, hired a courtesan named Habrotonon at twelve drakhmai a day to entertain and distract him (136–37).[2] Humor is provided by Pamphile's father, Smikrines, a miserly codger who arrives on the scene to complain equally about the plight of his daughter and the extravagance of Kharisios' entertainments.

In act 2, we learn that a slave shepherd named Daos has found the exposed infant and taken it home to rear, along with a necklace and other keepsakes adorning it. But the baby proves burdensome, and Daos gladly hands it over to a charcoal burner and slave of Khairestratos, Syriskos (or Syros) by name, who is eager to raise it, for he and his wife have but recently lost a child of their own. Later, Syriskos learns that Daos has retained possession of the trinkets left with the abandoned baby and demands them as the property of the child. Daos claims them as his own lucky find, and the two slaves turn to a bystander, who happens to be Pamphile's father, Smikrines, in order to arbitrate the issue (it is this scene that gives the play its title). Among other arguments, Syriskos appeals to the possibility that the jewelry may serve as recognition tokens (*gnorismata*, 303, 331, 341), citing mythological exempla to corroborate that exposed children have been rescued from humble obscurity and restored to their original free status thanks to items of this sort. An audience familiar with the conventions of New Comedy will have readily perceived that the tokens will serve just such a purpose in this case as well, and may also infer, if the facts have not already been set forth in a prologue (none survives), that the baby in question is none other than the child of Pamphile and, indeed, of Kharisios as well. That Smikrines, the child's grandfather, is judging the case adds an elegant touch of irony. Smikrines decides in favor of Syriskos, and before he exits he makes sure that the grumbling Daos hands over the ornaments.

Alone with his wife, Syriskos inspects the jewelry and has just begun examining an engraved ring as Onesimos, Kharisios' slave, comes on stage. Onesimos identifies the ring as belonging to his master and snatches it away. Both men enter Khairestratos' house, with the intention of putting the matter before Kharisios on the following day. However, Onesimos shrinks from showing his master the ring, because he fears it will stir up Kharisios' regrets over the separation from his wife, for which he is inclined to blame Onesimos' tattling; Onesimos even hints at the possibility of a reconciliation between husband and wife that would leave him out in the cold (425–27). When Syriskos takes him to task for stalling, Onesimos explains how Kharisios lost the ring at a nighttime women's festival, and surmises that he must have raped the girl who was the mother of the exposed child and who left the ring among the trinkets in its possession.

The problem is that the girl is unknown. However, the courtesan Habrotonon has overheard the conversation and reveals that she chanced to witness just such an assault at the very same festival, among a group of girls she was attending as a cithara player. She is confident she can recognize the unfortunate woman, who was of a wealthy family, and counsels Onesimos to make a clean breast of it with Kharisios, because if the mother of the child is of free status, there will be no cause for concealing the event (495–96). As Gomme and Sandbach explain, "Habrotonon will have it in mind that he might wish to repudiate Pamphile . . . and marry the other girl, obtaining what was always important to a Greek, a male heir" (ad 495–96; cf. 568–71, where Onesimos speculates along just these lines). However, Habrotonon declines to help find the girl as long as she is uncertain of the identity of her attacker. While she accepts that the ring is Kharisios', she has no way of being sure that he had not lent or lost it to some other man who then committed the rape, and she does not wish to upset the girl's family in such ambiguous circumstances. Instead, she proposes to wear the ring herself in the presence of Kharisios, and then pretend that it was she who was raped and who seized the ring on the fateful night. If Kharisios confesses to the deed, then will be the time to seek out the true mother. Act 3 ends with Smikrines still grumbling about the goings-on at Khairestratos' house—he seems to believe that his son-in-law has had a child by Habrotonon—and threatening vaguely to take his daughter home with him, dissolving the marriage with Kharisios (cf. Gomme and Sandbach [1973] ad 615–21, 632 ff., 637).

We come now to the crucial scenes. Smikrines pleads with his daughter to leave Kharisios, but Pamphile, in a badly damaged passage, defends her loyalty to her husband.[3] Habrotonon then emerges with the baby and recognizes Pamphile as the woman who was raped at the night festival (859–60), while Pamphile simultaneously notices a familiar token on the infant (865–66). Because Habrotonon has securely identified Kharisios as the father of the child, the women are now aware of its true parentage, and Habrotonon leads Pamphile indoors in order to go over the story in detail. At this point, Onesimos bursts on stage, excitedly remarking on his master's irrational behavior. I shall quote his monologue *in extenso,* along with that of Kharisios which follows, because they contain the nub of the issue we are considering. The translation is that of Geoffrey Arnott in the Loeb Library edition (the text of Arnott is identical here with that of Sandbach).[4] Onesimos explains that Kharisios overheard the dialogue between Pamphile and her father, and as he listened:

> "O my love, to speak
> Such words," he cried, and punched himself hard on
> His head.
>
> (898–90)

Onesimos continues reporting the reactions of his master:

> "What a wife
> I've married, and I'm in this wretched mess!"
> When finally he'd heard the whole tale out,
> He fled indoors. Then—wailing, tearing of
> Hair, raging lunacy within. He went
> On saying, "Look at me, the villain. I
> Myself commit a crime like this, and am
> The father of a bastard child. Yet I

Felt not a scrap of mercy, showed none to
That woman in the same sad fortune. I'm
A heartless brute." Fiercely he damns himself,
Eyes bloodshot, overwrought.

(890–900)

Onesimos is again in terror that Kharisios will hold him to blame for denouncing Pamphile, and he withdraws as Kharisios himself emerges. I quote his words up to the point at which the text becomes too mutilated to follow:

A faultless man, eyes fixed on his good name,
A judge of what is right and what is wrong
In his own life pure and beyond reproach—
My image, which some power above has well
And quite correctly shattered. Here I showed
That I was human. "Wretched worm {Kharisios imagines the *daimonion* saying}, in pose
And talk so bumptious, you won't tolerate
A woman's forced misfortune. I shall show
That you have stumbled just the same yourself.
Then *she* will treat you tenderly, while *you*
Insult her. You'll appear unlucky, rude,
A heartless brute, too, all at once." {Then in his own voice:} Did she
Address her father then [as] you'd have done?
"I'm here," [she said (?)], "to share his life. Mishaps
Occur. I mustn't run away." {To himself:} You're too Superior [

(908–22)

Kharisios' speech has appeared remarkable, and rightly so, I believe, for the way in which he seems here to judge himself by the same standard he has applied to Pamphile and has found himself wanting in humanity. Some scholars have seen in Kharisios' attitude a sign of Menander's self-conscious feminism. Thus P. Fossataro, writing in 1915: "It is a feminist thesis: a lapse in a woman must not be judged according to a different norm from a sensual offense on the part of a man."[5] And again, K. Stavenhagen, in a seminal article published in 1910: "Here for the first time a man treats his transgression as standing on the same plane as the fault of a girl."[6] Dario del Corno remarks in his edition and translation of the plays of Menander (1966): "In an ethical sense, the real resolution, in fact, of the crisis occurs when Kharisios decides to return to his wife while he is still in ignorance of the happy twist of fortune that has intended that the child that she conceived should be his own."[7]

In his 1925 edition of the play, Wilamowitz adopts a more sober tone: "A few generations ago, one would have asked about his [i.e., Menander's] meaning and have found it no doubt in this, that man and woman are measured pretty much by the same gauge. . . . But Kharisios draws no universally valid conclusion whatsoever [concerning the similarity of his situation to that of his wife], and we are not inclined to ask how he would have turned out in the long run, if he had had to forgive his wife a real fault."[8]

Other critics, however, have challenged the idea that there is anything resembling an egalitarian stance in Kharisios' self-reproach. Thus, Alain Blanchard, in 1983: "What used to be seen in the *Arbitration* was the expression of a feminist thesis: a fault in a woman must not be judged in a different manner from one in a man. Strange feminism, when one knows that Kharisios' fault is to have violated in the past the woman who subsequently became his wife, while the fault of the latter is simply the misfortune of having been violated."[9]

The crux of the matter has turned on Kharisios' conception of himself as the victim of misfortune (*atukhema*), as in the lines that he puts in the mouth of his imaginary *daimonion:* "You won't tolerate a woman's [*or* your wife's] forced misfortune [*akousion atukhema*]. I shall show that you have stumbled just the same yourself [*eis homoi' eptaikota*, literally: have stumbled into the same things or situation]" (914–15). Thus Wilamowitz (commenting on l. 918 in Sandbach's numeration) remarks: "It was considered very much from the man's point of view, since his guilt was supposed to be merely an *atukhema*, which is what had really happened to Pamphile."[10] Earlier, Kharisios speaks of his own wretched misfortune (*etukheka*, 891), though he has so fine a wife (Arnott translates: "I'm in this wretched mess"), and he then berates himself for hardheartedness toward "that woman in the same sad misfortune" (*atukhousei taut' ekeinei*, 898); that is, as his own. Edward Capps comments (1910): "Pamphile was the victim of the same outrage that he had committed—as he supposes—, upon another girl," in an apparent attempt to exonerate Kharisios at least here from his habit of self-exculpation by importing, quite gratuitously, a reference to the fortune of the girl he thinks he has raped.

Sandbach takes a sterner view. Of the first passage, he remarks (ad 891): "Probably *atukhein* is here used euphemistically for *harmatanein* ['to err']"; that is, Kharisios tries to gloss over his offense as a mere accident. Indeed, Kalbfleisch conjectured *edikeka* ["I committed a crime"] here, comparing fr. adesp. 221 Kock, and this was endorsed by Körte (see Sandbach 1990). Sandbach notes: "It gives something which Charisios might have said, if he had not preferred to say *etukheka*." Of the second passage, Sandbach observes (ad 898): "Again the euphemistic use of *atukhein* may be present. Charisios can conceive of his crime in getting Habrotonon with child (as he thinks) as an *atukhema:* whereas Pamphile had no responsibility for her motherhood, which was an *atukhema* in the proper sense of the word." Finally, on the passage that we mentioned first, Sandbach notes (ad 915, on the word *eptaikota*): " 'To have stumbled'; Charisios must use a somewhat euphemistic word since he is representing himself, as he did in 898, as being in the same position as his wife. He had had bad luck, like her, and she, as appears in 921, was prepared to treat his situation as a misfortune, not a crime."

Menander was perfectly well aware of the difference between an *atukhema* and an *adikema, as* frag. 359 Körte-Thierfelder clearly demonstrates ("There is a difference between a misfortune [*atukhema*] and a crime [*adikema*]: the one occurs by accident [*dia tukhen*], the other by choice"), and a suggestion on the part of Kharisios, that his rape of a woman was an "involuntary misfortune," sounds not so much euphemistic as downright hypocritical.[11] But is this what Kharisios is claiming? Let us look once again at his words, as quoted by Onesimos; I translate ll. 895–98 literally: "Having done such a deed myself, and become the father of a bastard child (*paidiou nothou*), I did not have or give a portion of forgiveness to her who was unfortunate in this same respect." Kharisios is comparing his situation as the father of a *nothos* (bastard), as he supposes, with that of Pamphile, who gave birth to a child as a result of the rape.[12] This is the misfortune of which he speaks, both in reference to her plight and to his own. Throughout, *atukhein* and *atukhema* refer to the circumstance of producing an illegitimate offspring, and this can, both in the case of Pamphile and of Kharisios himself, be described perfectly reasonably as an unintended piece of bad luck.

Indeed, Kharisios cannot very well mean at this point in the play to compare his rape of Habrotonon, as he supposes, with the fact that Pamphile has been raped. After all, he has known from the very beginning that he had raped *someone,* and there is no reason why at this moment he should suddenly be moved to recognize the analogy between his wife's circumstance as a victim of sexual violence and his own active commission of the very same crime.[13] Besides, the entire complicated plot of this play seems to have been constructed precisely in order to bring about the relatively unusual situation in which Kharisios knows (1) that his wife has borne a nothos, and (2) that he has been responsible for the birth of a nothos, without however yet being aware (3) that the two nothoi are one and the same.[14] This is the consequence of the extraordinary maneuver by which Habrotonon pretends that the baby is hers, on the grounds that she wants to be absolutely sure that Kharisios, rather than someone else who had somehow acquired his ring, was the author of the rape. The action seems organized just in order to allow Kharisios to recognize the identity of circumstance between his wife and himself in the fact of their both being parents of an illegitimate child, and his monologue is indeed, as del Corno observed, the ethical climax of the plot.

If this, however, is the plain meaning of the text, and if in addition the focus on the nothos both follows from the structure of the story and makes clear sense of the repeated use of the expression *atukhema* in reference to Kharisios as well as to Pamphile, why have so many excellent scholars missed the point and taken Kharisios' words as at best a self-exculpating euphemism for the act of rape? I think we can venture a plausible answer to this question. At the beginning of the play, Kharisios abandoned his wife because he had found out what had befallen her; in act 4, he perceives that he is in the same boat and prepares to return to her. If he left Pamphile because she had been sexually violated, then the reason why he subsequently changes his mind must be that he has come to take a more charitable view of such a misfortune in a woman, and this will be the result of reflection on his own wanton behavior. Whatever pain it causes him to think that she has been tainted by a prior sexual experience, he manages forgiveness because he can see his own responsibility as an aggressor. Such is the logic that has induced critics to read Kharisios' change of heart as a new-found capacity, however transient, to accept his wife despite her violated condition, a capacity that is helped along by the equation, albeit self-serving, of her experience with his own violent action in the past as involuntary misfortunes.

This line of reasoning is sound enough, if Kharisios can be said to have deserted his home because Pamphile had been raped. But was this his reason? Because the reversal in the drama centers on Kharisios' recognition that Pamphile's misfortune is analogous to his own, and that this misfortune is precisely that of having been responsible for the birth of a nothos, it is reasonable to suppose that the problem corresponds to the solution, and that Kharisios left his wife not because she had been raped as such, but rather because she had produced a bastard child, which is, after all, exactly what he learned from his slave Onesimos. If we understand that it is the fact of a nothos that moved Kharisios to abandon Pamphile, the climactic scene as we have interpreted it makes perfect sense. What is more, Kharisios' capacity to see the equivalence between his wife's misfortune in producing an illegitimate child and his own case no longer appears as a dishonest evasion of his responsibility for rape, but

DAVID KONSTAN

rather as an extraordinary rejection of the usual Athenian double standard for women and men in the sphere of sex and reproduction. On this
reading, then, we may recover a sense of the feminist or at least sexually
egalitarian implications of *Epitrepontes* that Stavenhagen and Fossataro
perceived, although their failure to distinguish the question of rape or
penetration from that of illegitimacy left Kharisios' great speech, with its
comparison between Pamphile's misfortune and his own, open to an
ironic interpretation.

I have been arguing that the issue between Kharisios and Pamphile in
Epitrepontes is that Pamphile has produced a nothos, not simply that she
has been violated. It is the child, and not the idea, for example, that
Pamphile has been polluted or contaminated by the sexual assault, that
causes Kharisios anguish in the first instance, and he is obliged to examine his reaction when he learns that he also is responsible for the birth of a
bastard. I am suggesting further that modern readers have mistakenly
ascribed to Kharisios a motive that is not his; namely, an anxiety that
centers upon sex rather than childbirth and legitimacy and that views a
woman who has had any kind of premarital sexual experience, whether
voluntary or not, as marred or corrupted. On the evidence of *Epitrepontes,* it seems to me that this was not how Menander expected his
Greek audience to respond. Rather, the hero's feelings about the premarital assault on his wife constellate precisely around the issue of children
and legitimacy. Anxieties about "damaged goods" and the like are irrelevant to his motivation.

Why critics today should have assumed that Kharisios or Menander
would be concerned primarily with the rape and sexual penetration of
Pamphile, rather than with the issue of a nothos, I shall not speculate
about here, save to say that it probably has to do with the nature of
contemporary male anxiety over women's sexuality, which is not entirely
congruent with the classical Athenian structure of feeling.[15] We may,
however, pursue further some of the implications of the interpretation I
have offered of Kharisios' motives in rejecting Pamphile.

To begin with, I wish to be clear about what I am not claiming. I do
not mean to suggest that Kharisios would be indifferent to the news that
his wife had had premarital sexual experience, even if it did not eventuate
in the production of a child. If, for example, he had learned that Pamphile
had conceived a passionate erotic attachment to a man which had culmi-
nated in sexual intercourse, he might have been troubled by this knowledge, even to the extent of rejecting her as his wife. Such a scenario is
irrelevant to Menander and to New Comedy in general, which never
ascribes *eros* or amatory passion to a citizen girl. Kharisios does not
wonder whether Pamphile sought out or enjoyed sex; it is not for him to

infer that a woman who has been raped was somehow inviting it. Pamphile reacted to the assault with tears, and tearing her hair, according to Habrotonon (487–88), and this response is typical in New Comedy (e.g., Terence's *Eunuch* 645–46, 820, based on a Menandrean original). Was Kharisios, then, wholly indifferent to the violation itself, apart from the consequence of the birth of an illegitimate child? It is impossible to know. What we can say is that the issue of the child is what is central to the play, and it displaces in Kharisios' mind any consideration of her technical virginity at the time of marriage.

In a way, it is not entirely surprising that the matter of the nothos should be of primary interest in the play. As many historians have argued in recent years, Greek law and custom seem to have been concerned above all to preserve the integrity of citizen households, in the first instance by insuring the legitimacy of the heirs. At least since Perikles' legislation of 451, it was necessary that a child be the offspring of two citizen parents (that is, an *astos* and an *aste*) in order to inherit, and the Greek idea of the nothos has to do not so much with our modern sense of illegitimacy as pertaining to a child borne out of legal wedlock, but refers rather to the status of the parents.[16] As long as the woman raped by Kharisios proves to be a citizen, the child will be *gnesios* (legitimate) rather than a nothos (at all events once the parents are wed and the child is acknowledged), irrespective of whether she turns out to be Pamphile or some other woman, as the play itself makes quite clear. Correspondingly, the reason why Kharisios believes that he has fathered a nothos is that Habrotonon is not an Athenian citizen, rather than that she is not his wife. In this context, then, it may seem natural that male feelings concerning the suitability of a citizen girl as wife, if she has been raped prior to marriage, should focus on the production of a child, whose status will, of course, be dubious. We may say that Kharisios seems to have internalized just the set of responses necessary to sustain and reproduce the social code that sought to guarantee the citizen line and its exclusive access to landed property.[17]

This sounds reasonable, and perhaps it is, but we must observe that Kharisios is not moved simply by a transparent desire to preserve the citizen status of his posterity. After all, he knows that Pamphile has exposed the child, and he has no reason to suspect that it will survive or be recognized as hers. Even if it were, he would not be obliged to treat it as his child, and it would be barred from inheriting in any case, for its father was unknown. I am suggesting that Kharisios' decision to leave Pamphile is not a gesture that sustains in some direct rational way the structure of the Athenian city-state as a closed consanguineous group. Whatever the nature of Kharisios' sentiment in rejecting his wife, it is manifestly in excess of what is required if we look to the preservation of the social code alone.

This does not mean that there is no connection between Kharisios' motives and the values of the city-state. I would offer as a general rule the proposition that there is always and necessarily a gap between the rules of a social system (or some particular formulation of these rules) and the ways in which those constraints (or at least some of them) are internalized and enter into a structure of anxieties and compulsions that motivate individuals in particular circumstances. Social codes are reproduced in a mediated way, processed through a thoroughly psychologized set of desires and inhibitions that ultimately reproduce, more or less efficiently and exactly, the system in which they are generated, but never correspond directly to the social imperatives. It is precisely in this space between society as a system of relations and the structure of motives that drive each individual that we may, perhaps, locate the play of ideology, which marks a dissonance or distance between the way society works and the way it presents itself to the subject's consciousness.[18] Kharisios was not worried for the purity of his line when he abandoned Pamphile. He was horrified at the thought that she had borne a nothos, and if this served, in the last analysis, to sustain the oikos system of Athens, it was, as far as Kharisios himself was concerned, an incidental consequence, and not apprehended as a personal motive.

Again, we ought not to be entirely surprised, perhaps, if a preoccupation with physical virginity that has peculiarly characterized our own society for at least a century was not equally central to another, and that this anxiety is not, accordingly, represented as the primary ingredient in Kharisios' motivation for rejecting his wife. We may remark, for example, that the Greek term *parthenos,* commonly translated "virgin," does not mean quite the same thing as the English noun. Rather, *parthenos* indicates in many contexts something like a social status, that of an unmarried girl, whose position will change to that of woman or *gune* at the time when she is given over to the authority of a citizen husband with the intention of producing children who are lawful heirs. A woman who had been raped might nevertheless be referred to as a parthenos, because she had not made the proper transition to the condition of gune. Thus, the poetic hypothesis to Menander's *Heros* informs us that "a *parthenos,* having borne a male and female child together, gave them to a guardian to rear, then later married the man who had violated her" (1–3). There is no suggestion here of a virgin birth, of course; *parthenos* means an unwed citizen girl.[19] Virginity in the modern sense was not the unique referent of the term most commonly employed to denote a maiden.

The Greeks in classical antiquity seem not to have known of the existence of the hymen in women. Bleeding at the occasion of a woman's first experience of intercourse was explained as a result of the readier flow of menstrual blood, which was partly blocked by the narrowness of the vaginal channel, until it was widened by penetration.[20] There was, accordingly, no tradition of exposing the wedding linens, or of digital testing, in order to determine the virginity of a bride. Greek popular beliefs, then, may not have focused so narrowly on physical virginity as modern attitudes might suggest.

If a Greek girl had been violated, the chief evidence would be, in the normal course of affairs, the birth of a child, since her family, and especially the women who would be most likely to be informed of the matter, would doubtless keep the event secret, as evidently happened in Pamphile's case and elsewhere in New Comedy. I assume this was accepted as normal; Kharisios, at all events, does not seem to hold Smikrines or anyone else to blame for having failed to inform him of the condition of Pamphile, and his slave Onesimos is in constant terror he will become the object of Kharisios' rage for having done precisely that.

Terence's *Hecyra* (*Mother-in-Law*), based on a Greek original by Apollodoros of Karystos, has obvious affinities with *Epitrepontes*. In Terence's play, the husband Pamphilus, who similarly rejects his wife when he discovers that she has borne a child conceived prior to wedlock, nevertheless agrees to keep the facts concealed so as not to compromise the girl's future chances at a respectable marriage (*Hecyra* 395–402). We may compare also Plautus' *Truculentus* (*Pugnacious*), where Callicles' daughter, who has been raped by Diniarchus, attempts to keep the birth of a child secret by having it exposed (797–98); her father has in the meantime betrothed her to a relative of his (848–49).[21] If the child can be concealed or disposed of, the fact of rape itself seems to pose no necessary obstacle to the girl's chances of finding a husband, at least in principle.[22] In practice, however, such situations are always resolved in New Comedy through the union of the original parents of the child, and *Hecyra* and *Truculentus* are no exceptions (it was Pamphilus who, all unknowing, raped the girl he later married).

A series of myths, brilliantly analyzed by Adele C. Scafuro, concerns women who have been raped by gods and who must face the wrath of their fathers upon the discovery that they have borne a nothos. Once again, the focus seems to be entirely upon the existence of the child rather than upon the sexual act per se.[23]

Theoretically, an anxiety over penetration among Athenian males might have served just as well as a concern with the birth of a nothos to preserve the integrity of the citizen household, by stigmatizing women who might have put in doubt the lineage of potential heirs. But perhaps the conditions of Athenian social life in practice discouraged an obsessive preoccupation with physical virginity at the time of marriage. Thus, there is no particular inhibition in New Comedy with regard to marrying a widow, irrespective of whether she has had children; Knemon, in *Duskolos* (*Grouch*), is a case in point. Given the continual warfare that characterized the Greek city-states, and the tendency for men to take brides much younger than themselves, young mothers must commonly have been available as potential brides, and bridegrooms may have learned to feel, in these circumstances, a keen difference between women who had conceived legitimate children in wedlock and those who had borne the offspring of a dubious or unknown father.[24]

From a different angle, though no less speculatively, we may reflect on whether differences, to the extent that they exist, between classical Greek and modern attitudes on the part of men toward the sexual experience of an unmarried girl might have something to do with the cultural paradigm of pederasty at Athens, at least among the middle and upper classes. Greek boys might be perceived by adult males as objects of love and sexual desire. A Greek man, accordingly, will have experienced (at least as a possibility) the asymmetrical structure of erotic relations from two sides, so to speak, both as active adult lover (*erastes*) and as passive or receptive beloved (*eromenos* or *paidika*).[25] It may be that, as a result, Greek men were less inclined to that mystification of female sexuality that informs modern male anxieties over virginity and penetration.[26] Correspondingly, male anger over adultery or the violation of a virgin girl seems to have been based as much on a sense of personal or proprietary injury as on feelings of jealousy and insecurity. The easy availability of courtesans, prostitutes, or slaves for the satisfaction of sexual desire may have helped condition the prevailing Greek view of sex as an appetite more or less like hunger, and comparable, when carried to excess, to gluttony.[27]

How Athenian males may have felt about the marriageability of citizen women who had been raped is not easy to assess, and inferences from contemporary social practices are extremely risky. We have seen that Menander constructed *Epitrepontes* (to return to our text) in such a way that the decision of the hero to be reconciled with his wife was predicated on the discovery that he, like her, had been responsible for the birth of a nothos, without reference to the matter of sexual penetration. No doubt Menander could count on the audience to recognize that the child was the main reason why Kharisios was upset and moved out of his house, and this tells us something about Athenian attitudes in such a pass. This is not to say that the rape itself was a matter of indifference to a girl's family: in *Eunuchus* (867–70), Thais laments that the violation of Pamphila has foiled her plan to win her recognition as a citizen, presumably on the grounds that Pamphila's brother will have no interest in acknowledging her when he learns of her ruined condition. However, we cannot conclude that the reason for her disqualification has to do with male anxieties over the sexuality of women, or that the experience of intercourse, willing or not, rendered women taboo or stained in the eyes of Athenian men. This is to project onto the Greeks attitudes inveterate to our own culture.

In Lysias' defense speech on the murder of Eratosthenes, the defendant remarks that the law inscribed in the Areopagos "judged that men who commit rape [tous biazomenous] deserve a lesser penalty than seducers [tous peithontas]." The reason alleged for this rule is that those who employ violence are detested by their victims, while seducers "corrupt the soul in such a way as to make other men's wives [allotrias gunaikas] care more for them than for their own husbands, and the whole household comes to depend on them, and it is uncertain whether the children are those of the husband or of the adulterer" (Lysias 1.32–33). The speaker has an interest in making adultery appear the gravest kind of offense, but he evidently counts on the jurors to agree that the physical violation of his wife is less momentous in and of itself than the threat to the integrity of his home and the legitimacy of his children (it is assumed, I suppose, that any issue resulting from rape will be exposed).[28]

That the sentiment here is a commonplace is apparent from a passage in Xenophon's *Hieron* in which the tyrant is represented as arguing against the poet Simonides that his life is the least pleasant of all. In particular, he urges that the tyrant is deprived of love or *philia*, which is reckoned the greatest of goods and cannot be forced. In evidence he cites the fact that adulterers are universally punished by death, because they corrupt "the love [*philias*] of wives for their husbands; for [*epei*] when a woman has sex as a result of some mishap [*aphrodisiasthei kata sumphoran tina*], their husbands esteem [*timosin*] them no less, provided that their love seems to remain uncontaminated" (*Hieron* 3.3–4).[29] Here, as in Lysias, the emphasis of the rhetorical trope is on the solidarity of the family rather than some possible pollution of the violated woman.

Having identified what is at stake in Kharisios' rejection of Pamphile in *Epitrepontes*, we may observe that Kharisios' recognition of the moral equivalence between himself and his wife in the matter of producing a nothos, which enables him to contemplate accepting her back, is distinct from and prior to the formal *anagnorisis* by which Kharisios discovers that the woman he raped and his wife are one and the same. The dutiful resolution, which bows to the apparent prohibition in New Comedy of marriage between a woman who has been violated and a citizen male, unless he turns out to be the author of the attack, seems an afterthought, normalizing the conclusion in accord with the conventions of the genre at the expense of the ethical significance of Kharisios' grand monologue. In this split or *décallage* between the narrative trajectory of the moral dilemma and the resolution of an extrinsic and independent social obstacle, the structure of *Epitrepontes* resembles that of other Menandrean comedies, above all *Cistellaria* (based on Menander's *Sunaristosai* [*Women at Breakfast*]), *Heauton Timorumenos* (*Self-Tormentor*), and *Perikeiromene* (*Shorn Girl*), with the difference that, in the last example, forgiveness and reconciliation are withheld prior to the elimination of the external barrier, while in *Epitrepontes* the point is that it is granted.[30] In all these comedies, the partial independence of the ethical plot or drama in respect to the formal denouement required by the genre opens up a space for the affirmation of the dignity and equality of women which they were denied in the civic world of the polis. The fissure in the structure of these plays testifies to the tension between women's role as moral agents and the constraints of status and sexual propriety, irrespective of character or intention, by which they were bound.

Notes

1. I chiefly follow Gomme and Sandbach 1973 for the reconstruction of the lost or fragmentary portions of the play.
2. The text is Sandbach 1990.
3. On the social basis for Smikrines' complaints and Pamphile's loyalty, see Williams 1961, who indicates parallels with the formulas in somewhat later marriage contracts from Hellenistic Egypt. For the text, see Sandbach 1990, 348–50.
4. Arnott 1979; inserts in curved brackets are my own.
5. Fossataro 1915, 305: "E una tesi femminista: il fallo d'una donna non deve giudicarsi a una stregua diversa dal trascorso sensuale dell'uomo," cit. Blanchard 1983, 334 n. 59.
6. Stavenhagen 1910, 581: "Hier zuerst betrachtet ein Mann sein Vergehen also aus gleicher Linie stehend mit dem Fehltritt eines Mädchens;" cit. Blanchard 1983, 334 n. 59.
7. Del Corno 1966, 179: "In realtà la soluzione autentica, in chiave etica, della vicenda si ha quando Carisio decide di ritornare presso la moglie, mentre ancora gli è ignoto il felice intrigo del caso, che ha voluto che il figlio da lei concepito fosse suo."
8. Wilamowitz 1925, 126: "Vor wenigen Menschenaltern würde man nach seiner Idee gefragt haben und hätte sie wohl darin gefunden, dass Mann und Frau einigermassen mit gleichem Masse gemessen werden. . . . Charisios zieht gar keine allgemeingültige Folgerung, und wir wollen nicht fragen, wie er sich auf die Dauer gestellt hätte, wenn er seiner Frau einen wirklichen Fehltritt hätte verzeihen müssen."
9. Blanchard 1983, 333–34: "Ce qu'on voyait dans l'*Arbitrage*, c'était l'ex-

pression d'une thèse féministe: la faute d'une femme ne doit pas être jugée de façon différente de celle d'un homme. Étrange féminisme quand on sait que la faute de Charisios est d'avoir violé jadis celle qui, depuis, est devenue sa femme, tandis que la faute de cette dernière, c'est seulement le malheur d'avoir été violée."

10. Wilamowitz 1925, 100: "Es war sehr im Sinne des Mannes gedacht, wenn seine Schuld nur ein *atukhema* sein sollte, wie es Pamphile wirklich betroffen hatte."

11. In his defense of Helen (19), Gorgias argued notoriously that *eros* or passion is godsent and that accordingly "it is not to be blamed as an error (*hamartema*) but rather to be considered as a misfortune (*atukhema*)." Aristotle acknowledges such sophistries (e.g., in the *Magna Moralia* 1.13.1188a 10–33), but states the ordinary view clearly: "Acts committed through sexual desire (*epithumia*) are not involuntary, but voluntary" (*Magna Moralia* 1.12.1188a 3–4); for the distinction between crimes and misfortunes, see also Aristotle *Rhetoric* 1.13.1374b 4–9.

12. The word *te* (and) is epexigetical: fathering the *nothos* specifies the nature of the deed in the previous clause.

13. *Contra* Wiles 1991, 3: "*The Arbitration* turns upon the young man's recognition that he has raped his own future bride, and that he is guilty of sexual double standards." Lowe 1987, 129 writes that "the *Epitrepontes* highlights the uncomfortable double standard of morality applied to judging the identical sexual offense in men and women," but does not specify the nature of the offense.

14. Cynthia Patterson informs me that the proper term for the illegitimate child of a woman is *parthenios* rather than *nothos;* cf. LSJ s.v. 1.2, citing *Iliad* 16.180. However, I shall continue to refer to the putatively illegitimate child of Pamphile as a nothos, both for the sake of convenience and in order to bring out the symmetry that Kharisios perceives between her situation and his own. See also n. 16 below.

15. The idea that a girl is "soiled" by sexual experience is frequently reported to be the view of men in modern Mediterranean communities; cf. D. Cohen 1991, 41 n. 19 for bibliography, and T. V. Cohen 1992 on the preoccupation with the sexual purity of marriageable women in Renaissance Rome. However, great caution is required in projecting such attitudes back to the city-state culture of classical Athens.

16. See Patterson 1990, 55: "The situation usually envisioned in discussions of *nothoi* is that of the child of adultery or premarital union, . . . but the offspring of such unions are not typically called *nothoi. Nothoi* were the offspring of *pallakai* or concubines, who generally in Athens were of slave or foreign origin. . . . Likewise in Menander's comedies . . . , premarital children are not called *nothoi.*" Patterson argues that the specific meaning of *nothos* is "the paternally recognized offspring of a mismatched or unequal union, which in Athens after 451/50 had both an *oikos* and a *polis* sense: 'man and concubine' and 'citizen and foreigner'" (56), and that "*nothoi* are a specifically recognized class of 'bastards with fathers,' or 'bastards with families'" (57).

On the legal status of the nothos, see also Just 1989, 50–60; and Sealey 1990, 12–19 and 32. On whether the offspring of an unmarried citizen couple was considered a nothos, see Cox 1989, 43 with n. 31.

17. On marriage and the oikos (household), see Just 1989, 89–95, with references there.

18. One may perhaps understand in this way the thesis of Althusser 1971, 164–65: "All ideology represents in its necessarily imaginary distortion not the existing relations of production (and the other relations that derive from them), but above all the (imaginary) relationship of individuals to the relations of production and the relations that derive from them. What is represented in ideology is therefore not the system of the real relations which govern the existence of individuals, but the imaginary relation of those individuals to the real relations in which they live." Althusser's analysis represents a partial and not wholly consistent attempt to ground a Marxist conception of ideology in a psychoanalytic (and, more particularly, a Lacanian) theory of the construction of the individual subject; see Smith 1984, 128–40. The idea of displacement or distortion distinguishes Althusser's approach from the theory of internalization developed by Talcott Parsons; cf. Habermas 1975, 95.

19. Cf. also Euripides' *Ion* 26, where Kreousa, who has been raped by Apollon and has borne a child, is referred to as *parthenos;* Owen 1939 ad v. 26 needlessly explains, "*parthenos* = 'like other maidens.'" Sissa 1990a, 73–86 discusses fully the arguments for a purely status-oriented or sociological interpretation of parthenos defended by Claude Calame and Angelo Brelich, and she gives them a qualified endorsement; Sissa argues that virginity was a sexual matter as well. Cf. also Dowden 1989, 2: "Although *parthenia* was perceived as adversely affected by premature sexual experience, . . . the real issue was marriageability and the real contrast was between *parthenos* and *gyne*, the married woman. A *parthenos* is a maiden, not a virgin."

20. On the physical signs of virginity, see Sissa 1990a, 105–24 and Sissa 1990b, 339–64; and Hanson 1990, 324–29 and 1989, with bibliography.

21. Sissa 1990a, 91 argues that an essential part of the stigma attaching to sexual relations on the part of an unmarried citizen girl was publicity: "Sexuality and virginity were compatible only if sexual activity remained secret." In *Hecyra*, the girl's mother proposes, should news of her daughter's pregnancy get out, to represent the child as Pamphilus', and then expose it (398–400). Clearly, the birth of a child conceived in wedlock with a citizen, though followed by immediate divorce, does not carry the same opprobrium as premarital rape by an unknown male. See, however, Scafuro's essay in this volume, with n. 58.

22. On the role of lying as part of a strategic manipulation of social norms, see D. Cohen 1991, 34 and 54–69.

23. Scafuro 1990; cf. Seaford 1990, 160–61.

24. In Isaeus 2.7–8, the speaker mentions approvingly that the aging Menekles gave up his young wife and bestowed her on another man in order to spare her the misery of childlessness; it is not imagined that the new husband

might entertain any objections to this transaction because he preferred a virgin bride. On the frequency of widowhood in Athens, cf. Gallant 1991, 26–27; and Seaford 1990, 170–71.

25. On Greek pederasty, see Halperin 1990, 29–40, with the copious references cited there.

26. Cf. Just 1989, 66: "The notion of 'living in sin,' or the mystical idea that a woman's essentially 'shameful' sexuality can find honourable accommodation only within the confines of legitimate marriage where it is somehow 'sanctified,' appear to have had little place in Athenian views of marriage. . . . The price paid by the woman for such [an informal] union was that she could not claim the veneration of being the producer of legitimate children. . . . [Formal] marriage by *engue* was seen for what it was—a means of ensuring the continuity of the oikos by the procreation of legitimate children acceptable to the state."

27. On the Greek ideal of self-mastery in relation to the appetites, see the seminal discussion by Foucault 1984, 111–40. Epicurus *Letter to Menoeceus* 131 illustrates nicely the casual inclusion of sexual desire among the appetites in general: "For what produces the pleasant life is not continuous drinking and parties or pederasty or womanizing or the enjoyment of fish and the other dishes of an expensive table, but sober reasoning which tracks down the causes of every choice and avoidance," trans. Long and Sedley 1987, 114; cf. Galen, *Peri ton idion hekastoi pathon kai hamartematon tes diagnoseos* 6.32 (Marquardt 1884): "Whatever one is in love with, he is pleased to make progress in it; and for this reason you can see drunkards feeling pleasure when they surpass their fellow drinkers, those who are gluttonous taking delight in the quantity of foodstuffs, and those who are gourmets in cakes and pans and dishes and sauces [reading *karukeiais* instead of the misprint *korukeiais*]. I have known some men who have even taken pride in the quantity of their sexual acts" (my translation; the entire treatise has been translated into English in Harkins 1963).

28. Harris 1990 challenges the claim that the Athenians regarded rape as a lesser crime than seduction, and he explains away the remark in Lysias 1 as "obviously the slanted interpretation of an advocate" (371; *contra* Cole 1984, 103, *et alii* cit. Harris 370 n. 2). Whatever the customary severity of punishment for the two offenses, however, the speaker surely expects that his argument will be received sympathetically by the male jury. Harris does not cite the analogous passage in Xenophon *Hieron* 3.

29. Marchant 1968, 22–23 n. 2 remarks that "*epei* should be rendered 'though,' not 'since' here, for it introduces a reason why one might suppose that there would be some restriction on the right to kill an adulterer, and *not* the reason why all adulterers may be killed with impunity." But the point is that Hieron is contrasting adultery, in which slaying the offender is permitted because it alienates the affection of a wife, with rape, which does not.

30. See Konstan 1983, 96–114; 1987; 1992, for detailed discussion of the plays mentioned.

Works Cited

Althusser, Louis. 1971. "Ideology and Ideological State Apparatuses (Notes towards an Investigation)." In *Lenin and Philosophy and Other Essays*, translated by Ben Brewster, 127–86. New York: Monthly Review Press.

Arnott, W. G., ed. 1979. *Menander.* Vol. 1. Cambridge, Mass.: Harvard University Press.

Blanchard, Alain. 1983. *Essai sur la composition des comédies de Ménandre.* Paris: Les Belles Lettres.

Capps, Edward, ed. 1910. *Four Plays of Menander.* Boston: Ginn and Co.

Cohen, David. 1991. *Law, Sexuality and Society: The Enforcement of Morals in Classical Athens.* Cambridge: Cambridge University Press.

Cohen, Thomas V. 1992. "Agostino Bonamore and the Secret Pigeon." In *Exploring and (Re)Defining Life Writing*, edited by Marlene Kadar, 94–112. Toronto: University of Toronto Press.

Cole, Susan G. 1974. "Greek Sanctions against Sexual Assault." *CP* 79:97–183.

Cox, Cheryl Anne. 1989. "Incest, Inheritance and the Political Forum in Fifth-Century Athens." *CJ* 85:34–46.

del Corno, Dario, ed. 1966. *Menandro: Le commedie.* Vol. 1. Milan: Istituto Editoriale Italiano.

Dowden, Ken. 1989. *Death and the Maiden: Girls' Initiation Rites in Greek Mythology.* London: Routledge and Kegan Paul.

Fossataro, P. 1915. "Gli 'Epitrepontes' di Menandro e l' 'Hecyra' terenziana." *Athenaeum* 3:305–18.

Foucault, Michel. 1984. *Histoire de la sexualité.* Vol. 2. *L'Usage des plaisirs.* Paris: Gallimard.

Gallant, Thomas W. 1991. *Risk Survival in Ancient Greece: Reconstructing the Rural Domestic Economy.* Cambridge, Mass.: Polity Press.

Gomme, A. W., and F. H. Sandbach, eds. 1973. *Menander: A Commentary.* Oxford: Oxford University Press.

Habermas, Jürgen. 1975. *Legitimation Crisis.* Translated by Thomas McCarthy. Boston: Beacon Press.

Halperin, David M. 1990. *One Hundred Years of Homosexuality and Other Essays on Greek Love.* New York and London: Routledge and Kegan Paul.

Hanson, Ann Ellis. 1989. "Greco-Roman Gynecology." *Newsletter of the Society for Ancient Medicine and Pharmacy* 17:83–92. Madison: American Institute of the History of Pharmacy.

———. 1990. "The Medical Writers' Woman." In *Before Sexuality*, edited by D. Halperin, J. J. Winkler, and F. I. Zeitlin, 309–39. Princeton: Princeton University Press.

Harkins, P. W. 1963. *Galen on the Passions and Errors of the Soul.* With Introduction and Interpretation by W. Riese. Columbus: Ohio State University Press.

Harris, Edward M. 1990. "Did the Athenians Regard Seduction as a Worse Crime Than Rape?" *CQ* 40:370–77.

Harrison, A. R. W. 1968. *The Law of Athens*. Vol. 1, *The Family and Property*. Oxford: Oxford University Press.

———. 1971. *The Law of Athens*. Vol. 2, *Procedure*. Oxford: Oxford University Press.

Just, Roger. 1989. *Women in Athenian Law and Life*. London: Routledge and Kegan Paul.

Konstan, David. 1983. *Roman Comedy*. Ithaca: Cornell University Press.

———. 1987. "Between Courtesan and Wife: A Study of Menander's *Perikeiromene*." *Phoenix* 41:121–39.

———. 1992. "The Young Concubine in Menandrean Comedy." In *Theater and Society in the Classical World*, edited by Ruth Scodel, 139–60. Ann Arbor: University of Michigan Press.

Long, A. A., and D. N. Sedley, eds. 1987. *The Hellenistic Philosophers*. Vol. 1. Cambridge: Cambridge University Press.

Lowe, N. J. 1987. "Tragic Space and Comic Timing in Menander's *Dyskolos*." *BICS* 34:126–38.

Marchant, E. C., ed. and trans. 1968. *Xenophon*. Vol. 7. Cambridge, Mass.: Harvard University Press (Loeb Library).

Marquardt, I., ed. 1884. *Galen: Scripta Minora*. Vol. 1. Leipzig: Teubner.

Owen, A. S. 1939. *Euripides' Ion*. Oxford: Clarendon Press.

Patterson, Cynthia B. 1990. "Those Athenian Bastards." *Classical Antiquity* 9:40–72.

Sandbach, F. H., ed. 1990. *Menandri reliquiae selectae*. Rev. ed. Oxford: Oxford University Press.

Scafuro, Adele C. 1990. "Discourses of Sexual Violation in Mythic Accounts and Dramatic Versions of 'The Girl's Tragedy.'" *Differences* 2.1:126–59.

Seaford, Richard. 1990. "The Structural Problems of Marriage in Euripides." In *Euripides, Women, and Sexuality*, edited by Anton Powell, 151–76. London: Routledge and Kegan Paul.

Sealey, Raphael. 1990. *Women and Law in Classical Greece*. Chapel Hill: University of North Carolina Press.

Sissa, Giulia. 1990a. *Greek Virginity*. Translated by Arthur Goldhammer. Cambridge, Mass.: Harvard University Press.

———. 1990b. "Maidenhood without Maidenhead: The Female Body in Ancient Greece." In *Before Sexuality*, edited by D. Halperin, J. J. Winkler, and F. I. Zeitlin, 339–64. Princeton: Princeton University Press.

Smith, Steven B. 1984. *Reading Althusser: An Essay on Structural Marxism*. Ithaca: Cornell University Press.

Stavenhagen, K. 1910. "Menanders Epitrepontes und Apollodors Hekyra." *Hermes* 45:564–82.

Wilamowitz-Moellendorff, Ulrich von, ed. 1925. *Das Schiedsgericht*. Berlin: Weidmann.

Wiles, David. 1991. *The Masks of Menander: Sign and Meaning in Greek and Roman Performance*. Cambridge: Cambridge University Press.

Williams, Thomas. 1961. "Menanders Epitrepontes im Spiegel der griechischen Eheverträge aus Ägypten." *WS* 74:43–58.

Notes on Contributors

ALAN L. BOEGEHOLD is Professor of Classics at Brown University and Chairman of the Managing Committee of the American School of Classical Studies at Athens. He has written numerous articles and reviews on Greek history, epigraphy, and law and has translated a selection of Cavafy's poems, *In Simple Clothes* (1991). He is the editor and major author of *Law Courts at Athens: Sites, Buildings, Equipment, Procedure and Testimonia* (1994). He is currently writing on nonverbal communication in ancient Greece.

W. ROBERT CONNOR was formerly Andrew Fleming West Professor of Classics at Princeton University; he has been the Director of the National Humanities Center in North Carolina since 1989, and was elected a Fellow of the American Academy of Arts and Sciences in 1992. He has written numerous articles on Greek history and historiography and is the author of *Theopompos and Fifth-Century Athens* (1968), *The New Politicians of Fifth-Century Athens* (1971), and *Thucydides* (1984). Recently, with C. L. Connor, he co-authored a study of the life of Saint Luke of Steiris.

FRANK J. FROST is Professor Emeritus of History at the University of California at Santa Barbara. He has written over forty articles on Athenian politics, Greek history, and archeology, including site reports from his dig at Phalasarna, Krete. His books include *Plutarch's Themistocles* (1980) and the popular textbook *Greek Society* (4th ed., 1992). He has been working on a book about Peisistratos and sixth-century Attika.

DAVID KONSTAN is John Rowe Workman Distinguished Professor of Classics and Chairman of the Department of Classics at Brown University. He has written numerous articles on Greek and Latin poetry and drama, Greek philosophy, and Marxist historiography of antiquity. He is the author of books on Epicurus, Catullus, Roman comedy, and the Greek novel, and he has translated Simplicius' commentary on Aristotle *Physics 6*. He is preparing a book on Greek comedy and another on ancient friendship.

PHILIP BROOK MANVILLE formerly taught ancient history at Northwestern University and is now a partner at McKinsey and Company, New York, where he leads the firm's Information and Technology function. He holds degrees in classics and history from Oxford and Yale and is the author of *The Origins of Citizenship in Ancient Athens* (1990). He has also written articles on Athenian law and history, as well as on information management and organizational change.

IAN MORRIS is Associate Professor of History and Classics at the University of Chicago. He is the author of *Burial and Ancient Society: The Rise of the Greek City-State* (1987) and *Death-Ritual and Social Structure in Classical Antiquity* (1992). He has edited a collection of essays, *Classical Greece: Ancient Histories and Modern Archaeologies*, and is preparing another book, *The Archaeology of Democracy*.

JOSIAH OBER is Magie Professor of Classics and Chairman of the Department of Classics at Princeton University. He has written numerous articles on Greek history and ancient political theory. He is the author of *Fortress Attica: Defense of the Athenian Land Frontier, 404–322* (1985) and *Mass and Elite in Democratic Athens: Rhetoric, Ideology and the Power of the People* (1989); the latter won the Goodwin Award for best book from the American Philological Association in 1989. He is preparing a book about Athenian critics of popular rule. He was Martin Lecturer at Oberlin College in 1993.

CYNTHIA PATTERSON is Assistant Professor of History at Emory University. She has written numerous articles on social institutions, law, and the status of women in ancient Greece. She is the author of *Pericles' Citizenship Law of 451/0 B.C.* (1981) and is currently writing a book entitled "The Family in Greek History." She is also preparing a translation of [Demosthenes] 59 *Neaera*.

ADELE C. SCAFURO is Associate Professor of Classics at Brown University. She has written articles on Attic law, drama, and Hellenistic historiography and, with Eva Stehle, edited two issues of *Helios* in 1989 devoted to Roman women. She is the author of *The Forensic Stage: Settling Disputes in Graeco-Roman New Comedy* (forthcoming).

ROBERT W. WALLACE is Associate Professor of Classics at Northwestern University. He has written articles on Greek history, law, and numismatics and, with B. MacLachlan, edited *Harmonia Mundi* (*QUCC* Supp. 5) in 1991. His book *The Areopagos Council, to 307 B.C.* (1989) won the Gustave Arlt Award in the Humanities in 1988 from the Council of Graduate Schools. He is preparing a book called "Music, Philosophy, and Politics in Fifth-Century Athens: A Study of Damon of Oa."